THE YEAR

2000

THE YEAR
2000

by
RAYMOND WILLIAMS

PANTHEON BOOKS
NEW YORK

All rights reserved under International and Pan-American Copyright
Conventions. Published in the United States by Pantheon Books, a
division of Random House, Inc., New York. Originally published as
Towards 2000 in Great Britain by Chatto & Windus/The Hogarth
Press, London.

Library of Congress Cataloging in Publication Data

Williams, Raymond.
The year 2000.

Previously published as: Towards 2000.
Includes index.
1. Twentieth century—Forecasts. 2. Twenty-first
century—Forecasts. I. Title.
CB161.W54   1983   303.4′909′05   83-21966
ISBN 0-394-53552-9
ISBN 0-394-72259-0 (pbk.)

Manufactured in the United States of America

First American Edition

Dyma ni yn awr ar daith ein gobaith
(Here we are now on the journey of our hope)
Morgan John Rhys, *Y Cylchgrawn Cymraeg,* 1795

. . . *Who holds that if way to the Better there be,
it exacts a full look at the worst.*
Thomas Hardy, *In Tenebris,* 1895

Acknowledgements

Early drafts of some of the material in this book appeared in *New Left Review*, *New Socialist*, *Socialist Register*, *Marxism Today*, *London Review of Books* and *The Forward March of Labour Halted?* I am grateful to my wife and to Neil Middleton for much detailed editorial help.

R.W.

CONTENTS

PREFACE TO
THE AMERICAN EDITION

More than we ever believe, we understand life from where we are. This book, written by a Welsh European, is an attempt to understand the forces and ideas which can influence our common life through the year 2000. Its perspective is intended to be general, but certain particularities are necessarily present. We take evidence from our own immediate social experience, even when we go on to broader themes and considerations. Moreover, when we are estimating possibilities, we have to work not only from the record but from a close sense of what the people we know believe to be possible. Even within a single society, there are many variations in this, and some absolute contrasts. But in another very different society there will be variations and contrasts which may be quite beyond our range. Introducing this book to American readers, I am very conscious of this possibility.

It is better to put it like that than to assume, as now regularly happens on both sides of the Atlantic, that we already have a common way of life and that every year makes it more so. I am perhaps especially aware of elements of this community: in the English language and in certain shared intellectual and literary traditions. Moreover, when I read eighteenth- or nineteenth-century contrasts of British and American life, by British authors, I am almost always on the American side: not through some alien attachment, but because what was then coming through in American popular and democratic practise was what my own people, a subordinated majority within the old British state, themselves believed. This historical attachment is still important to me.

Then there is another factor which often makes me feel especially close to some American colleagues. I have got used to being called, from across the Atlantic, an *English* author, or at best indiscriminate British. Yet my real social identity is, as I said, Welsh European. The Welsh element is very important in intellectual orientation, since in attitudes to popular democracy, culture, education and intellectual life it is radically different from the dominant English emphases. The European element is equally important, especially in its bearing on the human sciences, which have been more fundamentally accepted and more consciously developed in the rest of Europe than in an England or Britain governed by an old yet persistent kind of ruling-class amateurism. The large effect of this European element on American intellectual life, and then its own intensive development of it, has long made North America, for me, an intellectually congenial place. So that a Welsh European, consciously rejecting and resisting certain dominant English habits and prejudices, may feel in North America—but then too quickly—at home.

For what quite soon becomes clear, if the eyes and ears stay open, is not only the vast diversity of North American life which our selected elements of community have ignored. It is, as a fact less obvious and perhaps less welcome to North Americans, that the view east across the Atlantic is at least as selective and that in the current world-political situation this can be as disturbing as it is often dangerous. This needs to be very openly discussed.

Deeply attached as I am to certain shaping American ideas and feelings, I have to say also what it feels like, from a root in those ideas, to have to resist day by day the immense pressures on us to become, in effect, an American military, political and cultural dependency. I have mainly fought this battle in Britain, but the ground must be broadened. First, it has been literally disgusting to watch so many of my own generation, and more of a succeeding generation, turn and crawl and manoeuvre to the United States, not because of the real qualities of American life—for in private they often retain and cherish their insular sense of superiority, and in some American circles are even valued for such airs, as in one especially fashionable kind of Anglophilia —but because that is where the real money, the real power, the real careers now are. My ancestors watched the Welsh gentry go off with similar motives to the English court, but at least they were then largely rid of them. Now, what we have in Britain is a still nominally English or British group who in all their real interests and loyalties have become American.

That would be bad enough, but what is worse is that at the political and cultural levels this is rationalised as the new multinational democracy and modernism: a definition heavily promoted from the United States itself, which offers politically loaded universals as a way of establishing—as it were, innocently—a natural dominance. It really has to be spelled out that it is not only offensive but deeply injurious to democracy to have a president of the United States described—and believing himself correctly described—as the leader of the West or of the Free World. Yet, beyond such gross cases there are a thousand others, and it is where these bear on our common chances for a happy new year 2000 that they have most clearly to be identified.

The key political problem, discussed in this book in the chapters on disarmament and on the East-West contrast (Part Three, 2 and 3), lies in the complex of relations between Europe and the United States. It is ironic that many of us in Europe are described in that too popular formulation as 'anti-American' because we mean seriously to try to end the nuclear arms race, to get détente with Eastern Europe and to intervene in relations between the Third World and both the First and Second Worlds so that in everything we think and do we are on the side of its peoples rather than of our own ruling classes and definitions. Ironic, because a significant number of Americans agree with us. But not only ironic, since one of the now overpowering American universals is an absolute contrast between democracy and socialism, whereas we are not simply radicals or liberals but committed socialists, if in some ways of a new kind. This is now one of the hardest areas of intellectual negotiation across the Atlantic.

Since the late 1940s many liberal as well as reactionary Americans have been steadily telling us that socialism is at best an outdated, nineteenth-century idea, at worst a voluntary or involuntary conspiracy against freedom. Political groups in our own countries, often directly supported from the United States, have swelled this chorus. Every attempt is made to identify us with the ruling system and interests of the Soviet Union and its allies, though we have good reason to know what they actually think and say against us. As this debris is thrown at us it is not always easy to go on speaking steadily about extending our own democracy, about the real and equitable economic interests of our own peoples, about lifting the danger of locked-in nuclear-weapons systems and bases, about ending economic imperialism as it is practised from our own lands. Yet, speaking steadily about these matters is all we can now reasonably do. For things have been happening, especially in Britain, which make an older kind of confidence indeed outdated.

It was assumed until very recently—although not, as is clear in this book, by me—that there was a natural inbuilt British majority for democratic socialism, even if it was coming by instalments and in its own good time. No reasonable person in Britain can now believe this. In this respect at least we have come nearer to the situation of radicals and socialists in the United States. What we are faced with and governed by is no longer a traditional conservatism but an angry and destructive right-wing populism. Yet on this point especially I would ask American readers to consider, carefully, my arguments on class, politics and socialism (Part Two, 4). It was written before the 1983 election, though I was able to include some 1983 statistics in proof. Yet what it pointed to—and indeed what was pointed to in the 1959 essay in *The Long Revolution*—has now come openly through. Some friends, across the Atlantic and in the rest of Europe, see 'Britain' as now wholly or largely Thatcherite, though in fact this government got only a reduced vote, of some 42 percent, and only in our electoral system could gain its five-year monopoly of power. So that our friends elsewhere should at least remember the rest of us, still an actual majority.

But that is only half the story. What has really collapsed is the old Labour Party illusion that socialism would in effect come as a legacy, by some fortunate electoral result. Many people now throw this collapse at us as evidence that we should give up thinking about socialism. But the truth is quite the opposite. I am profoundly glad that long before this open collapse, and the crisis of ideas it is precipitating, I had begun work to try to go through and recast the whole argument: first in *Culture and Society* and *The Long Revolution*; then in this new book. For I have long believed that, whatever else we may do politically, we have also not only, as it is put, to 'win the intellectual argument' but even more—if anything serious is meant by that—to find out what, in modern conditions, the intellectual argument really is. A Left can survive for many years with what it believes to be a confident 'message'. But in the speed of change of the late twentieth century, it can be left with a 'message' and not much else, and the danger then is of a vacuum which will be quickly filled by the supposedly up-to-date universals, heavily funded as always, including directly from groups in the United States. The fact that some of these universals are just the old rubbish, reclaimed by command of money and power, is not reassuring. But what is worse is the development of a genuinely new kind of inhumane political rationalism: what I describe in my last chapter as the politics of Plan X. No received message can stand against that in the newly decisive areas of military technology, multinational corporations and the advanced technologies of modern culture and information.

This is why, in this book, I have deliberately chosen a future perspective. There are still many old and moribund ideas to oppose; but where I want to be, and where I have tried to put this book, is where the new ideas are forming, around new and in some ways unprecedented conditions and problems. There are then different intellectual enemies but also, I would hope, some new as well as many old intellectual friends. The year 2000, as I begin the book by recognising, is an arbitrary date. But the years between now and then will be critical and dangerous for all of us, in some common ways in spite of all our other differences. In asking American readers to look at how one Welsh European sees the coming years, and the different ideas and forces which can move through them, I have some confidence in that best part of the American tradition: the intellectual and imaginative ability to see a genuinely different future.

RAYMOND WILLIAMS
Craswall, 1983

I

TOWARDS 2000

TOWARDS 2000

I

We all think about the future, but in very diverse ways. In what we call the Western world, we are approaching one of the fascinating rounded numbers: 2000. This already has more than a numerical significance, for by the reckoning of the Christian era it is the second millennium, and such counting by thousands of years is loaded with cultural significance. The first millennium brought many expectations of the ending of the world and the second coming of Christ. In the extending irrationalities of our own time, many of them flourishing in the most developed centres of advanced industrial civilisation, we can already see some signs of this happening again, as the arbitrary date approaches. The danger of nuclear war is widely described, within an old scheme and vocabulary, as the threat of 'apocalypse'. Orwell's 1984, a numerical inversion from 1948 when he was writing his book, has become a date with tyranny. And beyond those who believe or half-believe in these arbitrary numerical significances, there is the deep habit of using some mark in time – a new year, a birthday, a millennium – to reflect and to look forward, to try to see where we are.

The arbitrariness has still to be noted. We are counting 2000 by the scheme of a Scythian monk of (by the reckoning he established) the sixth century Anno Domini. The chronologies of a developed industrial world still follow Dionysius Exiguus. Yet the dominance of this Western Christian dating coexists with the different numbering of other cultures: the Jewish sixth millennium; the long Chinese dynasties; the alternative Muslim era; and others. In the great diversity of recorded schemes for measuring time, there is still, however, a recurrence of significant periods and cycles. Schemes of history and of the future are made to emerge from the widely alternative numerical systems.

The millennium, within Western culture, has taken on secular as well as religious significance. Some millenarian visions by religious movements, breaking free of ties to an exact numbering, predicted and confidently expected the coming of Christ's kingdom on earth. Many were significantly active in times of major social disturbance and instability. There is then a clear cultural link to the secular millenarian visions, of the establishment of social justice, of liberty and plenty, in the world. Deep and stubborn beliefs in this coming time are easily mocked, as the dates pass and pass again. But perhaps more is lost than is gained when yet one more of the arbitrary dates is approached, by so many, as much with fear or hopelessness as with expectation. The settled pessimism of so much of the culture of the late twentieth century is in effect an absolute loss of the future: of any significant belief that it can be both different and better. The projection of dates is now more often an anxious calculation of the possibilities of mere survival.

We have again to remember the arbitrariness of the numbering. Beyond Dionysius Exiguus or any of the other traditional schemes, we have the modern reckoning of very much longer periods of development and of history. Thus we are in perhaps the thirty-seventh millennium since men and women quite like ourselves came into our kinds of land. We are in the always recalculated thousands of millennia since the development towards humanity began and can be visibly traced. The intense cultural interest of our own period in these longer spans of human time, which are so much more signi-ficant and more moving than any of the traditional schemes, is a new kind of assessment of the basic meanings of human history. The assessment is complex and self-conscious but also often anxious. Some people find reassurance in this long past, in which so much has been achieved, in so many different forms, and so many dangers and limitations have been surmounted. Others, in effect, escape into it, spinning time backwards from what they see as a hopeless present and a short and disastrous future.

There is little point in any recall of the millenarian spirit, though if we renounce the terms of its positive expectations we ought also to renounce the terms of the most common negative expectations. There are discovered and discoverable reasons, of a fully objective kind, for intense concern about the future of industrial civilisation and, beyond even that, about the future of the species and of the planet, under destructive forces that are already loose. But there are also discovered and discoverable reasons for a kind of hope which has accepted the facts underlying these fears and which can see ways beyond them which are fully within our capacity. A major element in what is going to happen is the state of mind of all of us who are in a position to intervene in its complex processes, and at best to determine them for the general good. It is these ways of thinking about the future, in their real sense as ways of making it, that we should now examine.

2

In intellectual analysis it is often forgotten that the most widespread and most practical thinking about the future is rooted in human and local continuities. We can feel the continuity of life to a child or a grandchild. We can care for land, or plant trees, in ways that both assure and depend on an expectation of future fertility. We can build in ways that are meant to last for coming lives to be lived in them.

It is true that all these ways have been weakened by particular kinds of society and economy, which set alternative priorities of quick satisfaction and return. Yet their impulses are still very strong. Beyond the snappy formulas of an instant and enclosed individualism; beyond the profitable fast exploitation of resources; beyond the market schemes of obsolescent durables; beyond the widespread and reckless borrowing from the future to solve some current difficulty without discomfort: beyond all these powerful and identifiable forces, these deeper impulses and reckonings persist. Yet just as they are often most actual in directly relating and local ways, so they can in practice be specialised to these: a family, a farm, an institution; getting these right, even if the world outside them is going to hell. What begins in a strong faith and a devotion to continuity can become at best isolated, at worst a form readily exploited by quite other feelings and interests.

There is no useful way of thinking about the future which is not based in these values of close continuity in life and the means of life. All the practical problems begin when these have to be related to other lives and other means, in an unavoidable and necessary diversity, and under the stresses of actual change. Most ways of thinking about the future jump from this practical level, where substantial feelings are deeply engaged, to what seem more realistic objective assessments, based on selected versions, often in fact contradictory, of these primary needs and desires.

This is most evident in a group of ways of thinking about the future which are now dominant in our culture. We can distinguish, within this group, between the forecasting model and the political programme. The former is apparently more objective. It is typically based on extrapolations from known laws or regularities. It projects, in what are often locally sophisticated ways, indices of general production, of employment and unemployment, of inflation, of demand. That there are rival and often significantly different forecasts is a fact about the type, but at another level no more than an indication of its inherent difficulty. It is common now to mock these statistical modes, and the diverse uses made of them by rival schools of economists, while at the same time in practice drawing general conclusions from them. This is unreasonable. It has been a fact about our kind of society, especially since the industrial revolution, that there are certain areas of reality which only statistics can recognise. Many events are too complex, too numerous, and too protracted to be seen at all, with any adequacy, by what some believe to be more reliable kinds of observation.

Much depends on the kinds of fact which are selected as statistically manageable. Similarly, the models of regularity or interaction which are applied for extrapolation are not often verifiable with anything like the precision of the founding records. Thus the past is littered with unrealised projections, in population figures and in production. The present is confused by sharply diverging forecasts, in a range of colours from black to pale grey or even the occasional white. Yet it would be folly for any of these reasons to renounce or to neglect the mode itself. The real questions about it relate to the models of regularity and interaction from which the forecasts are made. Interaction, especially, is an unusually obscure area, with comparatively sparse empirical data in its inevitably complex field, and carrying some of the most difficult theoretical problems.

It is then significant that the heaviest investment in the mode has been in terms of the existing kind of corporate market economy, neglecting wider forms of social interaction. It is for the investment decisions of productive corporations, or for the financial calculation of various kinds of unearned or indirectly earned income, that most of these forecasts are commissioned or compete. Thus the area of facts which they include is in the main ideologically determined. At the same time, because of their practical connection with actual dispositions of resources, many of these forecasts become plans and investment programmes, and can up to a point be self-fulfilling. New steel plants and tanker fleets and power stations materialise, on extrapolations which, however, later forecasts may revise or discard. In forms tied to this limited mode, there is often no real future but only a wasted present and past.

Yet some form of economic forecasting has been found to be necessary in the most widely divergent kinds of modern economy and society. It is obviously necessary in centrally planned economies, where it is integrally linked with centralised decisions about general provision and production. It is equally necessary, though with a different set of indices, in what are misleadingly called free economies, in which the most basic decisions are taken by various institutions of state and corporate power. The old kind of market, in relatively stable conditions with relatively few commodities, has been so largely replaced by the new kind of market, in which demand and preference have to be inquired into, predicted and where necessary (through advertising) formed, that a range of public and commercial forecasting is positively required.

The same or similar techniques are then applied, in capitalist societies, to the electoral system, through opinion-polling and issues-research. It is a fact against the centrally planned economies that except in certain standardised forms of production (such as basic electricity supply) a monopoly of research and prediction interlocks with a monopoly of decision-making to discredit and more seriously to limit planning itself. The inherent difficulties of prediction and forecasting are maximised by the fact of monopoly. It should be a central principle of any socially planned economy that there are always, as a matter of course, a number of model forecasts to be examined and publicly discussed, but this can only happen if there is no longer monopoly in the most general political decisions. Thus both the limited and the more extended forms of forecasting and planning are congruent, at every level, with the most general structures of a society. This is obvious, if only from the evidence of certain recurrent failures, in centrally planned economies. The forms of congruence in economies planned by a mixture of state and corporate power are equally close but less easy to see.

One significant form is the political manifesto, now one of the most widely distributed kinds of apparent thinking about the future. In its modern forms this is different from older kinds of manifesto, which were typically statements of general principle and intention. The more usual form, in contemporary party politics, is much nearer a commercial prospectus. It retains, in a general way, the rhetoric of principle and intention, but in substance it is a series of specific plans which (with an unintended but eventual irony) are also known as 'commitments'. In its most naive forms this is indeed little more than the 'shopping list' which it usually gets called by its opponents. 'Peace and prosperity' becomes the more itemised but not much more specific 'More jobs, lower prices, planned growth of incomes, improved social services, law and order, national security'. But then, if only from the rub of competition, there is an attempted interlock with the more rational if still limited models of economic forecasting. 'Every proposal in this manifesto has been carefully costed to prove its practicability.' 'The overall effect of these proposals has been carefully assessed, using the Treasury's own computerised model of the economy.' Not a prospectus then, but a future, and we might all hope that it could indeed be so. Yet any open-minded comparison of the manifestos and the actual governmental records of the relevant modern political parties shows a degree of disparity which is even more marked than the errors of simpler kinds of forecasting. Even when few of the details are remembered – and full manifestos are among the most unread writing of our time – a general public suspicion of the mode itself has become very widespread. The manifestos are still produced, but fewer and fewer people take them seriously. This may often be justified, but there is then, by the very prominence of this mode in the orthodox political process, a damaging loss of belief in the practicability of thinking and shaping the future.

What are the underlying reasons? One, evidently, is the simple fact of electoral competition, especially when it is between only two main parties. I remember speaking in support of a parliamentary candidate, in the sixties, who outlined, from the party manifesto, a whole series of desirable social measures which would not, however, require any increase in taxation, since they would all be paid for by a similarly projected annual increase of 3 per cent in national production. He seemed taken aback when a member of the audience suggested an obviously desirable social measure which happened not to be on the list. 'Don't you agree with it?' 'Certainly.' 'Then how will you pay for it?' At this point the candidate leaned across to me and said, in a whisper: 'Do you think the increase in production could be 3½ per cent?'

In practice, if we have had anything to do with electoral politics, we have all in some degree, actively or passively, taken part in this process. Even when there is an initial rational core in the programme, the competitive process of bid and counter-bid quickly pushes most people beyond it. A whole style of political consumerism, in which there need not be any hard choices, takes over as the essence of politics, and then has an evident congruence with the styles of commodity consumerism, similarly stimulated and financed by a manufactured credit. The tough talk about limits and choices, which should have been there from the beginning, is regularly reserved for a period some years into government, when various assumptions have been falsified and other structural constraints have emerged.

This is also true at an even earlier stage. A definition of politics as competing political leaderships exerts basic pressures on the inherently difficult process of forecasting and planning. People then blame the political leaderships, and for relief make jokes about them. But if we look at the whole process we have also to blame ourselves, for letting politics be like this. There is a widespread complacency of subordination, supported by cheap flattery of ourselves as voters, just waiting to be wooed, by a still better offer, for our precious cross. This has to be seen as contemptible. For it is this style of the whole culture, initially promoted by the techniques and relationships of modern corporate selling, which has reduced the only widely available form of positive thinking about the future, in the programmes of political parties, to a discredited game.

It is true that within this general style, formed by and actively contributing to it, the political leaderships still further compromise the available methods of rational forecasting. The major theoretical problems, of the indices to select, the diverse interactive relationships to assume, the timescale to work on, are again and again pushed aside for the selective presentation of forecasts that can be made compatible with a party tendency. The four- or five-year electoral rhythm determines one of the most crucial procedures, with special damage in a world in which only much longer timescales can reveal the full dimensions of the problems. While the failures can then be projected to the parties, the real failure is in the processes of common decision for which we continue to claim (but then as they fail to disclaim) responsibility.

3

A significant change is now happening. Intelligent politicians have noticed this depressing sequence. They know that the realistic choices, when a party enters government, are between (a) steady implementation of its promised programme or (b) an early transition to what is called, significantly, 'crisis-management' or (c) some mixture, in critically variable proportions, of (a) and (b).

It is very striking that (b) almost always happens, and that it determines the mixture in the eventual (c). But this is only to say that in any society (and especially in one so involved and exposed in a wider arena as Britain) the reality gap between a manifesto programme and a government is inevitably wide. Vietnam, Rhodesia and Northern Ireland has as much to do with the reality of the Labour governments from 1964 to 1970 as any programmes and policies which they had themselves foreseen or instituted. Renewed oil price rises, United States monetary policies and the crisis of the Falklands/Malvinas had similarly directive effects on the Conservative government elected in 1979. It is this regular experience which underlies the opportunism, the new rhetoric and even the open cynicism which are now endemic among most politicians with actual experience of governing. Many of them go on presenting detailed policies as if this were not so, but this means very little, and has the eventual effect, beyond them, of further sapping public belief in the possibility of planned, rational and deliberately selected change.

Yet those who have come to view government as crisis-management, with themselves as its self-evident crisis heroes, have in one way bridged the reality gap, by the practical cancellation of detailed, participating, consciously chosen planning. In the Centre this shows itself as a world-weary adaptation; on the Right as the abstraction of resolute leadership: in each case behind a screen of public relations. Yet these are more than the historical-occupational features of contemporary political leaders. They are also, for the rest of us, readily available responses to an actual and prolonged complexity of crisis: either sceptical resignation, or a willingness to leave matters to, even applaud, a strong leader.

To speak differently and positively is morally refreshing but is still on its own no alternative. It is not only that the reality gap is repeatedly ignored or denied, for what sound like good idealist reasons. It is also that by definition it cannot be bridged only by general positions or proposals, however internally convincing and coherent these may be. For the reality of what is called, with a certain heroic air, crisis-management is that the crises (including those which seem to take us by surprise) are simply exposures of existing real relations, as distinct from the presumed and limited relations within which most political programmes are formulated. Moreover, what is called management of the crisis is never a merely neutral process of local response, adjustment and negotiation. It is typically a practical disclosure of existing real forces and interests. Against such real pressures, not only public-relations manifestos but on their own even genuine locally-conceived programmes stand little chance of success. For these become, to the extent that they are serious, the crises that others, with all available real forces, move in to manage.

4

So the most widely practised form of general thinking about the future, in political programmes and manifestos, carries with it disadvantages which often lead to the abandonment of any real thinking about the future. The full scale of what can be rationally predicted, or at least of what has to be allowed for with some degree of possibility, is excluded or foreshortened to permit more persuasive or less disturbing short-term programmes. Or, through failure after failure, the idea of gaining some effective common controls of our future is steadily given up, leading on the one hand to a culture of nostalgia, on the other to the cruder politics of temporary tactical advantage. Yet at more serious levels there are other kinds of thinking about the future.

The most widely known is still called utopianism, though strictly Utopia is another place rather than another time. This whole mode is now again very active. There is an obvious relation between this revival and the recurrent disappointments and despairs of orthodox politics. It can then be readily seen as simple escapism, and excluded from practical thinking.

Yet it is necessary to distinguish two kinds of utopia, each of which can have specific strengths as well as specific weaknesses. The older kind of systematic utopia is now less popular. It was indeed heavily attacked, within its own form, by the systematic dystopia – the organised hell or vacuity – which has been much more common in the twentieth century. One simple ideological interpretation of this change is now fashionable: that the very attempt to achieve a systematic utopia leads straight to a systematic dystopia. Or, translated (for this is a very potent and apparently sophisticated argument among establishment intellectuals): the very attempt to make a new kind of society, more just, more rational and more humane, leads by its very processes and impulses, including above all planning, to the exact opposite, a more repressive, a more arbitrary, a more standardised and inhumane order.

This is a very powerful trick that has been turned. For where it is not simple assertion, the evidence that is used – of frustrated intentions, of contradictory results, of a liberation that becomes a tyranny – is not taken from the history of utopian attempts but from the very different practices of armed struggle and revolution. Most of the evidence is in fact from the history and consequences of the Bolshevik revolution, but whatever else may be said about that, it was never in any serious sense utopian; it was rooted, as were its complex consequences, in extending class struggle and the fight for a new social order. At a projected distance something like a systematic utopia was indeed in view, but the whole emphasis of the Bolshevik rejection of utopian thought was that what mattered was the road and the power.

There have been many devices of institution of a systematic utopia, from natural events to new technologies. A few have even included some form of transitional struggle, which, crucially for the form, are usually safely in the past. More typically, the new society has just happened; it is there or is come across. The Bolshevik rejection of this mode, because it encouraged abstract and idle dreaming, is directly comparable with other orthodox political rejections of it: 'it may sound very nice, but we have to live in the real world'.

This is often a reasonable rejection, but it overlooks a value which the systematic utopia can still have. It can envisage, in general structure but also in detail, a different and practical way of life, and therefore offers what can otherwise only be gained by the most general and universal (but then fully realistic) kind of history: the belief that human beings can live in radically different ways, by radically different values, in radically different kinds of social order. It is always the pressure not to believe this, by what is in the end a parochialism in time – a complacent projection of actual and historically instituted social orders as permanently necessary and exclusive – which most deeply discourages those who see very clearly that their own social order is in crisis. It may still be the case that they know there are alternatives but cannot believe that they will live to see them; this is a different and more limited kind of calculation. But what the systematic utopia offers, at its best, is an imaginative reminder of the nature of historical change: that major social orders do rise and fall, and that new social orders do succeed them. It is then mainly a matter of the general temper of the period whether the new order is seen as better or worse. There can be idle dreaming either way: the systematic nightmare no more and no less idle than the rosy fantasy. But the value of the systematic utopia is to lift our eyes beyond the short-term adjustments and changes which are the ordinary material of politics, and thus to insist, as a matter of general principle, that temporarily and locally incredible changes can and do happen.

The more admired contemporary utopian form is different. It is not based on a new system as a form of critique of an existing system, or as a whole worked-through alternative to it. Its purpose, instead, is to form desire. It is an imaginative encouragement to feel and to relate differently, or to strengthen and confirm existing feelings and relationships which are not at home in the existing order and cannot be lived through in it. This kind of heuristic utopia has much in common with the practical movements of alternative individual or small-communal lifestyles, and, crucially, with a significant and probably growing tendency in religious thought. Already, in its faith, the religious movement has an alternative body of values and, beyond the more secular tasks of witnessing and seeking to extend the faith, really can believe in the possibility or even the imminence of some general conversion.

The weaknesses of this mode are obvious. Its versions of desire, and of new feelings and relationships, are not only often vague but in their most subjective and private versions (as so often in the 1960s) are subject to capture by the existing social order, in some new phase, or even, in the worst cases, to actual marketing. On the other hand, when the alternative values run deep and include others, there is a persistence in this mode, if only among what are seen as negligible minorities, which certainly bears comparison with what are also the very small minorities still seriously set on a systematically new social order. There are signs, in the danger of the current crisis, that these two essentially different bodies of people are discovering the need, if not always as yet the means, to come together, by some form of mutual change.

Thus what can properly be called the utopian impulse still runs, not only against the disappointments of current politics or a more generalised despair, but also against the incorporated and marketed versions of a libertarian capitalist cornucopia (which, ironically, some of the earlier systematic utopias now strikingly resemble). Its strongest centre is still the conviction that people can live very differently, as distinct both from having different things and from becoming resigned to endless crises and wars. In a time of scarce resources, of any such kind, there can be no question of dispensing with it.

5

Yet it is necessary to think seriously about what is most deeply wrong with the utopian mode and about those more everyday forms which have important features in common with it. What is strongest about the systematic utopias is that they are formed by a kind of whole analysis and whole constructive formation. They may then be weak in their particularity or their narrow uniformity, but this procedure of whole analysis and whole formation is intellectually very important. What is most deficient in the strictly utopian mode is that this wholeness is essentially *projected*, to another place or time. What we have to learn, beyond utopian thinking, is this impulse to wholeness without the accompanying projection. Even to say this indicates its major difficulty, but new intellectual formations, centred on this intention, are in practise beginning to emerge.

The cultural analysis developed within and beyond Marxism in the last sixty years has rejected the idea of specialist 'areas' of society, each served by its specialist 'discipline'. It is a central achievement of this analysis that it has developed forms of attention to a whole social order without any dogmatic assignment of priority to this or that determining force. Yet what is often weak in this kind of analysis is that while it shows interactions, interconnections, even underlying structural forms, it usually cannot succeed in establishing, with any certainty, the real order of determination between different kinds of activity. That there always is such an order of determination cannot be doubted, from the historical evidence, though that it is not always the same order is equally clear. This is the necessary theoretical base for the recognition of genuinely different social orders. This point bears especially on the possible development of cultural analysis (always in practice pulled towards the manageable past) into constructive analysis of the present and of possible and probable futures, where its methods are especially necessary and where new practical formations might be found. For it is only by continuing to attend to a whole lived social order, and at the same time identifying the primary determining forces within it, that this kind of general humanist analysis can significantly contribute to thinking about the future.

Faced by this difficulty, it has been a welcome surprise to discover, within a wholly different intellectual tradition, kinds of analysis and projection which share the cultural emphasis on a whole order, but with radically different definitions and methods. It is significant that the methods of system dynamics, which in their early results became first generally known in the 1972 report *The Limits to Growth*, were widely overlooked by a transfer of attention to a version of the results themselves. The report concluded that there were systematic and unsurpassable limits to the kinds of exponential growth of industrial production, exploitation of resources and world population which seem to be inherent in the existing dominant social order. It indicated alternative models of a stable equilibrium. But while there was much to argue with in the report, its importance was always more in its methods, based on its insistence on the analysis of dynamic systems, than in any of its particular or general results.

The shift of emphasis in this kind of analysis has two main factors. First, it greatly extends the timescale by comparison with most economic and political forecasting. Second, it offers ways of measuring the complex and dynamic interactions between different kinds of activity, as distinct from studies which assess the problems of population or of resources or of production piecemeal. Extending the timescale is a fundamentally necessary move. It is inherent in the rhythms of both the market and the electoral processes that their significant timescales, governed by practical needs and urgencies, are relatively short (typically five or ten years at most). The difficulties of a longer timescale are obvious, since it is bound to increase the degree of uncertainty. Yet the relatively ungraspable date of 2050, for example, is within the normal lifespan of my grandchildren, and all more traditional ways of thinking about the future would certainly include this kind of natural human foresight and concern. The apparently more practical urgencies which foreshorten calculation, for temporary advantage, are in this respect as in others damaging to the most basic human order.

The insistence on analysing and trying to measure interactions, though its intellectual roots are different, has a comparable humane base. The deepest cultural damage of the ways of thinking promoted by industrial capitalism has been the isolation of certain activities, mainly economic, from the whole network of activities, interests and relationships within which they are inevitably carried on. A model of the system-dynamic kind has in its turn to abstract measurable activities, with observable effects on the political and cultural uses of the results. But its basic long-term selection, of the factors of population, food, capital, industrial production, mineral resources, and pollution and other 'by-products', takes us a very long way into the core of the existing dominant social order.

Some of the problems of such modelling and forecasting are strictly technical and professional; I can offer no useful opinion on them. But I have noticed in a much more accessible area how the central purpose of such a model has been either misunderstood or wilfully set aside. Thus it has been a common response to take, say, the projections on available mineral resources, to refute them in general or in detail by other estimates, or to update them by reference to new and probable discoveries, and then to suppose that the analysis itself has been refuted. A surprising number of otherwise well-informed people suppose that the systematic crisis has gone away because new oilfields have been discovered, or new energy sources, or new anti-pollution technologies, or simply because the economic depression since 1973 has reduced all the pressures. This is merely foolish. Every quantity and date in *The Limits to Growth* could be amended and yet the radical questions it poses would stand. Solving any one or two of the specific problems, on their own, is no kind of answer, because such 'solutions' necessarily exclude the certain or probable costs and effects of the localised solution within the system as a whole. Yet it has been by the loose recommendation of partial solutions, or by a silly reliance on 'something quite new turning up' (something new will almost certainly turn up, in many of these areas, but it has then to be shown that the new element will alter the *system* rather than merely the sector), that the urgency of the questions has been drained from current politics.

The five main propositions of *The Limits to Growth* seem to me to stand:

  (i)   that exponential growth is an inherent property of existing population and capital systems;

 (ii)   that there are unsurpassable physical limits to population and capital growth;

(iii)   that there are long delays in the feedback processes which are supposed to control the physical growth of the world system;

(iv)   that there are two possible responses to these limits to growth: either to reduce and redirect the exponential forces, or to act to reduce their symptoms, as a way of avoiding facing the question of limits;

 (v)   that the 'equilibrium state' – a self-renewable, self-controlling but also internally variable economic order – may be a desirable option, wherever the limits to growth may be.

What then follows, in detailed assessment of the interlocking problems, and in the necessary construction of alternative general policies, remains entirely open. But it is this framework of thinking which is bound, in my view, to govern all serious analysis of our material and therefore our political and social futures.

It is especially interesting, from a base in cultural analysis, to look at the problem of feedback. Within system-dynamics analysis, it is obvious that certain feedback processes are inherently subject to delay: high rates of growth in population are, by the time they can be measured, naturally subject to continuing high rates, for at least a generation; damaging pollution may only be identified when it has worked a certain way through the system, and may then be at least locally irreversible. But these, determined within the rationality of system dynamics, are not the only problems of feedback. It is very serious if necessary signals are late or too late in appearing. It is even more serious that within particular kinds of culture even the signals that appear may be not simply neglected but positively overridden.

What kind of culture is it, when some serious analysis appears and is almost at once placed as another instalment of 'doom and gloom'? What kind of culture is it which pushes distraction, in its ordinary selection even of news, to the point where there is hardly any sustained discussion of the central and interlocking issues of human survival? There are times, in the depth of the current crisis, when the image materialises of a cluttered room in which somebody is trying to think, while there is a fan-dance going on in one corner and a military band blasting away in the other. It is not the ordinary enjoyments of life that are diverting serious concern, as at times, in a natural human rhythm, they must and should. It is a systematic cacophony which may indeed not be bright enough to know that it is jamming and drowning the important signals, but which is nevertheless, and so far successfully, doing just that.

6

People don't want to hear bad news. But the kinds of analysis and proposal that are now being developed are in fact good news. It isn't the reality of major crisis that comes as a surprise to anyone, and its merely spectacular presentation, for the hundredth time, might persuade anyone to switch off. What is different in some of the new kinds of thinking is that, having sought to assess the full nature and depth of the interlocking problems, they begin also to offer ways of bringing them under control, by the development of specific kinds of information and intelligence. It is this development which is now being jammed.

The central need of the years towards 2000 is the discovery of adequate social and political agencies through which this urgent development can become generally available. Yet this is only one way of seeing the problem. What has also to be considered, and reconsidered, is the quality of the new information and intelligence, and of the kinds of connection they offer to our actual and usually crowded thinking. It is a question, that is to say, of how far any of us have got the analysis and therefore the signals right.

In 1959 I wrote an essay on Britain in the sixties, as the third part of my book *The Long Revolution*. The dates indicate the character of the essay: an assessment on the threshold of a new period. In our ordinary reckoning of time, that date and period are as far away from us as the date 2000 and the new millennium. Yet in another kind of reckoning there is no comparison. We so quickly absorb what has happened, as if it were some kind of datum, that simple numbering of the years loses much of its significance. The relatively few years that separate us from a new millennium are in this sense a vast unknown.

Yet there is then one interesting possibility. The prospective analysis can be looked at again, from a point on the far side of the period it was offering to interpret. This is not some process of checking predictions, since the essay was not of that kind. It was an attempt, through actual analysis, to interpret the underlying problems, forces and ideas, and to indicate some possible ways through them. Looking now at a new actual period, which in its real development has followed from that time, it should be possible not only to reconsider the analysis, to see how far it was adequate, but also to share some sense of how this kind of work can be done and be improved. It is quite common to let such work fade away, or silently adjust it to subsequent experience. But the point is not self-justification or some expedient amendment. It is to test and if possible improve the analysis from this position of special advantage: that a prospective analysis is on the record and that we can review and learn from it in the necessary work of a new prospective analysis. It is a matter of the content, but it is also a matter of the form.

What I propose is to reprint, as Part Two, the main sections of that essay and to use them as a starting point for an analysis towards 2000.

I shall take its four main themes and reconsider and rework them, in chapters on industrial and 'post-industrial' society; on contemporary and possible forms of democracy; on culture and its institutions and technologies; and on the relations between class and politics and their effects on the ideas and institutions of socialism. These chapters will form Part Three.

Part Four will enter new ground. The pivotal essay is on 'the culture of nations': in part a conscious revision of the perspective of the 1959 essay, in part a challenge to the controlling 'national' forms through which most of us still try to think. Much of the original essay is still relevant to the kind of society then being formed and still active in Britain. Moreover its main themes were always relevant to other societies in comparable stages of development. Yet while it was still just possible, at that time, to look at Britain in a relatively isolated if also representative way, it was clear soon after the essay was written that any such 'national' perspective is too narrow, even for the understanding of the nation concerned, and that this kind of narrowness has come to be a major component of the problems. Still in the eighties, in most orthodox writing and politics, that kind of isolating perspective is maintained. It is now very damaging, both to analysis and to politics. Yet it cannot be corrected by any simple move from 'national' to 'international' forms. That is why I follow the chapter on the culture of nations with an analysis of the orthodox international forms – East–West and North–South – which reproduce this perspective in a wider area. I try to offer an analysis which can take us beyond both the national and the international forms, in their ordinary currency. This connects with a third chapter: an analysis of the ways in which we think about the problems that now most often seem to stand between us and the possibility of 2000; problems of war and peace and disarmament.

Thus there is a sequence from the original analysis to its direct reconsideration and then its radical extension and revision. When I was writing in 1959 it was against the grain of what were then the dominant assumptions: the 'affluence' of the late fifties, with its assumption that the central economic problems of modern industrial societies had been solved; the related assumptions of 'the end of ideology' and of a new 'classlessness'; the consequent revision and dilution of ideas of socialism. My challenges to those assumptions or abandonments stand, in what is now a much less confident and much more unexpected world. Yet not much is to be learned if this is simply redirected into the kind of analysis of the 'decline of Britain' which became familiar soon after the original essay. The facts of such a decline are now obvious, but there are both old and new assumptions to challenge, still against the grain.

In much of this book I take my examples from Britain, and I am sometimes arguing close up to its specific circumstances. But the point, throughout, is to move on from these to much more general situations, in the crises of all industrial societies and of the world economy and politics. There are shifts of gear, in most of the essays, from closely analysed British situations to more general situations and the ideas necessary to interpret them. Wherever possible these shifts are noted, but it is worth emphasising at the outset that this is the character of the book.

My main hope is that there can be some sharing of this process of consideration, reconsideration and revision of outlook. This could be important beyond the book itself. I conclude it with an essay on 'Resources for a Journey of Hope': an examining but also a deliberately encouraging argument. From what began in 1959, as an idea of the long revolution, there is an intended and hopeful movement towards 2000.

II

THE 'LONG REVOLUTION' ANALYSIS

BRITAIN IN THE SIXTIES

(from The Long Revolution*)*

I

As we enter the 1960s, the effective historical patterns of British
society seem reasonably clear. The industrial revolution, in an
important technical phase, is continuing. The cultural expansion,
again with new technical developments, also continues. In the
democratic revolution, Britain has recently been mainly in a defensive position, as the colonial peoples move to emancipation. At
home it is generally assumed that the democratic process has been
essentially completed, with parliamentary and local government
solidly established on universal suffrage, and with the class system
apparently breaking up. Britain seems, from these patterns, a country with a fairly obvious future: industrially advanced, securely
democratic, and with a steadily rising general level of education and
culture.

There is substantial truth in this reading. It is not only the general
consensus, but most attempts to challenge it seem unreasonable;
even powerful local criticisms do not fundamentally disturb the sense
of steady and general advance. Yet in deeper ways, that have perhaps
not yet been articulated, this idea of a good society naturally
unfolding itself may be exceptionally misleading. It is perhaps an
intuitive sense of this that has given such emotional force to the total
denunciations, the sweeping rejections, so characteristic of recent
years, for even when these can be shown to be based on selective
evidence and particular minority tensions, the experience they attest
is still not easily set aside.

It seems to me that the first difficulty lies in the common habit of supposing our society to be governed by single patterns, arrived at by averaging the overall trends in familiar categories of economic activity, political behaviour and cultural development. As I see the situation, we need quite different forms of analysis, which would enable us to recognise the important contradictions within each of the patterns described, and, even more crucially, the contradictions between different parts of the general process of change. It is not only that the analysis should be more flexible, but that new categories and descriptions are needed, if all the facts are to be recognised. In particular fields we have made some progress with these, but in our most general descriptions we are all still visibly fumbling, leaving an uncertainty easily exploited by the blandest versions of a natural and healthy evolution, and certainly not redeemed by such general nostrums as the fight for socialism, which remains, after all, in terms of this country, almost wholly undefined.

We have to observe, for example, that the ordinary optimism about Britain's economic future can be reasonably seen as simple complacency. It is very far from certain that on present evidence and given likely developments the directions and rate of growth of the economy guarantee us, over say fifty years, a steadily rising standard of living in this economically exposed and crowded island. Both the rapid rate of economic growth elsewhere, and the certainty of steady industrialisation of many areas now undeveloped, seem ominous signs for a country so dependent on trade and in fact given its prosperity by its early industrial start (now being rapidly overtaken) and by its Empire (now either disappearing or changing its character). Long-term thinking of this kind is in fact beginning, but the gap between thinking and vigorous action to implement it seems no ordinary inertia, but the consequence of habits which, in other parts of our life, seem satisfactory and even admirable. The deep revulsion against general planning, which makes sense again and again in many details of our economic activity, may be really disabling in this long run. And this revulsion is itself in part a consequence of one aspect of the democratic revolution – the determination not to be regimented. Here is a substantial contradiction that I think now runs very deep. The very strong case for general planning, not simply to avoid waste but to promote essential development, research and reorganisation, is practically nullified by a wholly creditable emotion: that we reject the idea of this kind of economic system controlling our lives. True, we are controlled now and will continue to be controlled by a quite different system, with its own denials and rigidities, but in the first place this is very much harder to identify, and secondly, by its very structure and ideology, it appears to offer, and in just enough places does offer, the feeling of freedom. It seems unlikely that the case for general planning will ever be widely accepted until not only do its forms seem sensible, but also its methods seem compatible with just this feeling of freedom. Democratic planning is an easy phrase, but nobody really knows how it would work, and the spectacular successes of economic planning elsewhere have after all not co-existed with any general democracy. This is the severe damage of the contradiction, because it is then easy to suppose that we have found good reasons for not planning, when in fact the need remains urgent and the problems will not disappear because on balance we find them too difficult to solve.

It remains very difficult, in fact, to think about our general economic activity at all. Both its successes and its failures remain obstinately local, and to this kind of description (particular successes announced by their makers, particular failures not announced until they erupt in crisis) the only ordinary alternative is an almost useless measurement of total production, as if some single thing were being produced. Economists have done a good deal to make these questions significant, but in ordinary thinking it is either this success and that failure, or this misleadingly simple general graph. We can only think in real terms if we know what real things are being produced, and ask relevant questions about need and quality. Some part of the production may be truly unnecessary, but the more likely situation is that the balance between various kinds of production will be wrong or even absurd. The usual answer to this kind of question is a particular description, the market, which supposedly regulates questions of need and quality. 'It is needed because it is bought; if it were not bought, it would not be made'. Of course this leaves out one major consideration: whether need and ability to buy are matched. But in any case the description is crude, because it leaves out too much. To match the block figure of production, we are offered another block figure, the consumer. The popularity of 'consumer' as a contemporary term deserves some attention. It is significant because, first, it unconsciously expresses a really very odd and partial version of the purpose of economic activity (the image is drawn from the furnace or the stomach, yet how many things there are we neither eat nor burn), and, second, it materialises as an individual figure (perhaps monstrous in size but individual in behaviour) – the person with needs which he goes to the market to supply.

Why 'consumer', to take the first point? We have to go back to the idea of a market, to get this clear. A market is an obviously sensible place where certain necessary goods are made available, but the image of the place lingers when the process of supply and demand has in fact been transformed. We used to go to markets and shops as customers; why are we regarded now as consumers? The radical change is that increasingly, in the development of large scale 'industrial' production, it is necessary to plan ahead and to know the market demand. What we now call market research was intended as a reasonable provision for this: demand is discovered so that production can be organised. But in fact, since production is not generally planned, but the result of the decisions of many competing firms, market research has inevitably become involved with advertising, which has itself changed from the process of notifying a given supply to a system of stimulating and directing demand. Sometimes this stimulation is towards this version of a product rather than that (*Mountain Brand is Best*), but frequently it is stimulation of a new demand (*You Need Pocket Radio*) or revival of a flagging demand (*Drinka Pinta Milka Day*). In these changing circumstances, the simple idea of a market has gone: the huckster stands level with the supplier. It is then clear why 'consumer', as a description, is so popular, for while a large part of our economic activity is obviously devoted to supplying known needs, a considerable and increasing part of it goes to ensuring that we consume what industry finds it convenient to produce. As this tendency strengthens, it becomes increasingly obvious that society is not controlling its economic life, but is in part being controlled by it. The weakening of purposive social thinking is a direct consequence of this powerful experience, which seeks to reduce human activity to predictable patterns of demand. If we were not consumers, but users, we might look at society very differently, for the concept of use involves general human judgements – we need to know how to use things and what we are using them for, and also the effects of particular uses on our general life – whereas consumption, with its crude hand-to-mouth patterns, tends to cancel these questions, replacing them by the stimulated and controlled absorption of the products of an external and autonomous system. We have not gone all the way with this new tendency, and are still in a position to reverse it, but its persuasive patterns have much of the power of our society behind them.

An equally important effect of the 'consumer' description is that, in materialising an individual figure, it prevents us thinking adequately about the true range of uses of our economic activity. There are many things, of major importance, which we do not use or consume individually, in the ordinary sense, but socially. It is a poor way of life in which we cannot think of social use as one criterion of our economic activity, yet it is towards this that we are being pushed by the 'consumer' emphasis, by the supposed laws of the market, and by the system of production and distribution from which these derive. It is beginning to be widely recognised that a serious state of unbalance between provision for social and individual needs now exists and seems likely to increase. It is easy to get a sense of plenty from the shop windows of contemporary Britain, but if we look at the schools, the hospitals, the roads, the libraries, we find chronic shortages far too often. Even when things are factually connected, in direct daily experience, as in the spectacular example of the flood of new cars and the ludicrous inadequacy of our road system, the spell of this divided thinking seems too powerful to break. Crises of this kind seem certain to dominate our economy in the years ahead, for even when late, very late, we begin thinking about the social consequences of our individual patterns of use, to say nothing about social purposes in their own right, we seem to find it very difficult to think about social provision in a genuinely social way. Thus we think of our individual patterns of use in the favourable terms of spending and satisfaction, but of our social patterns of use in the unfavourable terms of deprivation and taxation. It seems a fundamental defect of our society that social purposes are largely financed out of individual incomes, by a method of rates and taxes which makes it very easy for us to feel that society is a thing that continually deprives and limits us – without this sytem we could all be profitably spending. Who has not heard that impassioned cry of the modern barricade: *but it's my money you're spending on all this; leave my money alone?* And it doesn't help much to point out that hardly any of us could get any money, or even live for more than a few days, except in terms of a highly organised social system which we too easily take for granted. I remember a miner saying to me, of someone we were discussing: 'He's the sort of man who gets up in the morning and presses a switch and expects the light to come on'. We are all, to some extent, in this position, in that our modes of thinking habitually suppress large areas of our real relationships, including our real dependences on others. We think of my money, my light, in these naïve terms, because parts of our very idea of society are withered at root. We can hardly have any conception, in our present system, of the financing of social purposes from the social product, a method which would continually show us, in real terms, what our society is and does. In a society whose products depend almost entirely on intricate and continuous co-operation and social organisation, we expect to consume as if we were isolated individuals, making our own way. We are then forced into stupid comparison of individual consumption and social taxation – one desirable and to be extended, the other regrettably necessary and to be limited. From this kind of thinking the physical unbalance follows inevitably.

Unless we achieve some realistic sense of community, our true standard of living will continue to be distorted. As it is, to think about economic activity in the limited terms of the consumer and the market actually disguises what many of us are doing, and how the pattern of economic life is in any case changing. Even now, one person in four of the working population is engaged neither in production nor in distribution, but in public administration and various forms of general service. For a long time this proportion has been steadily rising, and it seems certain that it will continue to rise. Yet it is a kind of economic activity which cannot be explained, though it may be distorted, by such descriptions as the consumer and the market. A further one in thirteen work in transport, and it is significant that the ordinary argument about our transport systems, especially the railways, is unusually difficult and confused, as the problem of finding any criterion more adequate than consumption, any method of accounting more realistic than direct profit and loss in the market, inevitably shows through. As for administration and general services, from medicine and education to art, sport, and entertainment, the argument is almost hopelessly confused. The product of this kind of work, which one in four of us give our time to, is almost wholly in terms of life and experience, as opposed to things. What kind of accounting is adequate here, for who can measure the value of a life and an experience? Some parts of the process can be reduced to more familiar terms: medicine saves working days, education produces working skills, sport creates fitness, entertainment keeps up morale. But we all know that every one of these services is directed, in the end, to larger purposes: doctors work just as hard to save the life of a man past working age; every school teaches more than direct working skills, and so on. To impose an accounting in market terms is not only silly but in the end impossible: many of the results of such effort are not only long-term and indirect, but in any case have no discoverable exchange value. The most enlightened ordinary reaction is to put these activities into a margin called 'life' or 'leisure', which will be determined as to size by the shape of 'ordinary' economic activity. On the other hand, if we started not from the market but from the needs of persons, not only could we understand this part of our working activity more clearly, but also we should have a means of judging the 'ordinary' economic activity itself. Questions not only of balance in the distribution of effort and resources, but also of the effects of certain kinds of work both on users and producers, might then be adequately negotiated. The danger now, as has been widely if obscurely recognised, is of fitting human beings to a system, rather than a system to human beings. The obscurity shows itself in wrong identification of the causes of this error: criticism of industrial production, for example, when in fact we should starve without it; criticism of large-scale organisation, when in fact this extension of communication is the substance of much of our growth; criticism, finally, of the pressures of society, when in fact it is precisely the lack of an adequate sense of society that is crippling us.

For my own part I am certain, as I review the evidence, that it is capitalism – a particular and temporary system of organising the industrial process – which is in fact confusing us. Capitalism's version of society can only be the market, for its purpose is profit in particular activities rather than any general conception of social use, and its concentration of ownership in sections of the community makes most common decisions, beyond those of the market, limited or impossible. Many industrial jobs, as now organised, are boring or frustrating, but the system of wage-labour, inherent in capitalism, necessarily tends to the reduction of the meaning of work to its wages alone. It is interesting that the main unrest of our society – the running battle which compromises any picture of a mainly contented and united country – is in this field of wages. Whenever there is an important strike, or threat of a strike, we tend to react by defining a different conception of work – service to the community, responsibility to others, pulling together. The reaction is quite right: work ought to mean these things. But it is hypocritical to pretend that it now does, all the way through. While the light comes on when we press the switch, we take for granted just these qualities, but ordinarily fail to acknowledge, with any depth, the needs of the man who made the light possible. If we want to stop strikes, we have to carry the reaction right through, for this system of bargaining for labour necessarily includes, as a last resort, as in all other bargaining, the seller's refusal of his labour at the price offered. Strikes are an integral part of the market society, and if you want the advantages you must take the disadvantages, even to the point of dislocation and chaos. While we still talk of a labour market, as despite long protest many of us continue to do, we must expect the behaviour appropriate to it, and not try to smuggle in, when it becomes inconvenient, the quite different conception of common interest and responsibility. The moral disapproval of strikers is shallow and stupid while the system of work is based on the very grounds of particular profit which we there condemn.

What is happening to capitalism in contemporary Britain? We are told that it is changing, but while this is obviously true it can be argued that the patterns of thinking and behaviour it promotes have never been more strong. To the reduction of use to consumption, already discussed, we must add the widespread extension of the 'selling' ethic – what sells goes, and to sell a thing is to validate it – and also, I think, the visible moral decline of the labour movement. Both politically and industrially, some sections of the labour movement have gone over, almost completely, to ways of thinking which they still formally oppose. The main challenge to capitalism was socialism, but this has almost wholly lost any contemporary meaning, and it is not surprising that many people now see in the Labour Party merely an alternative power-group, and in the trade-union movement merely a set of men playing the market in very much the terms of the employers they oppose. Any such development is generally damaging, for the society is unlikely to be able to grow significantly if it has no real alternative patterns as the ground of choice. I remember that I surprised many people, in *Culture and Society*, by claiming that the institutions of the Labour movement – the trade unions, the co-operatives, the Labour Party – were a great creative achievement of the working people and also the right basis for the whole organisation of any good society of the future. Am I now withdrawing this claim, in speaking of moral decline? The point is, as I see it, that my claim rested on the new social patterns these institutions offered. I recognise that the motives for their foundation, and consequently their practice, must be seen as mixed. Sectional defence and sectional self-interest undoubtedly played their part. But also there was this steady offering and discovery of ways of living that could be extended to the whole society, which could quite reasonably be organised on a basis of collective democratic institutions and the substitution of co-operative equality for competition as the principle of social and economic policy. In the actual history, there has been a steady pressure, from the existing organization of society, to convert these institutions to aims and patterns which would not offer this kind of challenge. The co-operatives should be simply trading organisations, the trade unions simply industrial organisations with no other interests, each union keeping to its own sphere, and the Labour Party simply an alternative government in the present system – the country needs an effective opposition. This pressure could not have been as successful as it has if just these aims had not been part of the original impetus of the institutions: certain elements in their patterns have been encouraged, certain elements steadily opposed and weakened. And in every case, of course, to accept the proposed limitation of aims may lead to important short-run gains in practical efficiency; the men within these institutions who accept the limitation often make more immediate sense. But it is quite clear, as we enter the 1960s, that the point has been reached when each of these institutions is discovering that the place in existing society proposed for it, if it agrees to limit its aims, is essentially subordinate: the wide challenge has been drained out, and what is left can be absorbed within existing terms. For many reasons this has sapped the morale of the institutions, but also, fortunately, led to crisis and argument within them. The choice as it presents itself is between qualified acceptance in a subordinate capacity or the renewal of an apparently hopeless challenge. The practical benefits of the former have to be balanced against the profound loss of inspiration in the absence of the latter. If I seem eccentric in continuing to look to these institutions for effective alternative patterns, while seeing all too clearly their present limitations, I can only repeat that they can go either way, and that their crisis is not yet permanently resolved.

The situation is complicated by the fact that real changes have occurred in the society, through the pressure of these institutions aided by reforming elements within the existing patterns. The extension of social services, including education, is an undoubted gain of this kind, which must not be underestimated by those who have simply inherited it. But it remains true not only that the social services are limited to operation in the interstices of a private-ownership society, but also that in their actual operation they remain limited by assumptions and regulations belonging not to the new society but the old. The other substantial change, the nationalisation of certain industries and services, has been even more deeply compromised. The old and valuable principle, of production for use and not for profit, has been fought to a standstill in just this field. The systems taken into public ownership were in fact those old systems no longer attractive in profit terms (coal, railways), new systems requiring heavy initial investment (airways) and systems formerly municipally or publicly developed (gas, electricity). Some of these systems have been much more successful than is generally allowed, but it remains true, first, that they have not only failed to alter the 'profit before use' emphasis in the general economy but have also been steadily themselves reduced to this old criterion; and, second, that they have reproduced, sometimes with appalling accuracy, the human patterns, in management and working relationships, of industries based on quite different social principles. The multiplication of such effects is indeed uninviting, and the easy identification of these institutions, as types of the supposed new society, has added to the general confusion. In being dragged back to the processes of the old system, yet at the same time offered as witnesses of the new, they have so deeply damaged any alternative principle in the economy as to have emptied British socialism of any effective meaning. The proposal to admit this formal vacuity, by detaching the Labour Party from any full commitment to socialism, then makes sense of a kind, the practical acknowledgement of an existing situation, until perhaps one remembers that the containment and eventual cancellation of any real challenge to capitalist society has been, for more than a century, the work of capitalist society itself.

These are major gains in capitalist ways of thinking, and it is easy to be overwhelmed by them. Meanwhile capitalism can point to its successes in expanding consumption, and to its extension of a huge system of consumer credit which, on its own terms, creates one kind of prosperity. With only the consumer in mind, as a point of economic reference, this is not easily challenged. Again, taking the point about restriction of ownership, capitalism has sought to extend ownership by promoting a wider holding of shares. This reply is characteristic, in that it misses the point of the criticism, and proposes reform in terms of the system criticised. The objection was only in part to restricted individual ownership (which in any case still holds); it was mainly to no social ownership. The extension of shareholding to about one in fifteen adults enables more of us to make money as a by-product of the system of satisfying our general needs (money made, in fact, out of the work of the other fourteen) but it does nothing to ensure that the needs are general or that the distribution of energy and resources is right in common terms. The latest device, of some limited control of this distribution by channelling public money into privately-owned systems, is only a further example of the way in which the very aspirations of the original challenge to capitalism are used as a means of strengthening it. Finally, capitalism (and its ex-socialist apologists) emphasises the decline in control by shareholders (an ironic comment, of course, on the extension of shares, which is then not a new kind of ownership but simply an extension of playing the market), and the rise in importance of the managers and technicians. In fact the economy, while not controlled by ordinary shareholders, is not controlled by managers and technicians either, but by powerful interlocking private institutions that in fact command what some Labour politicians still wistfully call 'the commanding heights of the economy'. Even if the managerial revolution had occurred (and the real revolution is the passing of power to financial institutions and self-financing corporations) the original challenge would still be lost, for the direction of our common economic life would have been reduced to a series of technical decisions, without anything more than a market reference to the kind of society the economy should sustain.

The central point, in this contentious field, is that the concepts of the organised market and the consumer now determine our economic life, and with it much of the rest of our society, and that challenges to them have been so effectively confused that hardly any principled opposition remains, only the perpetual haggling and bitterness of the wage claim and the strike. It is difficult to believe that we shall remain satisfied by this situation, which is continually setting us against each other and very rapidly promoting patterns of crude economic cynicism, yet to which no clear and practical alternative exists. The challenge to create new meanings, and to substantiate them, will have to be met if that apparently obvious future is in fact to be realised.

2

The progress of democracy in Britain is deeply affected by what is happening in the economy, but also by other factors. The aspiration to control the general directions of our economic life is an essential element of democratic growth, but is still very far from being realised. Beyond this general control lies a further aspiration, now equally distant and confused. It is difficult to feel that we are really governing ourselves if in so central a part of our living as our work most of us have no share in decisions that immediately affect us. The difficulties of a procedural kind in ensuring this share are indeed severe, and because of the variety of institutions in which we work there is no single answer. Yet if the impulse is there, some ways can be found, and steadily improved from experience. I know from my own experience, in helping to work out such ways in my own job, some of the difficulties yet also some of the real gains. From practical experience alone, I agree with Burke that

I have never yet seen any plan which has not been mended by the observations of those who were much inferior in understanding to the person who took the lead in the business.

Even the smallest human group produces leaders, though not always the same leaders for all projects. The difficulty lies in interpreting just what this leadership means. The majority patterns of our society, especially in work, offer an interpretation which not only fixes leaders, for all sorts of circumstances, but encourages them to believe that it is not only their right but their duty to make independent decisions and to be resolute in carrying them out. After all, a dog doesn't keep a man and then take the lead himself.

There are still many natural autocrats in our society, and the trouble they cause is beyond reckoning. More dangerous, perhaps, because less easily identified, are those skilled in what was called in the army 'man management'. The point here, as I remember, is that of course you have to command, but since a leader has to be followed he must be diligently attentive to the state of mind of those he is leading: must try to understand them, talk to them about their problems (not about his own, by the way), get a picture of their state of mind. Then, having taken these soundings, having really got the feel of his people, he will point the way forward.

I know few greater social pleasures, in contemporary Britain, than that of watching man-management, for indeed its practitioners are almost everywhere. It is true that they are usually very bad at it, although they invariably think themselves very good. The calmly appraising eyes (narrowed about an eighth of an inch; more would look suspicious), the gentle silences, the engaging process of drawing the man out: although I have watched these so often, I find them better than most plays. And these are the heroes of our public life, with a solid weight of mutual admiration behind them. An exceptionally large part of what passes for political commentary is now a public discussion of a party leader's command of this skill: how will the Prime Minister or the Leader of the Opposition 'handle' this or that 'awkward element'; how will he time his own intervention; if he says this, how can he avoid saying that? The really funny thing about this kind of commentary is that it is public; printed and distributed in millions of sheets; read by almost everybody, including the 'awkward elements'. The delicate art has become public myth, and it is rare to see it challenged. This, evidently, is what democratic leadership is supposed to be.

In fact, of course, it is the tactic of a defensive autocracy (and people do not have to be born into an autocracy to acquire its habits). The true process of democratic decision is that, with all the facts made available, the question is openly discussed and its resolution openly arrived at, either by simple majority vote or by a series of voluntary changes to arrive at a consensus. The skills of the good listener and the clarifier are indeed exceptionally necessary in such a process, but these are crucially different from the stance of the leader who is merely listening to the discussion to discover the terms in which he can get his own way. The intricate devices worked out by democratic organisations, to ensure the full record of facts, the freedom of general contribution, the true openness of decision, and the opportunity to review the ways in which decisions are executed, are indeed invaluable (some people thought I was joking when I mentioned committee procedure as part of our cultural heritage, but the joke is on them, if they are serious about democracy, for these are the means of its working). Yet just because they are intricate, they are easily abused by the man-managers: one even hears boasts about the ways in which this or that committee has been 'handled'. I would only say that I have never seen such handling, reputedly practised as a way of 'avoiding trouble', lead to anything but trouble. For once men are reasonably free, they will in the end assert their interests, and if these have not been truly involved in the decision (as opposed to collected and 'borne in mind') the real situation will eventually assert itself, often with a bitterness that shows how bad the man-managers really are. Our main trouble now is that we have many of the forms of democracy, but find these continually confused by the tactics of those who do not really believe in it, who are genuinely afraid of common decisions openly arrived at, and who have unfortunately partly succeeded in weakening the patterns of feeling of democracy which alone could substantiate the institutions.

We must add a note on the tones of contemporary discussion, if this situation is to be fully understood. Most people who pass through universities learn certain conventions of discussion which pass into the public process. The most important of these is a habit of tentative statement, characteristically introduced by such phrases as 'I should have thought that' or 'I don't know but it seems to me'. This manner is sometimes merely superficial, but elsewhere, for certain kinds of discussion, the conventions have their advantages. These can most easily be seen by contrast with the conventions of argument of many wage-earners (particularly manual workers, but not always trade union officers, who have sometimes learned tortuousness to a really amazing proficiency). At first, the bluntness of statement and assertion is refreshing after too long a course of 'I should have thought'. But one notices how easily, in such discussions, points of view become involved with the personal prestige of the speaker; the opinion cannot be attacked without attacking him as a man, and he cannot modify it without what looks like climbing down. I have listened in despair to many arguments of this kind, where in the end it would really be easier to adjourn and fight it out in the yard, all the signs of physical aggression and challenge being already more evident than the issues – except, of course, that tomorrow the discussion would only have to begin again. The value of the convention of tentative statement is that opinion can be reasonably detached from the personal prestige of the speaker, in a way that is ultimately necessary if a common opinion is to be arrived at. The frank speaking of the Labour movement has been, on balance, a great gain: the issues are forced into the open, away from the man-managers and the cupboarded autocrats. But at the same time the workings of democracy have been severely damaged by habits of aggressive assertion (personified in many a roaring old man at the rostrum) which must be seen quite clearly as pre-democratic: the language of unequals, shouting for their place in the world, and sometimes ensuring, by turning a common process into a series of personal demonstrations, that common improvement will not be got.

It is clear, on balance, that we do not get enough practice in the working of democracy, even where its forms exist. Most of us are not expected to be leaders, and are principally instructed, at school and elsewhere, in the values of discipline and loyalty, which are real values only if we share in the decisions to which they refer. Those who are expected to be leaders are mainly trained to the patterns of leadership I have been discussing, centred on the general development of confidence – but in fact that a leader should be self-confident enough to be capable of radical doubt is rarely mentioned and rarely taught. The necessary practice of the difficult processes of common decision and execution is left, on the whole, to hit or miss, and the result, not unexpectedly, is often both. A weakening of belief in the possibility of democracy is then inevitable, and we prefer to lament the 'general indiscipline' (trade-union leaders cannot control their members, party leaders are not firm enough; it is all sloppy discussion, endless talk, and then people behaving unreasonably) rather than nourishing and deepening the process to which in any case, in any probable future, we are committed.

The counterpart of this feeling, reinforced by the actual history of democratic institutions in this country, is an approach to government which in itself severely limits active democracy. A tightly organised party system and parliament seem to have converted the national franchise into the election of a court. As individuals we cast one national vote at intervals of several years, on a range of policies and particular decisions towards which it is virtually impossible to have one single attitude. From this necessarily crude process, a court of ministers emerges (in part drawn from people who have not been elected at all), and it is then very difficult for any of us to feel even the smallest direct share in the government of our affairs. Approaches through the party organisations, taking advantage of the fact that at least there are alternative courts, are more practicable, but not only is it generally true that inner-party democracy is exceptionally difficult in both large parties, it is also the case that the right not to be tied, not to be precisely committed, is increasingly claimed by both sets of leaders. The general influence of public opinion counts for something, since in the long run the court has to be re-elected. But the period is exceptionally long, given the rate and range of development in contemporary politics. In the four and a half years between the elections of 1955 and 1959 several wholly unforeseen major crises developed, and public opinion in fact violently fluctuated, to be met in general only by the bland confidence of the court in its own premises: that the duty of the government is to govern, for the Queen's government must be carried on. It is fair to say that this does not even sound like democracy, and we must be fair to our leaders, conceding them at least consistency, in their obvious assumption that direct popular government is not what democracy is about. It is true that any administration should have reasonable time to develop its policies, but this is not the same thing as the current uncritical belief in the importance of 'strong government': certainly one hopes that a good government will be strong, but a government that is both strong and bad (most people are agreed that we had such governments in the 1930s; I think we have had one or two since) is almost the worst possible public evil. I see no reason why two-year intervals of re-election of at least a substantial part of the House of Commons should not be our immediate objective, since it seems vital for the health of our democracy that more of us should feel directly involved in it. Such a change, coupled with working reforms now being canvassed in Parliament, and with an improvement of the democratic process within the parties, would be a substantial yet reasonable gain. The alternative is not only the rapid extension of man-management, monstrously magnified by the use of modern communications as its general device, but also the unpleasant development of organized pressure-groups, pushing into the anterooms of the court. One further necessary amendment seems to be a fixed date for the periodic elections, for to concede choice of this date to the court itself is psychologically quite wrong: we should not have to wait, within broad limits, for the court to ask our approval; the right of election is not theirs but ours.

These changes in themselves would make only a limited difference, but they would at least go some way towards altering the present atmosphre of British democracy, which seems increasingly formal and impersonal, and powered by little more than the belief that a choice of leaders should be periodically available. The next field of reform is obviously the electoral sytem, which seems designed to perpetuate the existing interpretations. Its most obvious characteristic is that it exaggerates, sometimes grossly, comparatively slight tendencies in opinion. Post-war electoral history suggests a violent fluctuation of opinion, from a very strong Labour to a very strong Conservative government. But actual opinion, reckoned in terms of people, has changed much less. What I notice most about current political commentary is that it is preoccupied by results at the level of the court, rather than by the registered opinion of actual persons; and this, however natural it may be to people who like living in anterooms, is quite undemocratic in spirit. I believe that the process of common decision, even as crudely registered by single occasional votes, must be carried through without distortion into the formal process of government, if we are to have any honest democracy. The weight of conventional thinking by politicians is against this tendency, but such conventional thinking, when it is traced to its sources, is again the tactical wisdom of a defensive autocracy, carried on, through inertia and lack of challenge, into what is claimed to be a very different society. It is difficult, as we look over this whole field, to assent even in passing to the ordinary proposition that the democratic revolution is virtually complete.

At this critical point, the relative absence of democracy in other large areas of our lives is especially relevant. The situation can be held as it is, not only because democracy has been limited at the national level to the process of electing a court, but also because our social organisation elsewhere is continually offering non-democratic patterns of decision. This is the real power of institutions, that they actively teach particular ways of feeling, and it is at once evident that we have not nearly enough institutions which practically teach democracy. The crucial area is in work, where in spite of limited experiments in 'joint consultation', the ordinary decision process is rooted in an exceptionally rigid and finely-scaled hierarchy, to which the only possible ordinary responses, of the great majority of us who are in no position to share in decisions, are apathy, the making of respectful petitions, or revolt. If we see a considerable number of strikes, as the evidence suggests, as revolts in this sense, we can see more clearly the stage of development we have reached. The defensive tactic, once again, is man-management, now more grandly renamed personnel management. This is an advance on simple autocracy, but as an answer to the problems of human relations at work only shows again how weakly the democratic impulse still runs.

It seems obvious that industrial democracy is deeply related to questions of ownership; the argument against the political vote was always that the new people voting, 'the masses', had no stake in the country. The development of new forms of ownership then seemed an essential part of any democratic advance, although in fact the political suffrage eventually broke ahead of this. The idea of public ownership seemed to be a solution, but there is some truth in the argument that little is gained by substituting a series of still largely authoritarian state monopolies for a series of private monopolies (something is gained, however, to the extent that the state is itself democratically directed). It is obvious that in a complex large-scale economy, many central decisions will have to be taken, and that their machinery easily becomes bureaucratic and protected from general control. At this level there can be no doubt that the separate democratic management of industry is unworkable. The true line of advance is making this machinery directly responsible to the elected government, probably through intermediate boards which combine representation of the industry or service with elected political representatives. With this framework set, as for example it is to some extent set in educational administration, the development of direct participation in the local decisions of particular enterprises could be attempted. The difficulties are severe, and there is no single solution. It seems to me that a government which was serious about this would initiate a series of varied experiments, in different kinds of concern, ranging from conventional methods such as the reform of company law, promoting actual and contractual membership, with definite investments and rights in the concern, to methods that would be possible in concerns already publicly owned, in which elected councils, either from a common roll or at first representing interests in an agreed proportion, would have powers of decision within the accepted national framework. It is commonly objected that modern work is too technical to be subjected to the democratic process, but it is significant that in certain fields, notably education and medicine, the necessarily complicated processes of involving members in self-government are already much further advanced than in work where the 'service' criterion is not accepted, though in fact it is claimed. Education and medicine are not less technical or specialised, but they have a less obvious class structure, which is undoubtedly important. The necessary principle is that workers of all kinds, including managers, should be guaranteed the necessary conditions, including both security and freedom, of their actual work, in precise ways that are perfectly compatible with general decisions about the overall direction of the enterprise. Boards of directors elected by shareholders now give such directions, ordinarily with less security and freedom for all kinds of workers, since these are not represented. In publicly owned industries and services, and in reformed companies, the principle of boards elected by the members of the industry or service, to operate within the agreed national framework, is surely not difficult. There would be a long and continuous process of setting-up and improving such machinery, and many serious and largely unforeseen problems would undoubtedly arise. But the basis of the whole argument for democracy is that the substance of these problems would in any case exist, and that participation in the processes of decision leads to more rational and responsible solutions than the old swing between apathy, concession, and revolt.

One other field in which the growth of democracy seems urgently necessary is the ordinary process of decision about the development of our communities. This has been approached, but is still very muddled, and it is unfortunately true that there is even more dissatisfaction, and consequent apathy, about local government than about the national court. Authoritarian patterns at the centre seem to be widely reproduced in our local councils, where much more of the process is in the open and within our ordinary experience, unfortunately in its ordinary course giving far too much evidence of how easily democracy is distorted. Still, the problems here are quite widely understood, and the active struggle against distortion is encouraging. More seriously, behind this struggle is a familiar inertia of old social forms. Housing is an excellent example, because the common provision of homes and estates is so obviously sensible, in principle, and is already extending beyond the mere relief of exceptional need. Why then does such an extension, or further extension, leave many of us quite cold? One answer, certainly, is the way such houses and estates are commonly managed, by supposedly democratic authorities. I have seen letters to tenants from council housing officials that almost made my hair stand on end, and the arbitrary and illiberal regulation of many such estates is justly notorious. While this can still be fairly said even of Labour authorities, it is difficult to feel that the spirit of democracy has been very deeply or widely learned. Why should a public official, often a perfectly pleasant man to meet, transform himself so often into the jack-in-office who has done extraordinary harm to the whole development of social provision? Partly, I suppose, because he sees so many jacks-in-office above him. More generally, I think, because the patterns and tones of leadership and administration are still pre-democratic. The businessman, dealing with customers, has learned to be pleasant; so, usually, has the public official, at that level. But there are public officials who regard such people as council-house tenants as natural inferiors, and they speak and write accordingly. The remedy, of course, is not to teach them man-management, but to try to develop democratic forms within these areas of public provision. Why should the management of a housing estate not be vested in a joint committee of representatives of the elected authority and elected representatives of the people who live on it? While general financial policy obviously rests with the whole community, there is a wide area of decision, on the way the houses are used and maintained, on estate facilities, and on any necessary regulations, which could be negotiated through such channels more amicably and I think more efficiently. If this experiment has been tried, we should know more about it and consider extending it. If it has not been tried, here is an immediate field in which the working of democratic participation could be tested. Labour councils, in particular, ought continually to be thinking in these ways, for there is great danger to the popular movement if its organisations are persistently defensive and negative (as in the ordinary Tenants' Association), and it is Labour which has most to lose if it allows democracy to dwindle to a series of defensive associations and the minimal machinery of a single elected administration. The pressure has been to define democracy as 'the right to vote', 'the right to free speech', and so on, in a pattern of feeling which is really that of the 'liberty of the subject' within an established authority. The pressure now, in a wide area of our social life, should be towards a participating democracy, in which the ways and means of involving people much more closely in the process of self-government can be learned and extended.

3

Behind any description of the patterns of our economy and of our political and social life lie ways of thinking about 'class', which in Britain in the 1960s seem exceptionally uncertain and confused. Here, as a matter of urgency, we must go back from our ordinary meanings to our experience.

I showed in *Culture and Society* that 'class', as a social term, came into ordinary English usage in the period of the effective beginning of the Industrial Revolution. Shaped by this particular history, it had from the first a confused reference, pointing to both social and economic facts in ways characteristic of a period of important transition. This confusion, unfortunately, has remained, and we are still not sure whether the determining factor, in our membership of a social class, is our birth or our adult work. 'Working class' has traditionally described the great body of wage-earners who came together in relation to the new methods of production. In much economic theory, this class is naturally contrasted with the propertied classes: people who own land, or other means of production, and employ wage-labour. Thus, on the one hand the working class could be contrasted with the land-owning aristocracy; on the other hand, and more usually, with the class of capitalists. But then who, socially, were the capitalists, since they were usually not aristocrats? And to what social class did small independent employers, shop-keepers, small farmers, and professional men belong? From these two questions came one answer: the 'middling classes', later settled as the 'middle classes'. But there were obviously very wide vari-ations here, from the large employer to the small shopkeeper, and from the successful professional man to the humble independent craftsman. Eventually, then, the middle class went into 'upper' and 'lower' divisions, but the upper division, as it became richer, was increasingly involved and mingled with the old aristocracy or 'upper' class. And movement between the working class and the lower-middle class was also fairly common, apart from the diffi-culty, as the character of work changed and many wage-earning jobs that were not in the old sense 'manual' were created, of drawing any clear line between the 'workers' and these 'lower-middle-class' wage-earners. These difficulties and complexities are all still with us today, and anyone who is used to either professional or amateur attempts at social classification will know how intricate it has all become. The question we need to ask however – and it is only rarely asked – is what all this classification is for, what actual purposes in the society it serves. Some people look forward to increasing accuracy in classification, and propose new formulas. Others speak of amending the old class descriptions to bring them into line with 'modern experience'. My own position is that we might get rid of most of this classification, and save ourselves much needless trouble, if we looked rigorously at what it is there to do.

Most people in Britain now think of themselves as 'middle class' or 'working class'. But the first point to make is that these are not true alternatives. The alternatives to 'middle' are 'lower' and 'upper'; the alternative to 'working' is 'independent' or 'propertied'. The wonderful muddle we are now in springs mainly from this confu-sion, that one term has a primarily social, the other a primarily economic reference. When people are asked if they belong to the working class many of them agree; when they are asked if they belong to the lower class many less agree. Yet the persistent sugges-tion of 'middle' is that the working class is 'lower', and it is hardly surprising that many wage-earners want to think of themselves as 'middle class' if 'lower' is explicitly or implicitly the alternative description. Again, many 'middle class' people are indignant at the suggestion or implication that they do not work because they do not belong to the 'working classes'. They are quite right to be indignant, but they have only themselves to blame if they have contributed in any way to the confusion between the economic description – the wage-earning 'working classes', and the social implication that these people are the 'lower' class. It seems that we have to ask not only what purposes are served by the classification, but also what purposes are served by so persistent a confusion.

The fact is that we are still in a stage of transition from a social stratification based on birth to one based on money and actual position. The drive towards the latter kind of society is very strong; it is both built into our economic system and continually stimulated by it. But we do not have to look far, in Britain, to find older ways of thinking. The principal function of the otherwise insignificant 'upper' class is to keep distinction by birth and family alive. A simple description of power in Britain might show the irrelevance of this, but there are still, after all, the monarchy, the House of Lords, and a system of honours involving change of family name and status. So far from these systems being regarded as merely the vestiges of an older society, they are now so intensively propagated that their practical effect is still considerable. By their very removal from the harsh and controversial open exercise of power, their social prestige is even enhanced. But why is this so, in a changing society? The intense propaganda of monarchy (by a shrewd mixture of magnificence and ordinariness which in its central incompatibility bears all the signs of functional magic) seems a conscious procedure against radical change. The emphasis on the unity, loyalty and family atmosphere of the Queen's subjects is not easy to reconcile with the facts of British life, but as an ideal, though silly, it catches just enough real desires, and just sufficiently confuses consciousness of real obstacles, to be a powerful reserve of feeling in favour of things as they are. This mellow dusk then spreads over the ancillary power system, still important in many areas of actual decision, in which people chosen by family status and not by the democratic process carry on in a special position, whether in the House of Lords or as chairmen of many official and unofficial but influential committes (a process still curiously known as voluntary public work, in which if the practitioners are discovered to have the common touch the magic is even more potent).

This could hardly have happened if the rising middle class had remained independent, or retained any real confidence in itself. Somewhere in the nineteenth century (though there are earlier signs) the English middle class lost its nerve, socially, and thoroughly compromised with the class it had virtually defeated. Directed personally towards the old system of family status, it adopted as its social ideal a definite class system, blurred at the top but clear below itself. The distinction of public schools from grammar schools led to a series of compromises: in the curriculum, where just enough new subjects were introduced to serve middle-class training, but just enough old subjects kept to preserve the old cultivation of gentlemen; and in social character, where just enough emphasis on the superiority of the whole class was shrewdly mixed with a rigorous training in concepts of authority and service, so that a formal system could be manned and yet not disturbed. The principal difficulty, in preserving this system, was that new middle-class groups kept rising behind those who had made their peace. However closely the grammar schools imitated those few of their number that had been renamed public schools, it was necessary for distances to be kept, and 'grammar school', in some ears, soon sounded like 'soup kitchen'. The principal tension, in recent English social life, has been between the fixed character of the arrived middle class, with its carefully conditioned ways of speaking and behaving, and the later arrivals or those still struggling to arrive. The worst snobberies still come, with an extraordinary self-revealing brashness, from people who, if family were really the social criterion, would be negligible. The compromise takes care of that, for it had included (what the aristocracy was not unwilling to learn) the accolade of respectability on work and especially the making of money by work. This enabled the pattern to be kept mobile, without altering its character. Distinctively, in Britain, the captain of industry provides himself with a family title and status expressing prestige in older terms. And since honours are easy, in the sense that they can be continually created and extended, it has been possible to work out a system whereby the results of individual effort and merit can be confirmed in terms of hereditary values. There is even a very nice grading, quite formalised in the public service, in which the particular point reached in climbing the bourgeois-democratic ladder is magically transformed into a particular feudal grade: a Prime Minister equals an Earl, a Permanent Secretary a Knight and so on. This fundamental class system, with the force of the rising middle class right behind it, requires a 'lower' class if it is to retain any social meaning. The people cast for this lower rôle keep turning round, it is true, and pointing the same finger at those below them. This is the basic unreality of the 'middle-class' in Britain, and also the explanation of its vagueness. I remember sitting with a group of small shopkeepers who were trying to explain to me how you could never trust 'that class of people' (shop assistants): it seemed, in the most colourful phrase, that they always had their fingers in the toffees. The particular climax of this discussion, for me, was a description of the group, by one of its members, as 'tip-top business men'; this went down very well. Here, in fact, was a solid assumption of middle-class membership and distinction by a group of people who if they moved only a little way up this same middle class would at once be placed and despised, much as the shop assistants were placed and despised (they would probably call the waitress 'Miss', which as the normal mode of address to a young unmarried woman by the eighteenth century gentry is of course now obviously 'low'). But so long as a group can find another group to turn round and point at, the contradictions seem hardly to be noticed. All class distinction in Britain is downward, under the mellow dusk from the very top. And it seems very doubtful if it will simply wither away, for the confusion noted earlier, between social and economic description, has, as explained, been built into the system. The drive for money, power and position, which might have created the separate ideal of self-made prestige, has been neatly directed into the older system, at a cost in confusion which we are all still paying.

In this respect, I belong to the awkward squad who have been discussed a good deal since the war. Many people have told us that the reason for our interest in class is that we are frustrated to find that educational mobility is not quite social mobility; that however far we have gone we still find an older system above us. This is a very revealing account of the class-feeling of someone born just too far down in the middle class but still accepting its ethos. That sense of differential mobility is just the confusion that many middle-class groups encounter, if they are thinking in their own class terms. I can only say for myself that I have never felt my own mobility in terms of a 'rise in the social scale', and certainly I have never felt that I wanted to go on climbing, resentful of old barriers in my way: where else is there to go, but into my own life? At the same time, the particular history of going from a wage-earning family to one of the old universities takes one on a very rapid traverse of this same social scale, which seems largely to survive with the confusions it now has because really, when it comes to it, movement along it is normally quite limited, and the divisions are quite carefully kept. It is then less the injustice of the British class system than its stupidity that really strikes one. People like to be respected, but this natural desire is now principally achieved by a system which defines respect in terms of despising someone else, and then in turn being inevitably despised. In my own traverse, I have seen so much of this, aware of the standards of one group while watching another, in a truly endless series, that I should have to be very odd indeed to be bitter: the predominant feeling is of pathos. The more widely this is experienced the better; we might even get back our nerve. But then we cannot stop at this stage of the analysis; we have still to look at what the system is for, in the actual running of our kind of society.

In part, as noted, it is for respect, though in making this respect differential it is often self-defeating. Still, as we move around in our own country, the operation of differential respect is evident enough to tempt some people into accepting the scale so long as they can improve their own position on it. Anyone who wants to experience the reality of the differential has only to put himself, physically, at a point on the scale other than that he is used to, changing some of the signals by which the ordinary exchange is operated, and he will feel the difference quickly enough. Let any middle-class man who thinks class distinction has died out put aside, if only for a day, his usual clothes, his car, his accent, and go to places where he is not known but where he knows how he would be normally received: he will learn the reality quickly enough. Let him go in the working clothes of a manual worker, but with his 'standard' accent, to a shop, an office, a pub, and watch the confusion as the contradictory signals are sorted out. In daily experience this complicated differential goes on, but we have to cross the borders to appreciate it fully, for we normally get used to the rate of respect our evident market value commands. Is this differential anything to worry about, though, in its patent hypocrisy? Not personally, of course, but it would be a change to have a community in which men and women were valued either as real individuals or, where that closeness is impossible, by a common general respect.

There are many signs that money, in the form of conspicuous possession of a range of objects of prestige, is rapidly driving out other forms of class distinction, and it is this change which is behind the argument that class distinction is diminishing. This is a simple confusion of meanings, for it is the reality of differential treatment, rather than the particular forms through which it operates, that makes a class system. The point is particularly important in that the money we earn, to set the differential system going, is itself subject to built-in differentials of an especially complicated kind. The differential for extra skill and extra responsibility is part of this system, but only part, and all arguments about pay become hopelessly confused if this basis of differential is assumed to be the only one generally operative. There is the first obvious fact that a radical differential is imposed by the general financial position of the industry or service in which a man is working. The teacher and the engine-driver start on different total scales, in services where money is short, from the copywriter or the car-assembly worker, where money is easier. And if standing in the community is increasingly assessed in straight money terms, this situation is a very serious distortion from the outset. The next radical differential is more closely tied to class. Most of us live by selling our labour, but in some cases the pay is called salary, in other cases a wage. In practice this is much more than a verbal difference: we hear of wage demands from one kind of man, but of requests for a review of remuneration from another. Public indignation, or what passes as such in the news-papers, is quite regularly reserved for the 'wage demands', while much larger 'adjustments' in the pay of salaried men pass with little comment. When workers in one industry agitate for more pay, there is too little comparison with the whole range of pay, and too much with other workers no better off. Or one reads the public dis-cussions, in some minority newspapers, of the level of percentage increase which wages can be confined to in a given year. In the same year quite different and much larger percentage increases are discus-sed in relation to salaries, but hardly ever within the same terms of reference. It is difficult to know what else to call this but a practical class system.

Many of the lower-salaried workers are in practice treated as wage-earners: there is great confusion at that point in the scale. But at a certain level a whole world of difference begins, not only in straight money, but in such critical factors as an automatic incremental scale, a contract of service conferring important rights in such things as payment in sickness and protection against dismissal, and differential facilities in many things from cups to carpets. The system is almost infinitely graded within itself, but the class-line, below which these benefits are not available, is ordinarily quite clear.

Once again, however, it is misleading to confine such analysis to comparison between salaried and wage-earning employment. Many salaried people consider themselves unjustly treated, in such matters as tax-relief for expenses, by comparison with salary-earners or employers in different parts of the economy. Between all these groups there is enough resentment to ensure a cynical community for generations. I support those economists who believe that in spite of the immense difficulties the attempt to establish some general principle of equity, to which particular arguments about pay can be referred, must be made. The present resentments, and the crude ways in which they are fought out, are more than a healthy community can afford.

Meanwhile, to finance the system of conspicuous expenditure, an extraordinary credit network has been set up, which, when considered, reveals much of our real class situation, and the ways in which it is changing. The earners of wages and salaries are alike in this, that most of them become quickly involved in a system of usury which spreads until it is virtually inescapable. How many supposedly middle-class people really own their houses, or their furniture, or their cars? Most of them are as radically unpropertied as the traditional working class, who are now increasingly involved in the same process of usury. In part it is the old exaction, by the propertied, from the needs of the unpropertied, and the ordinary middle-class talk of the property and independence which make them substantial citizens is an increasingly pathetic illusion. One factor in maintaining the illusion is that much of the capital needed to finance the ordinary buyer comes from his own pocket, through insurance and the like, and this can be made to look like the sensible process of accumulating social capital. What is not usually noticed is that established along the line of this process are a group of people using its complications to make substantial profit out of their neighbours' social needs. The ordinary salary-earner, thinking of himself as middle class because of the differences between himself and the wage-earners already noted, fails to notice this real class beyond him, by whom he is factually and continually exploited. Seeing class-distinction only in the limited terms of the open differential, he is acquiescing in the loss of his own freedom and even, by the usual upward identification with which the struggling middle class has always been trapped, underwriting his real exposure, as one of the unpropertied, as if it were his system and his pride.

As we move into this characteristic contemporary world, we can see the supposed new phenomenon of classlessness as simply a failure of consciousness. The public discussion is all at the level of the open differential and its complicated games, but if this were eventually resolved, into a more apparent equity, there would still be no real classlessness; indeed there can be none until social capital is socially owned.

It is in this context that the distinction between middle class and working class must always be considered. The line between them, always difficult to draw, is now blurred at many more points by a common involvement which the remaining distinctions not only disguise but in part are meant to disguise. Is the working class becoming middle class, as its conditions improve? It could as reasonably be said that most of the middle class have become working class, in the sense that they depend on selling their labour and are characteristically unpropertied in any important sense. The true description is one that recognises that the traditional definitions have broken down, and that the resulting confusion is a serious diminution of consciousness. New kinds of work, new forms of capital, new systems of ownership require new descriptions of men in their relations to them. Our true condition is that in relation to a complicated economic and social organisation which we have not learned to control, most of us are factually servants, allowed the ordinary grades of upper, middle, and lower, insistent on the marks of these grades or resentful of them, but, like most servants, taking the general establishment for granted and keeping our bickering within its terms.

This situation is clearly reflected in contemporary politics. The Conservative Party is still basically the party of the propertied and the controllers, with an old and natural genuflection to the mellow dusk in which these processes are blurred. But it is felt to be the party of most of those who still anxiously call themselves 'middle class', preoccupied as always with the upward identification and the downward keeping-in-place, the latter now fortunately expressible in precise wage percentages. The Labour Party, with vestigial ideas of a different system, offers little alternative to this structure of feeling, and upward identification, it is now learning, can spread a long way down. This is no sudden and dramatic change, though particular voting results may appear dramatically to reveal it. It is part of the logic of a particular system of society, which will operate so long as there is no adequate rise and extension of consciousness of what the system is and does.

Such consciousness is not helped by the ordinary kind of discussion which has followed Labour's third electoral defeat in 1959. The most popular formula has been that the defeat was inevitable because Labour is identified with the proletariat and the proletariat is breaking up. This is extremely doubtful. It is true, of course, that modern houses, modern furniture, television sets and washing machines and, in some cases, cars, are increasingly available to many wage-earners. But what is meant by calling this process 'deproletarianisation', as the *Economist*, following E. M. Durbin and others, has done? If the electoral decline of Labour in the 1950s is evidence of this, what are we to make of the fact that when working-class standards were low, as in the inter-war depression, and so when more 'proletarian' conditions might have been supposed to exist, many fewer people than now in fact voted Labour. Thus the Labour vote in 1959, in its third defeat, was nearly half as much again as it was in the worst periods of poverty and depression. In 1924 the Labour vote was 5½ million, in 1929 8½ million, in 1931 6½ million, in 1935 8½ million. In the famous victory of 1945, the Labour vote rose to 12 million, and a slump in the Conservative vote brought Labour a large parliamentary majority. After this peak, according to the popular formula, Labour lost electoral support because its first measures towards socialism were disliked. How curious, then, that in 1950 the Labour vote was 13,267,000, and in 1951 the highest figure ever polled by a British party, 13,949,105. The 'proletarian' situation of the depression had produced a maximum of 8½ million votes, the full-employment situation of 1951 nearly 14 million. It is a difficult situation to analyse, but we need not be hindered by myths of a 'proletariat' and 'deproletarianisation'.

The British working class, in the traditional sense of the great body of wage-earners and their families, has in fact never voted solidly Labour, as anyone who grew up in a wage-earning family would know without being told. If Labour had ever got a regular 70 per cent of these wage-earning voters, it would have been permanently in power. It is an extraordinary misunderstanding of politics to suppose that a man necessarily votes for a proletarian party because he was born in a proletarian position. The building of the labour movement, both industrially and politically, has been a continuous struggle to create a particular political and social consciousness. To the ordinary difficulties of education and propaganda has been added a continuous campaign, by other social groups, to check and confuse and sidetrack this movement. At times hardly any headway has been made; at times there have been real defeats; at times, again, important advances. Consider only, on the negative side, these statements:

Propose to a working man any great measure affecting the whole body, and he immediately asks himself the question, What am I to get by it? meaning, what at this instant am I to have in my hand or in my pocket? There he sticks.

Lancashire working men were in rags by thousands, and many of them lacked food. But their intelligence was demonstrated wherever you went. You would see them in groups discussing the great doctrines of political justice . . . or they were in earnest dispute respecting the teachings of socialism. *Now* you will see no such groups in Lancashire. But you will hear well-dressed working men talking, as they walk with their hands in their pockets, of Coops . . . and their shares in them or in building societies.

The difficulty of persuading workmen to listen to anything which does not concern pleasure or profit has long been acknowledged, and is, I think, even stronger than it used to be.

The people have all been busy getting on, some too busy to think of anything except their work, some too set on the pleasures now opened to them to care for knowledge.

Any of these statements might be made now, in the fashionable exposition of the 'I'm all right Jack' ideology of the workers. But their dates, respectively, are 1835, 1870, 1882, and 1900: spanning the years in which the labour movement's foundations were built. The ragged groups of our own century, discussing socialism, may have been similarly replaced by 'well-dressed working men talking of their shares', but this is no new phenomenon: the fluctuations are the real historical process, and in fact, as we have seen, there are more Labour voters in our own well-dressed times than in the days of the ragged groups of the 1930s. The fact is that there is no simple rising graph, for the process does not take place in a vacuum. It is profoundly affected by changing political conditions and by phases of change in the society as a whole. This is the real historical context from which any serious contemporary analysis must begin.

We have already rejected the ordinary explanation, of 'deproletarianisation': a proletariat may be factually created by an industrial system, but it is only politically created by political action, and in Britain this has never been fully achieved. Millions of wage-earners and their wives voted Conservative in 1959, as in previous elections. The significant questions are what kinds of people these were, and whether there are any new and permanent social patterns shaping them. It is difficult to answer these questions with any certainty, but one fact stands out. The division of votes by sex cuts right across the usual analysis by class, introducing questions which cannot be negotiated within our ordinary political categories. Thus, in the 1959 election, when the British people is supposed to have decisively endorsed conservatism, the votes of all men (according to poll analysis) resulted in a narrow majority for Labour. The figures were 51 per cent Labour against 49 per cent Conservative among men; 55 per cent Conservative against 45 per cent Labour among women. This male Labour majority has been normal since the war, though it is also significant that it narrowed during the fifties, and that the Conservative majority among women has also been narrowing. The reasons, in each case, are still speculative, but at least it is impossible to analyse the distribution of the wage-earning vote without serious allowance for this difference by sex. In 1955, for example, the wage-earning vote split 55½ per cent to Labour, 40½ per cent to Conservatives, while all men split 50 per cent Labour to 45½ per cent

Conservative, all women 54 per cent Conservative to 42 per cent Labour. It is then highly probable that in addition to wage-earning Conservative families, there were many Conservative wives of Labour husbands. Given actual trends, it is very difficult to see any radically new pattern in this complex, especially if we are rid of the 'proletarian' myth that before 1939 almost all wage-earners and their wives voted Labour as a matter of course. Labour gets a higher percentage of the total vote in the period of washing-machines and television than in the period of high unemployment, and the adjustments within this are obviously too complicated for any single explanation.

Another possible line of approach is in terms of new kinds of community. If we look at a political map of Britain, over the century, we see an important relation between kinds of community and political representation, and this seems a real clue to understanding contemporary change. A map of Labour representation is virtually a map of the coalfields and the great towns, with the significant exception of some of the 'Celtic' areas, where English social patterns are less marked and where Labour can win even in scattered rural constituencies. Conservatism is strong in almost all the English counties, some Scottish counties, Northern Ireland (where English politics are confused by questions of religion and partition) and the smaller English towns. This diversity is the reality, which is masked by overall counts and the exaggerations of the present electoral system. In 'Conservative Britain', in 1960, Wales is strongly Labour, Scotland has a Labour majority for the first time, and, to take only the outstanding cases, there is a Labour London, a Labour Birmingham, a Labour Manchester, and a Labour Glasgow. Thus in the heavy industrial areas and in the great towns the wage-earning identification with Labour remains high, though in no sense total or even nearly so. Similarly, in other easily identified communities, such as the English rural counties, and the traditional 'residential' resorts, popular support of the Conservatives is high, as it has traditionally been. It is in other kinds of community, between these extremes, that the difficult social analysis begins.

We think of the new housing-estates, the new suburbs and the new towns as characteristic of the new Britain, and on the whole it is in these areas that Labour hopes are now most regularly disappointed. This is the living-space of that other popular figure of contemporary analysis, the 'semi-detached proletariat'. But in fact people of many different kinds live in these places, which also between themselves have important differences. Attention has been concentrated on the break-up of old community patterns, by such physical removal, but this needs discriminating description. There is social variation, all the way from the estate still mainly serving a single works to the new town wholly mixed in origins and centres of work. There is also historical variation, from the first-generation estate in which social relations are still at the level of casual neighbourly contact, to the second-generation estate on which people have been born, grown up and married. The disruption of extended families noted in some removals is in itself a temporary phenomenon: all first-generation estates will become second and third-generation, though not necessarily with exactly the same family patterns. We cannot be sure what will happen, but it would be rash to assume that all former patterns are permanently gone. The old working-class communities grew, over a century, from a situation of removal and exposure fully comparable in effect to the present phase. When the temporary and artificial nature of the newest communities has been allowed for, and when we have overcome the simple determinism of supposing that things (whether houses or washing-machines) shape men, we shall perhaps be more cautious in assuming that there are wholly new permanent patterns, and in particular that we know what these are. All that can reasonably be noted at the present stage is that these communities were not planned by the people who live in them; but by others with their own versions of what these people needed and what a society or a community is. Again there is variation, but in many places certain patterns of thinking are now on the ground – as they were in the terrace-barracks of the first industrial towns – and these, characteristically, are a cheap version of recent middle-class provision for itself. Thus the houses or flats have more space around them, which is a gain, and have hardly any social buildings ancillary to them, which I think is a loss. A social pattern of a particular kind is thus built into the provision of better housing; you take the one with the other, and the housing, giving previous conditions, you must take. At the same time, new communication systems, built on old social patterns but on a very wide scale, are immediately accessible: the cheap national newspaper, the woman's magazine, television. It is not that these external systems are new in kind, though certainly in scale. It is that their growth interlocks with the uncertainties of the general transition, among which there is less to countervail. A new and uncertain factor, in those new communities where work is very mixed, is the degree of interaction between social consciousness gained at work – a classic centre of the growth of Labour consciousness – and social consciousness gained in the community. It is too early to say anything definite about this, since both elements in the interaction are themselves changing, but I am interested in some evidence of a split between trade-union consciousness (the simplest thing learned at work) and Labour consciousness in the wider sense, which has to be in terms of a mixed community and a whole society. Since it is in some groups' interests to encourage this split we must not take such signs of it as there are as an act of God (the 'American future', which this is also sometimes called, would be very much an act of men). At the same time, the conditions for this kind of change exist, indeed have been created. Caught in these many currents, the men and women of the newer communities are living out, explicitly, a pattern of learning and response which is also involving the society as a whole. I am not greatly surprised that contemporary Conservatism, in part directing just this complex, makes sense as an interpretation of it to very many people. For at just this point, Labour seems to have very little to offer. A different version of community, a pattern of new consciousness, it has not been able to give. Its compromise policies combine the two irrelevant elements of appeal to old and fading habits and memories, and of cultural adjustment to the present social confusion. Old Left and New Right in the Labour Party are unconscious allies in delaying any relevant analysis and challenge. The invocation of old habits, which to some extent people are bound to change and reject, combines with the rejection of socialism as a radically different human order, to leave the ruling interpretations and directions essentially unchallenged. Thus the complex and uneven growth of consciousness, most marked in the new communities but present almost everywhere in the society, is left with too few channels through it which can be politically expressed. This cannot be a permanent situation. Men and women do not wait for ever on established systems. New learning, new response, will work through, perhaps in forms we cannot yet envisage (already the Aldermaston marches seem to me new in spirit, whatever their final implications). For the one absolute fact about the men and women of the new communities, as of the new kinds of society everywhere in the world, is that they are created in a human image, and not in the image of anybody's version of them. The 'telly-glued masses' do not exist; they are the bad fiction of our second-rate social analysts. What the masses, old or new, might do is anybody's guess. But the actual men and women, under permanent kinds of difficulty, will observe and learn, and I do not think that in the long run they will be anybody's windfall.

The received descriptions of social classes have been at their most confusing, in just this new situation. How is anyone to know, in a new town or on a new housing estate, if he or she belongs to the 'working' or the 'middle' class? The traditional meanings that come through are not in economic terms (where, as we have seen, the working class-middle class description is very difficult to draw) but in terms of style of life and behaviour. 'Working class', for very many people, is simply a memory of poverty, bad housing, and exposure, while 'middle class' is a name for money to spend, better housing, and a more furnished and controllable life. Since the styles of living of the whole society are in any case changing, this contrast very easily becomes one between past and present: 'working class' is the old style, that people are steadily moving away from; 'middle class' is the new 'contemporary' style. It is easy to point out that by this time these terms have lost any relevant meaning, as descriptions of actual social organisation, but their emotional charge is no less powerful for that. 'Working class and proud of it' may last in the older communities, and in some politically active individuals, but in most cases it is now deeply confused: on the one hand, 'I work for my living' (which almost everyone does); on the other hand, the strong social sense of 'working' = 'lower' class, with inferiorities and deprivations to which nobody in his senses wants to return. I have the impression that when socialists speak now of the working class, they attract to themselves natural resentments against the whole idea of class and inferiority. In its social sense, most people only talk about class when they are anxious, and often want to get rid of the feeling that there are these kinds of distinctions between people. I think this desire should be respected, for it is an exceptionally valuable piece of social growth and maturity. But the point has been reached where the growing feeling that class is out of date and doesn't matter is being used to ratify a social system which in other terms than those now visibly breaking down is still essentially based on economic classes.

To perpetuate the present confusion is to guarantee a minimal social consciousness. We have instead to concentrate on two general facts: the open differential, and the ownership and control of social capital. If the open differential, which still gives some reality, though confused and confusing, to the working class-middle class distinction, is discussed on its own, the society cannot be understood. The differential is merely an operative function of a particular kind of society, and to promote an even more tense competition within it, setting one kind of worker against another, has the effect of directing social consciousness into forms that simply perpetuate the overall system. It is certainly my view that the differential will have to be revised, but the only possible basis for this is a real feeling of community – the true knowledge that we are working for ourselves and for each other – which, though present now as an ideal, is continually confused and in some cases cancelled by the plain fact that most of us do not own or control the means and the product of our work. In an industrial economy, social production will either be owned or controlled by the whole society, or by a part of it which then employs the rest. The decision between these alternatives is the critical decision about class, and if we are serious about ending the class system we must clear away the survivals, the irrelevancies, and the confusion of other kinds of distinction, until we see the hard economic centre which finally sustains them. With that basic inequality isolated we could stop the irrelevant discussion of class, of which most of us are truly sick and tired, and let through the more interesting discussion of human differences, between real people and real communities living in their valuably various ways.

4

The extension of culture has to be considered within the real social context of our economic and political life. In the 1960s, the rate of growth seems promising, and we are busy with plans to maintain and increase it. Yet here, very clearly, is a major contradiction easily overlooked by following a simple rising graph, for while real art and argument are being more widely enjoyed, the distribution of a bewildering variety of bad art and bad argument is increasing even more rapidly. We are reaching the point where the contradiction between these different lines and rates of growth is serious and inescapable, yet even those who see this situation feel particularly uncertain about what can be done.

We must look first at a particular and local contradiction which can quickly confuse any such discussion. If someone proposes ways of extending good art and argument, and of diminishing their worst counterparts, someone else usually answers that we mustn't be snobs: that football, after all, is as good as chess; that jazz is a real musical form; that gardening and homemaking are also important. Who exactly is someone like this arguing with, since it is usually obvious that he is not really arguing with the man to whom he replies? Unfortunately he is arguing with actual people and a familiar way of feeling. It is true that certain cultural forms have been used as a way of asserting social distinction, and that much wholesale condemnation of new forms has been a way of demonstrating the inferiority of those two groups who have regularly to be put in their (lower) place: the masses and the young. This habit has to be resisted, but there is equal danger in a popular form of demagogy which, by the use of selective examples, succeeds in avoiding the problem of bad culture altogether. Can we agree, perhaps, before passing to the more difficult questions, that football is indeed a wonderful game, that jazz is a real musical form and that gardening and homemaking are indeed important? Can we also agree, though, that the horror-film, the rape-novel, the Sunday strip-paper and the latest Tin-Pan drool are not exactly in the same world, and that the nice magazine romance, the manly adventure story (straight to the point of the jaw) and the pretty, clever television advertisement are not in it either? The argument against these things, and the immense profits gained by their calculated dissemination, cannot afford to be confused by the collateral point that a good living culture is various and changing, that the need for sport and entertainment is a real as the need for art, and that the public display of 'taste', as a form of social distinction, is merely vulgar.

In a rapidly changing and therefore confused society, in which cultural forms will in any case change but in which little is done by way of education to deepen and refine the capacity for significant response, the problems that confront us are inevitably difficult.

Two parallel efforts are necessary: on the one hand the maximum encouragement of artists who are seriously trying to create new forms or do significant work in traditional forms; on the other hand, the steady offering and discussion of this work, including real criticism and therefore its distinction at least from calculated and indifferent manipulation. It would be wrong to say that these efforts are not being made: some help, though still inadequate, is being given to the arts; some responsible offering and discussion are publicly underwritten. These policies fall within the evolutionary conception: a steady encouragement of elements of valuable growth. But while supporting them, and certainly wishing to see them extended, I find it difficult to feel that they go to the root of the problem. For it is usually not recognised that inferior and destructive elements are being much more actively propagated: that more is spent, for example, on advertising a new soap, and imprinting a jingle attached to it, than on supporting an orchestra or a picture gallery; and that in launching two new magazines, one trying to do a serious new job, the other simply competing to capture a share of a known popular market, the ratio of comparative investment is ludicrous, for hardly anything is behind the former, while huge sums of money are poured out on the latter. The condition of cultural growth must be that varying elements are at least equally available, and that new and unfamiliar things must be offered steadily over a long period, if they are to have a reasonable chance of acceptance. Policies of this degree of responsibility seem impossible in our present cultural organisation. The encouragement of valuable elements is restricted to what is little more than a defensive holding operation, which of course is better than nothing but which is hardly likely to make any general change. The rest of the field is left to the market, and not even to the free play of the market, for the amounts of capital involved in financing our major cultural institutions restrict entry to a comparatively few powerful groups, so that both production and distribution are effectively in very few hands. The serious new magazine referred to, usually the result of a major voluntary effort by a group of dedicated people, is unlikely to be even available for buying, in the sense of lying ready on the average bookstall where somebody might try it, while the new commercial magazine will be so widely displayed that it can hardly be avoided. It is then stupid and even vicious, when it is clear that no real competition exists, to use the evidence of immediate results as proof of the unalterable vulgarity of the public. Instead of the ritual indignation and despair at the cultural condition of 'the masses' (now increasingly uttered even by their supposed friends) it is necessary to break through to the central fact that most of our cultural institutions are in the hands of speculators, interested not in the health and growth of the society, but in the quick profits that can be made by exploiting inexperience. True, under attack, these speculators, or some of them, will concede limited policies of a different kind, which they significantly call 'prestige'; that is to say, enough to preserve a limited public respectability so that they will be allowed to continue to operate. But the real question is whether a society can afford to leave its cultural apparatus in such irresponsible hands.

Now I think many people feel the strength of this question, but feel even more strongly the difficulties of any possible alternative. Steady and particular encouragement, in the obvious limited fields, is quite widely approved, but any attempt to tackle the whole situation runs into major difficulties. For it is obvious that the amount of capital and effort required, to make any substantial change, can come only from public sources, and to this there are two objections. The first is the question whether such resources are really available, on the scale required. This goes back to the difficulty discussed earlier: that we find it almost impossible to conceive the financing of social policy out of the social product, and have never learned a system of accounting which would make this possible or even visible. For it is true, of course, that the present investment comes from the society and economy as a whole. The supply of advertising money (the contemporary equivalent of manna) can only come in the end from us, as workers and buyers, though it is now routed through channels that give control of this social capital to very few groups. If we can realise that we are paying for the existing cultural system, by one kind of organisation of the economy, we need not be frightened by the scale of resources required, since that organisation is in fact subject to change. We should be much clearer about these cultural questions if we saw them as a consequence of a basically capitalist organisation, and I at least know no better reason for capitalism to be ended. It is significant that the liveliest revolt against the existing system, particularly among the new young generation, is in precisely these cultural terms.

But then the second objection is deeply involved with this point.

What is the alternative to capitalism? Socialism. What is a socialist culture? State control. There are many good liberals, and many anxious socialists, who draw back if this is the prospect. Better even the speculators, they say, than the inevitable horde of bureaucrats, official bodies, and quite probably censorship.

This difficulty has a representative significance. It is not only in cultural questions, but in the whole area of thinking about change in our society, that this knot is tied. Here is the deepest difficulty in the whole development of our democracy: that we seem reduced to a choice between speculator and bureaucrat, and while we do not like the speculator, the bureaucrat is not exactly inviting either. In such a situation, energy is sapped, hope weakens, and of course the present compromise between the speculators and the bureaucrats remains unchallenged.

Democratic policies are made by open discussion and open voting. In relatively small bodies, contact between members and policies can be close, though even here some responsibility for decisions will be passed to elected representatives rather than to members as a whole, and where much administrative work is necessary will also be passed to officials. The principle of the official in a democratic organisation is quite clear: he administers within an elected policy, and is responsible to the membership for his actions. The practice, we all know, can be otherwise, but given an adequate constitution and genuine equality of membership it is still the best and most responsible system known.

There are strong arguments for the national organisation of the means of cultural exchange, but the persistent danger, even in a democratic country, is that too large an organisation becomes rigid and in a sense impenetrable. Any adequate cultural organisation must be open, flexible and committed to genuine variety of expression. It would seem simple to say that the best people to run the various cultural organisations are those who use them for the production of their own work, for here is the deepest and most practical interest in keeping the organisation flexible and open. Yet it is equally clear that the actual producers of cultural work cannot, from their own resources, command the ownership of any but the simplest means. Where indeed they can do so, no change is necessary. But in the press, in broadcasting and television, in the cinema and theatre it is obvious that this simple co-operative ownership is impossible. This ought not then to mean, however, that the control of these expensive means should be made available to the highest bidder, especially when he is not even particularly interested in the actual work but mainly in its financial possibilities. The signs are, in contemporary Britain, that this worst of all arrangements is becoming normal, with a dominant policy criterion of profit and with the producers turned into employees within this emphasis. In press and television this is especially the case, and powerful interests are working to extend the same system to broadcasting. It is urgent to define the alternative principle, which I think can only be that when the producers cannot themselves own the means of their work, these must be owned by the community in trust for the producers, and an administration set up which is capable of maintaining this trust. The difficulties here are obvious, but all administration and constitution-making in fact proceed from an emphasis of what is desirable, and I believe that if we can agree that this end is desirable, no society is better qualified from experience to devise adequate practical methods.

In the drama, for example, it would be possible for most theatres to be publicly owned, preferably by local authorities though perhaps with a small national network in addition, and then licensed to companies of actors. It would then be possible for these companies, through open regional and national organisations which they would be free to join or not as they decided, to pursue reasonably long-term policies on the guarantee that a particular production would go to a series of theatres, when financially necessary. Similar arrangements could be made, through permanent and regular liaison, with the broadcasting and television services. The advantages to the drama of permanent companies creating their own varying traditions, in a context of adequate professional security, would undoubtedly be great: almost all the good work we now have in the theatre comes from such companies, which are left, though, to struggle on as best they can with the hope of being eventually hired by the speculators who control the big national theatres. If we are serious about freedom in the arts, we can give it, in this way, to actual artists.

In the cinema, a related system is possible. As things now are, the makers of films are almost wholly in the hands of the distributors, who decide, by certain crude tests, whether a film is worth making before it is made. This is the freedom of the artist which our liberals so complacently defend. It is clear that the number of cinemas is in any case going to decline. The opportunity this presents of a sensible reorganisation ought not to be missed. The cinemas should become publicly owned and vested in an independent public authority. There should be at least two or three circuits, including one specialised circuit, to ensure alternatives. Production should be in the hands of independent permanent companies, which as in the case of the theatre would have to satisfy the public authority of their professional competence. Public money should then be made available to these companies, for the making of films which would be guaranteed exhibition on one of the circuits. The more independent companies there are the better, and it would be encouraging to see some links between some of these and the theatre companies already referred to. A possible organisation of the independent authority would be joint representation between officers appointed by and responsible to Parliament and representatives elected by the permanent companies.

In the case of books, we already have a good range of independent publishers, though the pressures on them to surrender independent policies are severe. A rapid process of amalgamation (often retaining apparently independent imprints) seems to be under way, and new kinds of owner, often little concerned with literature, are becoming more common. With high costs, and the wide opportunities of the 'paperback revolution', it seems that a stage has been reached very similar to that in newspapers at the turn of the century. The quantitative thinking that can follow from such a system would be disastrous to publishing, past a certain point, and I think the time has come for an inquiry into the facts of recent changes and possible courses of action. Meanwhile it is of vital importance that publishers who pursue, as now, responsible and therefore varying policies should be given all possible help. This can probably best be done in the now chaotic field of distribution. It is a standing disgrace that there should be hundreds of towns without anything that can be called a decent bookshop. The good independent bookseller performs an especially valuable service, but unless he is lucky in his locality he will often go under. The existing chain shops apply to books and periodicals simple tests of quantity: below a certain figure they do not consider particular items worth handling. Is this any kind of freedom, or free availability? I think we could set up a Books Council, representative on the one hand of publishers, booksellers and authors, on the other hand of Parliament, which would have the duty of ensuring the continued independence of publication, and at the same time the best possible distribution of books and periodicals here and overseas. The pressure to reduce publications to a limited number of standard items, easily sold in quantity, should be resisted as a matter of public policy. Such a Council could review existing bookselling arrangements, and wherever it found (as it would now widely find) that the real range of books and periodicals is not offered, it would have power to establish and guarantee independent enterprises committed to the policy outlined. It is very odd that we have accepted this principle, in the public library service, for the borrowing of books, but are still so far short of it in terms of books that readers can buy and keep.

In the case of newspapers and magazines, we have to deal with a situation in which control is passing into fewer and fewer hands, within a policy dedicated not to the quality of newspapers and magazines but to their profitability. The criterion of profitability is being raised to absurd levels, in which for example a daily newspaper may have to cease publication if less than a million people buy it, and in which a steady decline in the number of newspapers and magazines seems assured. Again, is this freedom, or free availability? The quality of newspapers is unlikely to be raised either by exhortation or censorship. Experience in all other fields suggests that standards in a profession rise when they are in the control of members of that profession. Such professional responsibility is now virtually impossible, as a permanent and consistent policy, since the whole organisation of the press (like the organisation of the cinema and the theatre) creates a different atmosphere, in which standards are set by the controllers, on an estimate of likely profit, and the actual producers instead of feeling a common responsibility to their work are encouraged, in far too many cases, to compete with each other in supplying a pre-determined article. Personal standards will always vary, but it is a poor society which creates institutions that give success to the least scrupulous and the least concerned. Any attempt to reform these institutions, though, is met with prolonged abuse and misrepresentation. Obviously we do not want a state-owned press, but I think we have reached the point where we need a new Press Council, including public and elected journalist representatives, charged with the maintenance and extension of genuinely independent newspapers and magazines. We need in particular to ensure the survival of local newspapers, and I think it is essential that these should become locally owned and managed, as very few of them now are. There are serious objections to involving local authorities in the ownership of local newspapers, though in certain cases this might be done. More generally, the guarantee of independence, and any necessary provision of capital, should be accepted as a public service at national level, through a Press Council including, as defined, journalist representatives. The same public service principle should be applied to magazines, on terms guaranteeing independence to professionally recognised editorial bodies. With experience, this principle could be extended to the national press. I do not see why the editorial bodies of any newspaper or magazine should not be free, by their own democratic decision, to apply to such a Press Council to be recognised as an independent enterprise, which would then be guaranteed freedom from any external private financial control. The terms on which this recognition and support would be granted would be the producers' own definition of policy. There might be cases when the Council, including public and professional representatives, would be unwilling to underwrite a particular policy proposed, but in such cases we should be no worse off than we are now: such a policy could be tried on the market, or financed much as now, for of course there can be no question of any newspaper or magazine being forbidden to publish. I think that with experience and goodwill a majority of professionally responsible independent papers could be built up, and even if we did not achieve a majority, we should at least have ensured that no newspaper or magazine could be killed by a financial organisation indifferent to quality and interested only in immediate profit. Reform can only come from within, in such a field, if it is publicly supported.

In broadcasting and television we see an imperfect but still generally responsible public authority, the BBC, powerfully challenged by new kinds of organisation. It is obvious, as these services extend, that we need the continual extension of choice, but it is doubtful if we shall get this, on any responsible basis, if we construe independence as the possession of working capital from elsewhere (mainly, as now, from advertising). There might well be two or more public authorities owning the technical means of distribution, but the same principle holds as before: policy can be generally defined by the public authorities, but the provision of actual work must be in the hands of the real producers. Practical networks exist, and their wide use is clearly desirable, but what one would like to see serving them is a variety of independent groups, with genuine local affiliations and alternative policies. The existing programme companies, in commercial television, are hardly ever of this kind, but are essentially a congeries of financial interests employing the real producers. It should be a matter of public policy to encourage the formation of professional companies to whom the technical means of distribution would be made available by the public authorities. The core of such groups would be the professional broadcasting and television producers, who would work out means of association with other professional companies in the theatre, the cinema and the press, with orchestras and other similar institutions in their region, and with wider local organisations, including education committees and the great voluntary societies. In this way the dangers both of a central monopoly and of simple surrender to the speculators could be avoided.

I am very much aware, in putting forward these outline proposals, that much remains to be done, in detailed planning and in improvement, by discussion between all those with relevant experience. I do not suppose that any of these measures of reorganisation would be easy, but I do claim, emphatically, that we can envisage a cultural organisation which would greatly extend the freedom of the cultural producers, by the sensible application of public resources to cut out their present dependence on dominant but essentially functionless financial groups, and by forms of contract which while preserving responsibility in the spending of public money would give the producers control over their actual work. This is surely a hopeful way forward, and constitutions can in fact always be devised if there is substantial agreement on principles.

The matter is now urgent, for while some liberals still shy away from reform in the name of the freedom of the artist, or argue that culture in any case can never be organised (the spirit bloweth where it listeth), a very rapid reorganisation of a different kind is in fact going on, with the area of real ownership and independence shrinking in every part of our culture, and seeming certain to continue to do so. I must plainly ask such liberals what they are really defending, for there seems little in common between the freedom they value and the actual freedom described recently by an owner of a television service and a great chain of newspapers as 'a licence to print your own money'. We have reached a crisis in which freedom and independence can only be saved if they are publicly assured and guaranteed, and the ways I propose seem a working basis for this, taking care as they do to avoid or minimize the real dangers of bureaucracy and state control.

Would the quality of our cultural life be improved by such measures? I feel certain that it would, in the real energies that would be released, but I am not thinking in terms of any overnight transformation. I say only that the channels would be more open, that the pressure for quick profit would be lifted, and that a more genuine range of choices would be made available. My whole case about social change is, moreover, that the interdependence of elements which I described as a matter of theory is an argument for conceiving change on the widest possible front: the changes in emphasis in our economy, in our ordinary working relationships, in our democratic institutions, and in education are all relevant to cultural change in this more explicit field. I would repeat my emphasis on the overriding educational problem: the provision of new kinds of education for the now neglected majority between fifteen and twenty-one. The growth of adult education is also relevant: much more could be done to house this increasing work properly, at the centre of its communities, and to improve its connections with the wider cultural services.

A particular job is waiting in relation to information about the quality and use of the new range of goods now available. We are spending £400,000,000 annually on an advertising system which, instead of performing this rational service, lives in a world of suggestion and magic. The existing 'consumers' advice' associations should certainly be encouraged, but characteristically, like most existing encouragement of the arts, they serve only a limited public. Could we not then have a public research and information service, with adequate offices and showrooms in every town, where genuine choice could be made available to the ordinary buyer? This could be done on the present expenditure on the antiquated system of advertising, which is simply a pre-democratic form of manipulation of a public regarded as 'masses'. And the more all this new work could be brought together, so that these new kinds of community service could be seen as factually linked – buying and learning, using and

appreciating, sharing and discriminating – the more likely a healthy
cultural growth would be.

5

The human energy of the long revolution springs from the conviction that men can direct their own lives, by breaking through the
pressures and restrictions of older forms of society, and by discovering new common institutions. This process necessarily includes both
success and failure. If we look back over recent centuries, the
successes are truly spectacular, and we ought to keep reminding
ourselves of them, and of the incomprehension, the confusion, and
the distaste with which the proposals for things now the most
ordinary parts of reality were received. At the same time the failures
are evident: not only the challenging failures, as new and unrealised
complexities are revealed, but also the straight failures, as particular
changes are dragged back into old systems, and as ways of thinking
deeply learned in previous experience persist and limit the possibility
of change. We tend to absorb the successes and then to be preoccupied by the hard knots of failure. Or as we approach the failures, to
see if anything can be done, we are distracted by the chorus of
success.

I am told by friends in the United States that in effect the
revolution is halted: that my sense of possibility in its continued
creative energy is a generous but misleading aspiration, for they in
America are in touch with the future, and it does not work – the
extension of industry, democracy and communications leads only to
what is called the massification of society. A different stance is then
required: not that of the revolutionary but of the dissenter who
though he cannot reverse the trends keeps an alternative vision alive.
I hear this also in Britain, where the same patterns are evident, and it
is true that in a large part of recent Western literature this is the
significant response: the society is doomed, or in any event damned,
but by passion or irony the individual or the group may preserve a
human enclave. Meanwhile I am told by friends in the Soviet Union
that the decisive battle of the revolution has been won in nearly half
the world, and that the communist future is evident. I listen to this
with respect, but I think they have quite as much still to do as we
have, and that a feeling that the revolution is over can be quite as

disabling as the feeling that in any case it is pointless. To suppose that the ways have all been discovered, and that therefore one can give a simple affiliation to a system, is as difficult, as I see it, as to perform the comparable act of ingratiation in Western societies: either the majority formula of complacency, or the minority announcement (tough, hard, realistic) that we are heroically damned.

In the long revolution we are making our own scale, and the problem of expectations seems crucial in every society that has entered it. 'That's enough now' is the repeated whisper, and as we turn to identify the voice we see that it is not only that of the rich, the dominant and the powerful, who want change to stop or slow down, but also that of many others, who have no further bearings and are unwilling to risk their real gains. 'That's enough now; we've got rid of poverty, we've got the vote, every child can be educated.' And there it all is, for once these were all seemingly impossible expectations. Even to shape them took many men's lives, and to realise them took the work of many generations. 'But that's enough now; let's tidy up and consolidate.'

We have to distinguish three kinds of thinking by which the long revolution is continually limited and opposed. The first and most important, though it is often left unnoticed, is the steady resistance of privileged groups of many kinds to any extension of wealth, democracy, education or culture which would affect their exceptional status. In the early stages this is usually quite open, but later it becomes a very delicate strategy, using the advances that have been gained as reasons for doing no more, and above all creating the maximum of delay. It is because of the existence of this conscious and highly skilled opposition that the process is still as much a revolution, though in different forms, as when earlier expectations were met with open violence. Recent arguments and measures against African democracy are very similar to the history of early nineteenth-century Britain, but a further relation is even more important, that the arguments and measures against, say, the extension of education in Britain on any adequate scale are part of the same historical process. This strategy must obviously be defined and opposed at every stage.

Yet the privileged groups, again at all stages, find strange allies. The ordinary tactic of attaching the leaders of one phase to its achievements, and encouraging them to identify with the existing order, is extremely successful. The history of the labour movement is full of such cases, in which former leaders become determined opponents of further change, and give much of their energy to fighting new elements coming up through their own movement. This is still going on, in very much its old forms, though the reality of what such men are doing is usually not generally recognised until they are dead. In our own generation we have a new class of the same kind: the young men and women who have benefited by the extension of public education and who, in surprising numbers, identify with the world into which they have been admitted, and spend much of their time, to the applause of their new peers, expounding and documenting the hopeless vulgarity of the people they have left: the one thing that is necessary, now, to weaken belief in the practicability of further educational extension. They could find plenty of vulgarity and narrowness where they are, if they had the nerve to look, just as the knighted trade-union leader, indignant about shop-stewards and communists and all kinds of disruptive elements, could find plenty of arbitrary and ignorant power and conscious intrigue in the world in which he now moves. In our own period it is impossible to overlook this body of people who are effectively limiting and opposing the revolution by which they themselves have benefited.

The third kind of thinking which limits and opposes is much the most difficult to understand. What the Americans call the 'massification' of society can only happen, however hard the new élites may work, if a majority of the people whom they regard as 'the masses' accept this version of themselves. But then it is a fact that for long periods, given sufficient skill in the élites in confusing and flattering, such a majority can for practical purposes be got. I remember watching in a backstreet fish-and-chip shop, the man and his wife, obviously not well off, with obvious local accents, looking in, with what seemed pleasure, at a television play in which people like themselves and their customers, with the same local accent, were made nonsense of, as a class of obviously ignorant clowns. This is not an isolated example of a human version of ordinary people which is regularly and widely presented for the enjoyment of the very people whom the version misrepresents and insults. It is from evidence like this that some people resign themselves to 'massification': the masses will create themselves, take any inferior position that is offered them, and that is the end of any hope of change. I am conscious of the weight of the evidence, but I think it is ordinarily misinterpreted. There is a very skilful obliquity in all such versions: it is always other people who are inferior, the practical identification is never with oneself. While no significant version of other people is there as an alternative, the degrading version makes easy headway. But this version of other people is, precisely, a social expectation. The version of ordinary people as masses is not only the conscious creation of the elites (who work very hard at it, by the way). It is also a conclusion from actual experience within the forms of a society which requires the existence of masses. The framing of different expectations of others has to be carried out, always, against the pressures of an existing culture which is teaching, often very deeply, incompatible patterns. A good example of this is the popularity of 'I'm all right, Jack' as an interpretation of our majority social feelings. Whatever moral notes may be added on the selfishness of this attitude, the fact is that this is a version of ordinary people which the terms of our society need people to accept: if everyone is only out for himself, why bother about social change? Very few people, however, would accept this attitude as an adequate description of their *own* feelings. It is how the others are, and the irony is that some real behaviour in the society, against which there might otherwise be principled protest, feeds in to this cynical version to promote and confirm the safe attitudes it embodies.

The central problem is that of expectations. I do not think the 'I'm all right, Jack' attitude correctly describes our majority social feelings; it is, rather, a skilful stabilisation of achieved expectations. Facing real contradictions, which cannot be argued away but need long and difficult effort for any solution, it makes sense to very many of us to concentrate on an area of immediate living where the relation between desire and achievement is straight and practical. If you accept your place and work hard at your job, you *can* make a big improvement in your life, as things now are. Any alternative effort will not only make less visible progress, but it is by no means clear what in fact the effort would be for. The main pressure of the last three generations of social criticism has been towards the abolition of individual poverty, and the point has now been reached where the social conditions for this have been largely achieved, and can then be taken for granted, the immediate climb from poverty seeming now an individual effort. And the point is not so much to remind ourselves that unless the social effort had been made the individual effort, as in the past, would have been normally fruitless. Most people, understandably, will not take much notice of the past. The point is always to frame new expectations, in terms of a continuing version of what life could be. Thus the crucial definition, in the coming generation, is that of social poverty, which in overcrowded hospitals and classrooms, inadequate and dangerous roads, ugly and dirty towns, is as evident in a supposedly prosperous Britain as were the rags and hunger we have abolished. But it is characteristic of all cultural growth that the intensity with which the old patterns have been learned is itself a barrier to the communication of new patterns. Everything will in any case be done, by those opposed to social change, to keep the old patterns alive, even if originally these were bitterly opposed in their turn. And since these patterns are not abstractions, but deeply learned ways of thinking and feeling and forms of behaviour, it is not surprising that for some time a majority in their favour can usually be got. The long effort to communicate new patterns must continue, but it can be cut short and weakened if, falling into old types of despair, those who wish to communicate them dismiss other people, who are under real pressures, as the ignorant and selfish masses who are deliberately prolonging their own condition.

The definition of social poverty, and the revolt against it, have in fact already begun. Parallel definitions of cultural poverty and of inadequate democracy are also being actively shaped. These ways of thinking require not only new kinds of analysis of the society, but also new versions of relationship and new feelings in human expectation. Characteristically, much of the first phase of this growth of consciousness has been negative. The new feelings of the middle 1950s were not in themselves creative; they were a stage of dissent from old formulations, and contempt, sickness and anger were the predominant impressions. These feelings, rooted in a brittle boredom, were indeed strange counterparts of the more general reasoned catalogues of an achieved Utopia. It was comparatively easy to isolate this kind of protest, and to discount it as the expression of an eccentric minority out of touch with the mood of a society which had gathered its energies to a pattern of known expectations. Yet the patterns of real communication in a society are always changing, and people thinking in the old ways suddenly found that a generation had grown up behind them which was similarly isolated, and which found little meaning in the achieved patterns that had seemed so satisfactory. The new feelings, if still only at the stage of disbelief, boredom and contempt, were getting through with surprising speed. New areas of feeling and expectation were being actively reached, if only in the sense of the touching of an exposed nerve. As this was realised, the old kind of attempt to dilute, contain and direct the new feelings was hurriedly made. 'Youth' became a problem, and the more this was said the more contemptuous and insulted most young people felt: 'Can't they see that they're a problem too?' A process very familiar to any historian of cultural change emerged with unusual clarity. People tied to the old definitions and expectations assumed, as always, that the new feelings were either irresponsible or a misunderstanding. 'Perhaps we ought to explain to them that people are earning good wages, that every child gets his chance in education, that we all have the right to vote. Men struggled for these things, so can't these young people show a bit of respect?' 'Or if we trained them more carefully, some wiser investment in qualified leadership perhaps, until they share our values.' But this kind of reaction, characteristically passed through many committees, is in fact useless. Consciousness really does change, and new experience finds new interpretations: this is the permanent creative process. If the existing meanings and values could serve the new energies, there would be no problem. The widespread dissent, and growing revolt, of the new young generation are in fact the growth of the society, and no reaction is relevant unless conceived in these terms. The most useful service already performed by the new generation is its challenge to the society to compare its ideals and its practice. This comparison, as we saw earlier, is the first stage of new learning. People get a sense of reality, and of their own attitudes to it, from what they learn of a whole environment. It is one thing to offer certain meanings and values and ask people to consider and if possible accept them. Yet we all naturally look, not only at the meanings and values, but at their real context. If, for example, we are to be co-operative, responsible, non-violent, where exactly, in our actual world, are we expected to live? Is the economy co-operative, is the culture responsible, are the politics non-violent? If these questions are not honestly answered, propagation of the values as such will have little effect. The degree of evasion will be matched by a degree of contempt, and this can as easily degenerate into cynical apathy as grow into protest and new construction. The only useful social argument is that which follows the meanings and values through to the point where real contradictions are disturbing or denying them. Then, with the real situation admitted, the stage of contemptuous comparison and dissent may pass into constructive energy. For my own part, I see the present situation as a very critical phase in the long revolution, because it is by no means certain, in the short run, whether the new and constructive stage will be reached in time. There are many warning signs of dissent and boredom being capitalised, as a new kind of distraction. The cult of the criminal, the racketeer, the outsider, as relevant heroes of our society, is exceptionally dangerous, because it catches up just enough real feelings to make the heroism seem substantial, yet channels them towards those parodies of revolution often achieved in modern history in the delinquent gang or even in fascism. These destructive expressions can only occur when, in the widest sense, the society is in a revolutionary phase. It is not time then for the reasoned catalogues of sober achievement, but for new creative definitions. The contradiction between an apparently contented society and a deep current of discontent emerging mainly in irrational and ugly ways is our immediate and inescapable challenge.

A growing number of people, in recent years, have been trying to describe new approaches and to make them practical. They have, of course, been widely dismissed as utopians or extremists. But how did they seem at the time, those men we look back to who 'in opposition to the public opinion of the day', 'outraging their contemporaries', 'challenging the general complacency', somehow live with us and even seem tame and 'limited by their period'? Working for something new, a writer or thinker easily identifies with these men, and of course may be wholly wrong: not everything new is in fact communicated and lived. But the reasonable man, tolerantly docketing the extremists of his day: who is he exactly? For he too identifies with these figures from the past; it is usually where he learned to be reasonable. And then who is left for that broad empty margin, the 'public opinion of the day'?

I think we are all in this margin: it is what we have learned and where we live. But unevenly, tentatively, we get a sense of movement, and the meanings and values extend. I have tried to describe some possible ways forward, and ask only for these to be considered and improved. But what I mainly offer is this sense of the process: what I have called the long revolution. Here, if the meaning communicates, is the ratifying sense of movement, and the necessary sense of direction. The nature of the process indicates a perhaps unusual revolutionary activity: open discussion, extending relationships, the practical shaping of institutions. But it indicates also a necessary strength: against arbitrary power whether of arms or of money, against all conscious confusion and weakening of this long and difficult human effort, and for and with the people who in many different ways are keeping the revolution going.

III

THE ANALYSIS RECONSIDERED

'INDUSTRIAL' AND
'POST-INDUSTRIAL' SOCIETY

'The industrial revolution, in an important technical phase, is continuing.' We can say that again. In the last quarter-century, the speed and extent of technical change have been remarkable in themselves but even more remarkable, especially in recent years, in their effects on habits and kinds of work. In the further development of these changes, persistent mass unemployment, of a structural kind, based in the further industrialisation of many existing kinds of work, has been widely predicted. Yet at the same time it is common to talk of these changes as leading to a 'post-industrial' society.

All the terms of this discussion need some new analysis. It has become common, in orthodox accounts, to refer not only to 'the industrial revolution' but to second and third industrial revolutions. The first industrial revolution, from the 1780s to the 1840s, is seen as based on the application of steam power. The second, between 1860 and 1910, is seen as based on the application of new forms of power from oil and electricity. In this kind of classification, the third industrial revolution has been seen as based on the new power of nuclear energy, from the 1950s, but a more familiar scheme, shifting the point of reference, defines it as the application of electronic systems – computers, automation, microchips – to widening areas of production and control.

The material significance of each of these major shifts is beyond question. Yet it is obvious that each of the descriptions depends on a solely technical sense of 'industrial revolution'. In fact, if we were to take this full emphasis, and enter the real history of the many major technologies, we would find such a sequence too simple and too abbreviated. We would have to speak of one, two, three, many industrial revolutions.

What has really to be said is very different. The full significance of the industrial revolution is not to be found only in the introduction and development of new *forces* of production. What began to be changed, from the 1780s, was the whole set of *relations* of production, which eventually constituted a new social order. It is obvious that there has been a close relation, from the beginning, between the new forces and the new relations of production. But it is a very weak kind of thinking to abstract the technical and technological changes and to explain the widespread social, economic and cultural changes as determined by them. This error, now identified as 'technological determinism', bears with particular weight on interpretation of all the later stages of industrialisation. It is especially misleading in descriptions and predictions of a 'post-industrial' society. For in the end it is impossible to understand the industrial revolution, in any of its phases, including the most recent and most imminent, by reference to the changes in the forces of production alone.

Consider first another sequence that could be as reasonably proposed: the institution of a capital market; the transformation of land ownership, leading to the displacement of millions of small farmers and agricultural labourers; the beginning of joint-stock companies; the institution of free trade; the organisation of corporations and cartels; the development of new international monetary systems; the growth of multinational companies. Each of these events and their combined sequence (which again, to be complete, would require many more entries) affected the development of modern society as fundamentally as any of the major changes in techniques of production. It is only in the weak intellectual form of technological determinism, or in the established ideological form in which industrialisation is presented without reference to its historically inextricable capitalism, that the familiar reduced and excluding senses of 'industrial revolution' are possible.

There is a major problem, to which we must return in detail, in diagnosing the relations between industrial production and capitalism. Historically they have been so closely linked that they can often be seen as dependent on each other. Yet most modern socialists have believed that it would be possible to have modern industrial production without capitalism. Indeed in Eastern Europe this has been widely attempted and, as some would say, achieved. The results, however, both there and in more limited kinds of what has been called socialism in Western Europe, are still matters of basic dispute. This is not an intellectual problem for those who isolate the development of the forces of industrial production. Moreover, those who support and advocate capitalism have their own version of the fundamental relationship; it is, they say, the institutions and incentives of capitalism which develop the productive forces, and there is no other practicable way. For socialists, however, who typically believe that the forces and the relations of production are integrally connected and indeed mutually dependent, the proposition of modern forms of industrial production without capitalism has far more difficulties than are usually or at all admitted. This point is of intense practical significance in the historical phase which we have recently entered, under the heavy pressure of the latest changes in both technology and capitalism.

2

The point of entry for an analysis, either of the fundamental nature of the industrial revolution or of the severe crisis of industrial society which we are now beginning to experience, is the idea of *employment*. This goes beyond the earlier analysis in terms of the 'consumer' and the 'market'. There is now a regular association of *employment* with *work*. For most people of working age, it is widely believed, to be not employed is to be not working. A woman doing long and often heavy or demanding work in a home and family is said to be not a working woman, but if she is employed, in any capacity, she becomes one. So prepotent is this idea that even those people who work on their own account, as independent craftsmen, consultant professionals, freelances, contractors, owner-occupier farmers and so on, are said to be *self-employed*. A legal fiction, of an employer who employs himself, is invented to conform to the predominant idea that all work is employment.

The industrial revolution did not invent the institution or the idea of work as employment, but it powerfully strengthened both, and in its full development made them overwhelmingly dominant. In previous social orders millions of men and women had been practically subject, for their means of livelihood, to the controls of power and property. Yet the emergence of employment, in its basic sense of a contract of labour for a wage, and especially for a regular wage, is a major qualitative change. It is evident, in its early forms, for several centuries before anything that can be called an industrial revolution. Yet it is clear that the full development of the factory system, steadily displacing earlier forms of domestic and small-workshop production, greatly generalised the regular wage relationship. At the same time, and indeed earlier, several forms of rural livelihood, in small areas of land or in access to commons, were made marginal or were extinguished. The development of new forms of government, of commerce, of larger companies and of the money market itself produced new major areas of employment. It is only as these changes develop that we begin to hear of *employment* in that special sense indicated by its converse, *unemployment*, which in the course of the nineteenth century became a condition seen as outside the now normal and expected social organisation of work. It is this normalisation, the inner core of modern industrial society, which is now in its turn threatened by further major developments in the forces of production, most obviously in the introduction of newly automated systems.

Yet employment in this sense, of the regular contract for wage labour, while dominant, has never been anything like total. In the 1980s most industrial societies are suffering from mass unemployment, but most are also still characterised by mass *employment*, at historically high levels. If employment is expressed as a percentage of people of working age, the current figure in Britain is just below 70 per cent, as compared with below 60 per cent at the beginning of the 1930s (source: H. Neuburger, *Guardian* 21.7.82). The employment of men, at 80 per cent at the beginning of the 1930s, has now dipped below 80 per cent; the general difference is accounted for by the increased employment of women, from 36 per cent to 61 per cent. However, within this general movement, there are periodic and perhaps unrepeatable high points, reaching over 90 per cent for men in the 1950s and 1960s, and over 65 per cent for women in the 1970s. In this as in several other respects, modern industrial society, in its assumed norms, seems to have peaked in the major period of growth between the 1950s and the 1970s. The processes of centralising and rationalising production, begun in systematic ways in the first decades of the industrial revoltuion, brought with them a dominant definition of work as employment within these productive forms. It is ironic that the logic of their own further development has come to disturb and to threaten the very norm of employment on which the social order has come to depend.

Again this is more than a series of technical changes: the coming of robots or microchips or whatever. The purpose of these processes of centralising and rationalising production was not then and is not now the general welfare of all the people in the society. The benefits of increased production and of regular and rising wages have been real. But whenever the choice has had to be made between the true primary purposes – increase of production, reduction of costs, thus success in the market and higher returns on invested capital – and the variable secondary effects – increased employment, rising living standards for wage-earners, even overall levels of common wealth – there has never been any real doubt which way it would go. It is in this fundamental sense that we have still to speak of 'the industrial revolution', and more specifically of the revolution of industrial capitalism, in and through all its important technical and institutional changes. 'Structural unemployment' – that key phenomenon of the late twentieth century – is never only a 'technological' development; it is always also a function of the general relations of production, both within and between specific capitalist economies. This then has special effect on the orthodox prediction of a coming 'post-industrial' society.

3

The marks of a 'post-industrial' society are usually specified in terms of changes in 'work'. Manufacturing employment is seen as in major decline, especially in the old industrial countries. Service employment is seen as in major growth, in the same countries. New forms of service employment, in relation to collecting, processing and distributing information, are seen as becoming dominant. Indeed the 'post-industrial' society is often also called the 'information society'.

Real and major changes are being registered in this analysis, but in intellectually confused ways. The very facts that are produced to inform and illustrate the analysis are themselves subject to ideological presumptions which belong to the social order which the analysis both partly illuminates and partly obscures. We can see this most clearly in the founding definitions of categories of work.

There has been since the 1930s an orthodox tripartite division of kinds of work. This begins with a primary sector, in agriculture and the gaining of raw materials. There is then a secondary sector, in which goods (commodities) are manufactured. This is followed by a tertiary sector, often headlined as 'service industries', in which, within the orthodox definition of employment, everything else is done. Given these categories, it can be shown that the primary sector has dramatically declined: in the whole period of the industrial revolution from well over 50 per cent to under 10 per cent. The secondary sector, manufacturing, rose in the same period to a peak of more than 35 per cent but is now falling towards 20 per cent. The miscellaneous tertiary sector, quoted as 'services', provides the residual figures, and is now evidently, in these terms, an actual majority. This is then taken to be the nature of a 'post-industrial' economy.

This confusion has to be tackled at several levels. First, it has been shown by several recent analysts (cf. B. Jones, *Sleepers, Wake!*, 1982) that the orthodox tertiary sector is absurd. It includes work as diverse as building, construction and transport on the one hand and professional, commercial and entertainment employment on the other. Evidently some of these 'services' are the necessary infrastructure of manufacturing distribution; others are agencies of the public order; others again are services provided for individuals. In all of these, in fact, the growth of 'information' employment is marked; it has been aggregated at more than 50 per cent of all employment, in the most developed industrial societies.

But this kind of aggregation, within the received overall categories, is misleading. The special problems of what has been called the 'information society', and its major new technologies, will be examined more closely in the chapter on 'Culture and Technology'. What must be noted at this stage is the extent to which this classification of work is confused by the ideology of work as employment, within market terms. The three-sector model in fact reproduces the stages of production for a market within industrial capitalism, though by some residual traces from the real world it then succeeds in confusing them.

At its simplest, the model presupposes the gaining of raw materials, their manufacture as commodities, and then their distribution. A scheme of production for the market has then substituted itself for a society, even a society conceived primarily in terms of work. All that work which is the nurture and care of human beings, on whom the entire system depends, is excluded unless it is paid employment. All social development and education is either excluded or is relegated to the tertiary sector, where it can be seen as dependent on what have been defined as primary and secondary, although in reality all are mutually interdependent. Again, the care of people, in all phases of life but especially in sickness and age, becomes, in the model, what is attended to after the primary raw material and secondary manufacturing processes have been completed. This set of relegations and exclusions, in the interest of a scheme of increased and profitable production, is the inner history of industrial capitalist society. It has never in practice been able to shift all human priorities and interests into its desired ordering, but it has established itself as systematically dominant. It has done this by its control of the means and resources of production, which prevents all but a small minority from gaining their livelihood with their own means and resources, and which forces them into available employment.

There is a further point about orthodox classifications of work, as conceived within the assumptions of industrial capitalism. One of the delusions of modern production is its definition of *skill*, which appears in the occupational categories as *skilled*, *semi-skilled* and *unskilled*. One of the first extraordinary effects of this is that, interacting as it does with the definition of work as employment, it relegates most of the fundamental forms of human work to the *unskilled*. All the ordinary nurture and care of people, and all ordinary homemaking and preparation of food, are in this lowest category or beneath it. Then, even within employment, the old skills of farming, gardening, fishing, lumbering are written down as unskilled. Harry Braverman, who initiated analysis of this fantastic distortion (in *Labor and Monopoly Capital*, 1974), goes on to show in clear detail how the category of the *semi-skilled*, defined by routine operations with machines, has been used to support a quite false assertion of the increase of skilled labour in industrial production. It is not only, for example, that the deep skills of tending land and growing food are categorically reduced by comparison with relatively quickly learned operations with machines (a typical training for these is from a few weeks to a few months). It is also that the general tendency of industrial production has been to displace or reduce the industrially skilled craftsmen, whose apprenticed trades, on which all early mechanical production absolutely depended, may often be cut out by centrally automated processes. The confusion about skills is especially marked in the supposed tertiary sector, which manages to include some of the longest periods of formal training, a large number of relatively quickly learned routines, and those traditional skills which, dependent primarily on experience, have been ideologically classed as unskilled.

It is of course true at the same time that the development and application of advanced technology, in an increasing number of kinds of work, requires a growing number of very highly skilled workers, typically with theoretical as well as practical knowledge. But it is an outcome of the same process that there is a steady polarisation between this important group and an increasing majority of workers whose means of livelihood depend on the maintenance and reproduction of existing working routines: routines, however, which it is one of the central purposes of increasingly rationalised production to reduce or abolish. This is the crisis of employment which will dominate the coming generations. It can be summed up in the word which is now the battlecry of the directors of industrial capitalist production: *overmanning*. As labour processes are rationalised, and costs in a competitive market pressed to be reduced, this social order of work is saying to the people of the society not only that in this or that industry the workforce must be reduced but that, taken as a whole, the society itself is overmanned. It is this disastrous and ultimately fatal conclusion which is the true crisis of industrial capitalism, which in its own terms can think and act in no other ways.

4

Or are there other ways? The hope that there might be, within the existing kind of social and economic order, underlies the proposition of a 'post-industrial' society. It is believed that as the workforce in agriculture and manufacturing continues its steep decline, the transfer to 'service' employment, already strongly under way, and especially to 'information employment', will simply redistribute jobs. This belief in 'transfer', historically based on the entry of the displaced farm labourers into the factories, is uncritically extended to what are in fact quite new social conditions.

For, first, in much service employment (as in the techniques of 'fast food') and especially in information employment (computers, teletext, word-processors as against bookkeeping, typing and filing) the same processes of capital intensity and labour reduction are now being very strongly developed. Professional work of all kinds is unlikely to be reduced for any technical reasons, but already its natural growth is being restrained by problems of funding (as in medicine and edcucation) within the priorities of a capitalist economy. The one great area of work that will never be made redundant, though it may continue to gain useful technical supports, is in the nurture and lifelong care of people. The permanent need for such work, often now dramatised by its relative neglect under other pressures and priorities, makes it nonsense to say that in any future society there will not be enough work to go round. At different phases of life, but especially in infancy, sickness, disability and old age, the ratio of work is never less than one to one and can be as high as three to one, if it is to be properly carried out. But then it is precisely in this area of permanent need that the category of 'employment' exerts its worst distortions. Within the terms of a capitalist economy, the raising and care of healthy and capable human beings is emphatically not seen as 'the creation of wealth'.

Yet it has been widely hoped that the results of labour-saving could be used to create a new kind of society. It would be one in which the worst physical burdens were lifted, in which working years and hours could be dramatically shortened, and in which – in that highly significant phrase, expressing a permanent response to the social order of capitalist employment – people could have 'more time to themselves'. These are reasonable hopes. The technical conditions for them already exist. But then everything depends on which of the two meanings of 'labour-saving' we choose.

The humane choice is clear enough. Nobody who for any length of time has done heavy, dirty or dangerous labour, or for that matter endlessly repetitive routine impersonal tasks, could wish for any-thing but the further development of true labour-saving. Some critics of industrial production or electronic technology as such, usually writing at comfortable distances from the actual labour these replace, have lost human contact with most actual people. It is true that there are better kinds of work than either, and that in very diverse ways most of us would like to have more time for them. But the only way in which enough or all of us can get such conditions of choice is through the further development of all real labour-saving, in all necessary burdensome, fatiguing or boring work.

On the other hand the dominant meaning of 'labour-saving' is now very different. It is not so much the labour that will be saved as the labourers: the 'employees'; the 'labour costs'; the payroll. This connects with an important retrospective argument about the in-dustrial revolution itself. It has been widely argued recently that (all) critics of the industrial revolution have been hostile to progress and production. It has even been said that there is some element in English culture which makes it resistant to such progress, and which is now responsible for the British industrial decline. This is an intolerable confusion. The element in English culture which has been hostile to production and trade has a precise location in a *rentier* sector and in its supporting writers and thinkers. This sector, living on rents from land or on profits from internal and external produc-tion and trade, has kept its physical distance from both agricultural and industrial development. Yet for all its expansion of an almost wholly monetary world it has forged significant cultural con-tinuities with the older culture of the landed gentry, in carefully preserved and imitated styles and titles and rituals. Essentially defined by privileged money, it has of course theoretically opposed production and trade. Its main demand has been that they should be profitably (to itself) carried on by others and as far away as possible – a condition which the export of productive capital is well on its way to realising.

But this sector is a world away from those others who are now loosely called Luddites. The actual Luddites were engaged in one of the first crises of the meaning of 'labour-saving'. Few working men and women have ever wanted to refuse machines or methods which would reduce their labour. Indeed their positive commitment to them is a major impulse which the industrial capitalist order has abused. What they have resisted, and continue to resist, is the introduction of machines and methods which will take away their employment and therefore, in conditions in which the means of independent production have been sharply reduced or altogether taken away, their income, their means of livelihood. It is an abuse of reason to confuse such men and women with the privileged distastes of the *rentiers*. Moreover it is now an ideological abuse, since it is used to block thought about the one necessary question. Are the new means of labour-saving to be used for the general wellbeing? If so, this absolutely includes the wellbeing of all those people whom the new machines and methods displace. Yet the common practice now is that they are from the beginning, in market terms, used to reduce costs, to dispense with large numbers of workers, and so to restore or maximise the profits of production. The basic choice is very clear, but it has been intolerably muddled by false ideas of work and of its possible and variable social ordering.

How does this bear on the idea of a 'post-industrial' society? To begin with, the society that is now emerging is in no sense 'post-industrial'. Indeed, in its increasingly advanced technologies, it is a specific and probably absolute climax of industrialism itself. What is often loosely meant is the declining relative importance of manufacturing, which is due to follow agriculture into being a small-minority sector of employment. The decline itself is real, in some societies, though even there its assessment is confused by tendencies in the export of manufacturing, within a world capitalist system, to countries with much lower labour costs and little or no working-class organisation. This aspect of the problem will be discussed further in the essay on 'Class, Politics, and Socialism'. Yet at this stage it is necessary to insist that a decline in manufacturing is not a decline in 'industrialism', and certainly not in industrial capitalism. The system of rationalised production by increasing applications of technology, within a system of regular wage-labour hired by the owners of the means of production, is not weakened but in its immediate terms strengthened when smaller and smaller numbers of workers are required to operate it. Moreover, service employment of a related kind, in distribution and checking, including the distribution and checking of information, is itself caught up in the same process, and is not, in its usual terms, the great residual to which the unwanted will transfer. The only available area for transfer, which is also the ground for great hope, is that of relatively direct human work and activity, for which, however, the market has no time except as a margin or an unavoidable residue.

It is by no means certain how fast a 'post-industrial' society, of this reduced market kind within the existing social order, will develop in practice. There are many centres of resistance to it, not only in trade unions but in habits of expectation of regular paid employment, which are still electorally powerful. There is also resistance of a deeper kind, from habits of work which have survived or developed within many of the most regulated systems. To the despair and anger of the great rationalisers of production, many people still spend a lot of their time at work talking to other people about other things, or in a host of marginal and unpaid activities. It is easy to say that these are compensatory activities; that people have to be there, for the money, but then make the best of it. It can be argued that it would be better to have much shorter hours and all go off home. But many people need a workplace just because it gives them these varied social relationships. In real terms these are choices for actual people to make. Much of the evidence so far, including the behaviour of those who are theoretically the great rationalisers, suggests a wealth of human ingenuity in finding something to do which appears to make a job indispensable. Of course, as most notably near the top of modern industry and services, this can become decadent. In some circumstances, under relatively tough conditions, it can even destroy the valued place. But taken together with what may be, for a time, the electorally enforceable demand for regular employment income or its direct substitutes, and with the stubborn though now in most conditions less enforceable resistance of the unions, concerned with simple job preservation, the introduction of this technically possible and (by its directors) theoretically desired economy may be slower in coming to completion than simple technical analysis suggests.

At some points, however, and in certain variable degrees, it is already making its mark. What then needs to be looked at is the major problem of the future of income and means of livelihood as the old employment system is steadily reduced. But before this, we should look at an important alternative account of what appears to be the same general process: not the coming of a 'post-industrial' society but, as in countries like Britain, a damaging and even frightening 'deindustrialisation'.

4

Everyone seems to be saying that the British economy is being 'deindustrialised', but what this means is not clear. Should 'deindustrialisation' mean a decline in the total of industrial production, for example, or a decline in the total or the proportion of industrial workers? As it happens the British economy has recently experienced both, but it is still a key question to ask which is meant, and which matters more. In simple market terms, and within the habit of measuring production as an undiscriminated general total, it is obvious that the level of production matters more. The same or increased production, with fewer workers, is a sacred capitalist intention. At the same time falls in production, whether generally or in particular sectors, are usually bad news, since in conditions of stable or increasing demand they mean, as is now widely the case in Britain, that a greater share of production is being taken by competitors including crucially foreign competitors. In conditions of reduced demand, these competitive pressures are even heavier.

On the other hand, reduced industrial employment may be either an index of reduced production or a result of technical change. It is in practice very difficult, when both conditions are present, to analyse and assign figures to these distinguishable causes. Almost the whole of current politics circles around these questions, and in some cases is based on genuine concern. Those who choose the level of production as primary are determined, by a whole range of measures, including typically the reduction of 'overmanning', to make industry more competitive and in that way raise production again. Others, in a plausible option, choose both at once: more production *and* more jobs of an existing kind. Very few of us, faced with the urgency of these questions, can really see the argument through. Most of the choices involved are too radically disturbing, and even if they can be made in the head they become very different on the ground and with actual people.

What then most needs to be said is that the industrial revolution has not been a process of a single economy, and that at every stage it is insufficient or actually misleading to isolate an economy within national borders and propose policies within those unrealistic terms. It is true that there are periods of relative advantage and disadvantage between economies considered nationally. Diverse national policies and changing objective conditions have observable major effects.

Yet what in its full development the industrial revolution created was not only a world market – some of the conditions for that had been created before general industrial production – but an interlocking, interdependent and (in national terms) interpenetrating world market. The current crises of both industrial production and industrial employment, on a world scale, show this underlying and persistent reality very clearly. Within it, all the time, there are ups and downs, shifts of advantage and disadvantage, but it is always the general process that is finally dominant. And what has then to be said, not as paradox, is that the various forms of local and national deindustrialisation have, as one of their principal causes, the general process of industrialisation itself.

It has always to some extent been so. By its inherent processes of centralising and rationalising production, the industrial capitalist system has been socially and economically uneven in its effects. When it was still only a matter of a single nation, disadvantaged and peripheral regions and smaller and more traditional types of production were steadily and at times ruthlessly marginalised or excluded. In a developing world trade, the same things were done to other societies and their native modes of production. As the whole process was generalised, and became ever more intense, a worldwide scramble for productive advantage and for markets was unleashed. Production was no longer defined by socially determined needs, but by the constant move outwards, leaving behind any worked-out areas or unprofitable communities. The deindustrialisation of certain sectors, regions, countries was thus a wholly predictable result of this ever more dominant mode of production.

It is hard when it happens to your own people: no harder, but more actual, than when it happens to others. Yet the only intelligent response is not then a further intensification of this at once necessarily productive and destructive process, but a search for the means of its rational control. This is not now what is generally happening. Within particular economies, most discussion is centred on the drive for competitive advantage, currently at the cost of mass unemployment and the impoverishment of all other parts of the society. It may seem for a time to make sense, until you realise that *everyone*, every economy, is doing this. I know that I have gone from reading the English newspapers on these familiar themes and then read for some weeks the French or the Italian or the German newspapers only to realise, beyond the differences of language, that the same analyses were being applied, the same remedies proposed, as if each were the only people in the world. This talk is described by its practitioners as tough and realistic, but even where it is benevolent it is a fantasy. It could only be by some almost inconceivable expansion of world trade, surpassing not only the probable limits of natural resources but also the hitherto intractable problems of the poverty and lack of buying-power of those most in need, that the aggregated export plans of the old industrial countries, the newly industrialising countries and those now planning industrialisation could possibly be realised, or come anywhere near their projections. However, instead of recognising this, the silly tough talk goes on. It is fully in the spirit of the history of industrial capitalism that its vocabulary is violent: 'aggressive marketing', 'market penetration', 'consumer impact'. Yet most of this talk is by smooth men in sleek offices taking no significant risks. The real toughness is all at the other end: where caring and efficient production can be ruined by the arbitrary exploitation of temporary advantages; where the edge of the most currently competitive economies (at whatever costs to their own workers and citizens) can cut into other societies and depress or ruin them; or where, within a currently uncompetitive economy, millions are out of work while millions are in need.

There will be 'deindustrialisation', in certain sectors, just as there will be new industrialisation in others. But the only attainable general solution is some form of reconstruction of the basic mode of production itself. This can only be on the principle of combining necessary domestic production with planned foreign trade. The principle of a society sustained by its economy has to replace the practice of a society determined by a market.

There are then vast practical problems. The definition of the appropriate size of such a society is among the first. The obvious definition, in the nation-state, is inadequate in both directions. It includes, internally, depressed and marginalised regions, their production determined by the larger forces elsewhere. At the same time, in the actual diversity of resources and skills, it is often too small to sustain a stable and adequate economy from its own production. But then none of the economic problems is soluble, in any new ways, unless we begin from some realistic definition of a society and then directly determine its necessary production and trade, rather than as now, with increasing hopelessness, taking such society as is left after the operations of the international market.

5

Within any reconstruction of the mode of production, certain basic problems of work and income persist. Yet some already possible solutions come into view, and only come into view, when this major reconstruction has been begun. Within the terms of the capitalist market, and within the imposition of free trade by the temporarily strongest economies, necessary domestic production can not even be defined. The cheapest or most available or most recent products will be bought from anywhere, often financed by debt. Foreign trade, meanwhile, is not a matter of mutual and stable advantage, but an arbitrary interpenetrating process within an inherently unequal world economy. To draw back and begin to determine production and trade from the whole needs of the people of a society requires, evidently, first limiting and then breaking the arbitrary power of capital: increasingly, in practice, of international capital.

It is the detailed practicability of what could and would then happen that is now in question. The will to challenge and defeat the arbitrariness of capital is almost wholly dependent on a belief that the rest of us could in practice manage our own affairs, and that there is some other future than being its declining but inevitable employees.

At the most general level the reality of the hope can not be doubted. Freed from random external forces, a society could make its own patterns of production and use, its own scales and rhythms of work, within the material limits from which every society must in reality define itself. The possible arrangements are then very diverse. There is, to begin with, the choice within the range of effective societies: the range, for example, from Wales to Western Europe. There are major advantages in the larger societies, both in diversity of resources and in the capacity to sustain a stable economy in a world market which will not change all at once. At the same time, as my own land, Wales, has repeatedly experienced, a real society, deciding its own production and trade, can be lost along the way to some larger political unit. These problems and choices are discussed again in the essay on 'The Culture of Nations'.

More generally, and quite as hard to solve, there is the problem of the relation between work and income. It will be one of the main advantages of changing the mode of production that people, rather than only employers, will be able to decide, in specific cases, what amount and type of real labour-saving will be introduced, in relation both to its advantages and to its effects on available work. Nobody can predict how all these choices would come out, but it seems likely that the amount of necessary work, certainly in manufacturing and distribution, would decline. It is then obviously possible to share this, in each sector, by shorter working lives and hours, but of course what will also have to be shared is the income, the share of production. Moreover, given the probable and necessary increase in work directly concerned with people rather than with goods, there are quite new problems of determining value and therefore income, in work which by definition is not marketed. Again, beyond these different kinds of active workers, there is the problem of determining the level of transfer of the means of livelihood to those who are not working, by reason of age, sickness or disability, or who (as in proposals for a general minimum income unrelated to work) are for other reasons out of the work-income relationship. This problem will also materialise, at a very different level, in the changes already under way in both the idea and the practice of the family as a 'unit of household income'. The more diverse primary relationships which people seem likely to choose (and it is this diversity and relative freedom of choice which needs to be emphasised, rather than any new single pattern) will encounter some quite new conditions of material livelihood and relationship as the full-employment pattern weakens. Some new and renewed kinds of positive bonding, as distinct from the liberal 'independence' apparently offered by employment, are certain to be necessary.

If then the first problem of the coming economy is the recovery of control of our own production, the second problem is that of the politics and culture of income and transfer. It is true that the absolute link between employment and income has already been broken. Not only in the provision of public education and health services, but more directly in the extension of benefits to citizens rather than only to workers, the crude market principle has already been refined. Yet it would be stupid not to notice that this regulated distribution of benefits, in much the same way as the contested distribution of incomes, has produced many destructive confusions and resentments. In a society which did not yet fully control its own production, these might actually increase, in conditions of declining marketable employment. Certainly one common current projection, of skilled and highly skilled minorities very actively engaged at work, and of a majority not employed in profitable work but sustained from the energy and resources of the others, is wholly unrealistic and unstable. Its most likely product would be a more actively authoritarian and more criminal society.

It is only by a full recovery of control of production, and therefore of the fully social means of determining shares of work and of livelihood, that these problems can be solved, and even then only by very advanced forms of democratic discussion and decision. The current political market, like the economic market from which it in some respects derives, is altogether too crude for their complex resolution. What was argued in 1959, that the 'social services . . . remain limited by assumptions and regulations belonging not to the new society but the old', is still true but incomplete. There was never any way in which the genuinely new ideas and provisions for a caring society could persist as an *exceptional* sector, contradicted by systematic inequality and competition everywhere else. In fact the models of 'relief' and 'insurance', from the old order, provided a base from which, in a period of rising incomes, the idea of common social provision was steadily weakened and interpreted as selective 'entitlement' and burdensome 'cost'. It is not by bureaucratic regulation, however complex, but only by direct communal administration, that an idea of common welfare can become actual.

At the same time it is impossible that any of these problems can be solved by measures based on the kind of fantasy which has grown in the shadow of the capitalist ideal of ever-expanding, ever-competitive, ever-successful production. The kinder-sounding fantasy of giving everybody more and more, so that no choices need ever be made, is the death-cry of an old social democracy. The world is not only as tough as the capitalists keep telling us; it is very much tougher. There are hard material limits, wherever they may finally and unevenly fall, on the indefinite production and consumption of goods which the capitalist system and its political junior partners have assumed and promised. Real sharing will have to occur, in some cases within increased production and available time, in other cases within stable or actually reduced resources and availabilities. The profound political problems of sharing, which if it succeeds can take us beyond an industrial capitalist order, can be neither evaded nor postponed by the old fable of the cake. A sharing society, in any case, has to begin by really sharing what it has, or all its talk of sharing is false or at best marginal. Moreover, sharing is not only at the receiving end; it is also, from the beginning, a matter of shared effort and responsibility. These are the only conditions for anything but an imposed and arbitrary stability, or an unstable chaos.

6

What has finally to be said, though, is that the major changes in work and production which are now happening and which are only weakly interpreted by the received ideas of both industrial and post-industrial society, are evidence as much of opportunity as of danger. It is only within a false and unnecessary system that there can ever really be over-production, or unwanted work, or what are called, cruelly, 'redundancy' and 'overmanning'. In the reality of labour saving, and in the availability of new skills and activities, we could, quite practically, enter a new world of human work. Sharing the political effort to make it like that is then in practice our first task.

DEMOCRACY OLD AND NEW

I

Many basic changes in the organisation of work and in the distribution of income and resources will happen whatever political choices we may make. Yet politics can be either a limping follower, trying to tidy up and adjust to the economic and social consequences, or an active common effort to foresee and direct all necessary changes, in the general interest. In *The Long Revolution* I argued the need for an educated and participating democracy. I intended an equal emphasis on each condition. General participation in common decisions can be argued on grounds of principle. It is, after all, the deepest principle of democracy itself. But it has also still to be argued in terms of efficiency. In a complex and interdependent society, sustained effective decisions require positive general involvement and consent. At the same time the nature of the decisions now being presented to us, involving not only general redirections of policy but very sensitive and flexible forms of negotiation of detailed changes, innovations and adjustments, all in matters requiring the fullest available knowledge, increases the emphasis on education and information in the most urgent practical ways.

Yet many people – some reluctantly, some cynically – are now losing faith in or actually rejecting democracy. The necessary decisions, it is said, are too complex and too dependent on specialised knowledge. The electoral rhythm, with its crude swings of opinion, prevents the sustained execution of any long-term rational policy. It is not clear, in most such arguments, what then follows. There are fantasies and indeed some planning of more efficient forms of expert administration, either removed or better shielded from the electoral process. There are some uglier ideas of an effective imposition of new kinds of authoritative regime: constitutional if possible, based on the manipulation of government within existing electoral systems; unconstitutional if necessary, in the form of direct controls by an alliance of administrators, financial institutions, the police and military, and 'impartial' or 'national' political leaders and figureheads.

Each of these tendencies, it is true, has existed in various forms throughout modern political history. Some of them, usually disastrously, have actually been put into practice. Yet what is most worrying now is that versions of such directions, and especially the first, are coming not only from the traditional enemies of democracy but from some of those who most clearly realise the nature and depth of the crisis we are entering. Such people have convinced themselves, on apparently rational grounds, that the kinds of decisions that are going to have to be made – in the management of scarce resources within tight limits of growth; in the unprecedented problems of transfer of income within quite different patterns of employment and non-employment – are beyond the understanding but even more beyond the wills and interests of the ordinary electoral process. It will then be a choice, the best of them say, between new kinds of decision-making or relatively rapid disintegration and decline. The worst of them, meanwhile, await just such a moment, when they will be called to institute their programmes of authoritarian salvation.

It would be very much easier if we could say that such people are simply wrong. That is, in effect, what is said by what remains of the old liberal consensus, in which either the market or the existing forms of parliamentary democracy, or as in common practice the two in general combination, will solve these problems in the future as they have solved them in the past. It is a familiar and reassuring response. Hands still get raised for it. But what more and more people now see, as often in merely cynical as in any serious and constructive ways, is that it has been this precise combination of the market and old-style representative democracy which has led us into these major problems, or has at best proved incapable of preventing or resolving them. The grounds for certain kinds of authoritarian alternative are then being steadily consolidated and extended. Indeed the combination of seemingly insoluble economic crises and of contempt for politicians is just such a ground.

It is against these dangers (either a continuation of the present orthodox drift, with all the social and economic failures it is certain to lead to; or the impatient move or relapse to more shielded and authoritarian forms) that the case for an educated and participating democracy has again to be made. The phrase itself, though not really the case, was widely repeated in the 1960s, and can still sometimes be heard. It appeared in many places in carefully diluted forms, as new procedures of consultation, new arrangements for communication, within relatively unchanged structures of decision and control. But these, however locally desirable, are not what was meant. What was and is meant is the institution and extension of quite new forms of decision-making, and of the processes of information which are necessary for such decisions.

I have of course been told, repeatedly, that people are just not interested enough – even, behind the hand, not intelligent enough – to make these new institutions and processes work. The usual evidence offered is the cynicism and apathy surrounding existing electoral and democratic forms. None of us can ignore this, yet equally none of us can know how much of it is the predictable consequence of merely *apparent* involvement in decision-making. Too many familiar current processes frustrate or default on actual decisions, or somehow lose them in the carefully protected intricacies of reference elsewhere. There is now so much of this, and so much that appears systematic, that anyone can feel discouraged. But it would be absurd to reject new principles and practices on the evidence of the very faults of those older principles and practices which now make changes necessary. In truth nobody can know exactly how any of it would work, until some of it has been tried. And it has certainly not, in any general way, been tried.

One central reason for not trying it is the hysterically defensive response to any such proposals from the existing representative institutions. It is understandable and welcome that there should be vigorous defences of parliamentary democracy against the strong current tendencies to bureaucratic or authoritarian solutions. There are plenty of examples, all over the world, to show us the deficiencies and the evils – often both – of such forms. But it will not then do to abstract 'parliamentary democracy', in its simple and just comparison with those authoritarian forms, and go on to use the mere phrase, in hypnotic or self-hypnotic ways, against quite different tendencies of a democratic kind. For it is precisely the existence of major and increasing bureaucratic and authoritarian practices, within and alongside the institutions of parliamentary democracy, which has led to these new democratic proposals and campaigns. This is not only some abstract or theoretical argument. The scale of the general crisis now developing is such that it is virtually certain that there will be changes in one direction or another: either more democratic or more authoritarian. Failure to make any changes is almost certain to lead to continued social and economic decline and disintegration, or indeed to worse.

Thus the argument must be resumed, and first, because it is where the mental blocks are now in place, on the nature of parliamentary democracy.

2

What sort of definition is 'parliamentary democracy'? Is 'parliamentary' a qualifying adjective, to indicate one kind of democracy but also to admit that there are other kinds? Or is it, in effect, an excluding adjective, to indicate that there is only one real kind of democracy, which operates through the procedures of a parliament? This second answer often carries a further implication: that a parliament is not only a necessary but a sufficient condition of democracy. If you have a parliament, you have a democracy.

The difficulty with any such conclusion is, of course, that there have been several kinds of parliament in societies which hardly anyone would consider to be democracies. The English medieval *parlement* or *parliamentum* was a meeting of the king in council, to which judges were summoned. One of the same words, *parliamentum*, was later applied to what was also called a *colloquium*, a meeting of the king in council, to which peers, or the higher clergy, or representatives of counties and boroughs, were summoned for specific business. Later again, such a *parlement* – still then a general word for a meeting and discussion – became more regular, and was distinguished from the king's council. Eventually there was a definition of two 'houses', of lords and commons, which could enact legislation and pass it to the king's council for assent. All these and later developments are important stages in the movement from an absolute to a constitutional monarchy, but none of them, as yet defined, are or were ever claimed to be elements of a *democracy*.

But if a parliament is not a sufficient condition for a democracy, should the definition then be taken as a whole: *parliamentary democracy* or, as we now often hear, 'parliamentary democracy as we know it'. The crucial condition then becomes a process of *election* of the representatives gathered in a parliament. This is widely and reasonably believed, but the problem then is how we identify and date it. The two elements of the definition, *parliament* and *democracy*, are not only run together but are often confused. Thus 'the English parliamentary tradition' can be given an historical ancestry of some seven hundred years, but the element of 'democracy' has a more arguable but in any case much shorter ancestry: from at most, say, a hundred and fifty years (the Reform of 1832), down to little more than fifty, when all adult women were at last given the vote (1928). The electorate as a percentage of the adult population (over 20) ranged from 4.4 per cent in 1831 to 16.4 per cent in 1868 to 30 per cent in 1914 to 74 per cent in 1921 to 96.9 per cent in 1931. As matters of history these are important and complex changes, but they are often overridden by a sweeping invocation of 'the tradition of parliamentary democracy', running these diverse and often contrasting elements into a general and even 'immemorial' haze.

But that, it is regularly said, is the past. What is at issue, now, is the system of parliamentary democracy 'as we know it'. Yet this, also, requires scrutiny. Suppose we begin not historically but formally, and define parliamentary democracy and its conditions. We must recognise some diversity of arrangements, in different national traditions, but we can probably agree on the most general features. Consider this definition:

A parliamentary democracy is a system in which the whole government of a society is determined by a representative assembly, elected in secret ballot by all adult members of the society, at stated and regular intervals, for which any adult member of the society may be an open and equal candidate.

All formal definitions have their difficulties, but this seems fairly to represent the general idea of parliamentary democracy which is now current.

We can then ask three questions. To what extent, in the terms of this definition, is Britain, today, a parliamentary democracy? More generally, to what extent can any parliamentary democracy be said to determine the whole government of a modern society? Finally, what are the relations between parliamentary democracy, in this agreed general sense, and other actual and possible ideas of institutions of democracy?

3

It is taken for granted, in current arguments, that Britain is a parliamentary democracy. But this assumption can be shown to depend on running the two elements of the definition together, unargued. We indeed have a parliament. We also have a system of general election, by universal adult suffrage. This system is supported by general customs and conventions of free speech and free assembly.

These are very important and valuable conditions of British society. It is necessary to support and defend them, most specifically against those elements of the Right who talk of the society as 'ungovernable' and of the 'crisis of democracy'. Yet to defend the real values which they embody or partly embody, we have to take the claim to 'parliamentary democracy', and especially to 'parliamentary democracy as we know it', at something more than face value.

For, first, the British Parliament, strictly speaking, is not an institution but an assembly of three bodies, of which only one is elected. The House of Commons is elected by all adult members of the society who wish to participate, and candidacy to it is (with some marginal exceptions) open to any adult member. It is not in fact elected at stated and regular intervals, but in terms of a maximum duration (five years); the date of an election, within this limit, is determined not by law but by the political decision of the head of the existing government. Its representative composition is determined by electoral procedures which need not (and in fact normally do not) correspond directly or even closely with the actual distribution of votes. Nevertheless, it is an elected assembly, and is often, as such, called 'Parliament'.

Yet Parliament in Britain, both formally and practically, contains only this one elected element. A second house of the assembled parliament, the Lords, is composed by inheritance in certain ranks of the peerage, by appointment to certain state offices, and by royal and political patronage. The distribution of powers between these two houses has a long and contentious history. In the twentieth century the House of Commons has achieved substantial predominance. Yet Parliament is still, formally and practically, and for all legislation, these two elements acting together and in relation to the third: 'royal assent' by the hereditary monarch:

Be it enacted by the Queen's most excellent Majesty, by and with the advice and consent of the Lords Spiritual and Temporal, and Commons, in this present Parliament assembled, and by the authority of the same.

Indeed Parliament is only fully constituted when it is assembled in this way: the 'Crown in Parliament', as at the 'Queen's Speech', when the Commons are summoned to the Lords to hear the monarch.

It is hardly necessary to argue that this does not sound like the language and procedures of modern electoral democracy. Of course some aspects of this real situation are treated, in practice, as if they were merely ceremonial: what Bagehot called the theatrical elements of the constitution. Certainly some of them are so. It is well known that the 'Queen's Speech' is determined and written by the government which commands a majority in the Commons. The elaborate fancy dress and ceremonies, on such occasions, are also evidently theatrical and decorative. Yet it would be a serious mistake to suppose that this actual constitution of the true Parliament is only a picturesque survival. The House of Lords, controlled by heredity rather than by election, is often seen as residual: a contradiction of the ideology of electoral democracy. It is indeed a contradiction of the ideology, but in terms of the actual constitution it may be not the House of Lords but the House of Commons that is anomalous. For the sovereignty of the British State is not in the British people, as in most electoral democracies, but in this special definition of the

'Crown in Parliament'. British adults are not citizens but, legally, *subjects*, in that old term derived from absolute monarchy. The powers of the often unregarded third element, in the Palace and also in the Privy Council, are legally very extensive, though conventionally only exercised formally and in certain limited areas (such as universities). When the House of Commons is functioning in what have come in the twentieth century to be regarded as 'normal' ways – for example with an evident Prime Minister with a majority in the Commons – the powers are indeed only formal. But in either of two possible cases, in changing political conditions – failure of parties to agree, in a House of Commons with no single party majority; or a more general state of civil emergency – the powers are there and ready to be exercised.

Such powers are in any case backed by an alternative ideology, which runs in a crazy parallel with the ideology of electoral democracy. For all British Ministers are Ministers of the Crown, Her Majesty's Ministers. Even the Opposition is Her Majesty's Opposition: a phrase first used in the nineteenth century as a joke. The state bureaucracy is a Civil Service, the armed forces the Military Services, of this same 'Crown' or 'Crown in Parliament'. The constant reinforcement of this level of authority, locally theatrical but then undoubtedly culturally powerful, can never reasonably be seen as politically neutral. Attempts to assimilate the Second Chamber to the electoral ideology – for example by a general or Commons vote to abolish or radically to reform the House of Lords – would encounter, at every stage of its legislation, the entrenched powers of the legal constitution of Parliament, to the point where it could indeed be the case that the electoral process and the elected Commons were seen as anomalous and practically, within existing terms, ineffective. A majority of practising politicians seem already willing to back off when they see this forbidding range ahead of them, for it may in practice be very much easier to override an electoral mandate (the normal ideological appeal for legitimacy) than to sustain a conflict with these entrenched powers.

Thus it matters a good deal, in current arguments in Britain, whether the appeal is to 'parliamentary democracy' or to 'parliamentary democracy as we know it'. For the latter, with its deeply conservative implications, has to be sharply distinguished from the former, as generally understood. Indeed there would seem to be three minimum conditions for Britain to become a modern parliamentary democracy:

 (i) the transfer of legal sovereignty to the people or to their elected parliament;
 (ii) abolition of the second chamber now based on heredity and patronage, and its replacement by a differently constituted body, based on election;
(iii) adoption of an electoral system which would determine the composition of an elected parliament in terms of the actual distribution of popular votes.

It is perfectly possible to argue against any or all of these changes, by other political criteria. What is really disreputable is to argue against any of them in the name of representative or parliamentary democracy. The details of such changes, including the necessary choices between available and possible alternative procedures within these conditions, can be separately argued. But it is necessary at the outset to reject the current orthodox cant and to place the whole argument on its real ground, which is that if Britain wants a system of full parliamentary democracy, it still has some distance to go.

4

The defects of British 'parliamentary democracy as we know it' can be seen as archaic and residual, to be remedied by modernising reforms or by the adoption of models from other democratic societies. Yet there is another dimension of argument (often in practice used to defend or rationalise the residual elements in Britain) which turns on the broader question of 'representation', 'parliamentary democracy' then being a special form of the more general principle of 'representative democracy'.

'Representation' is at first sight a very simple idea. In societies which have too many people to be able, practically, to meet together and take decisions, representatives of various localities, various interests, various opinions, are in some way appointed or elected to meet and conduct the necessary business.

This is so obviously necessary, in all ordinary contemporary circumstances, that it acquires the status of common sense, and is then used to justify, in what are often very sweeping ways, many kinds of political system which describe themselves as 'representative'.

Yet if we look back at the definition just given, and think about it, many problems soon appear. 'Various localities . . . interests . . . opinions': there, for a start, are three quite different bases of representation. 'In some way appointed or elected': there, in practice, is a diverse and often fiercely contested political history. 'The necessary business': there is the problem of defining the scope and powers of 'representatives'.

Before entering the detail of such problems, it is necessary above all to be aware of the different actual meanings of this important group of words: *represent, representation, representative*. From very early in their history there are two related but distinguishable lines of meaning: on the one hand the process of 'making present'; on the other hand the process of 'symbolisation'. The political uses are often confused across this range.

What does it mean, for example, when the successful candidate, in a contested parliamentary election, says, as is now customary after the result, that he intends to represent all electors in his constituency, and not just those who voted for him? This can sound absurd or offensive, especially to those who have just given much time and energy to rejecting him. How can this person whose policies they have bitterly opposed now 'represent' their views in parliament? There is some element of attempted unification and consensus, after the electoral battle, but the main ground of the idea is different and in its own way rational, because it rests on one selected idea of 'representation'. What is being claimed, and is usually honoured in practice, is that the elected person will take up cases and problems on behalf of any of his constituents, whether or not they voted for him. This is a use very similar to that in 'legal representative', when a competent person acts on another's behalf. Parliamentary representatives, in current practice, act for constituents in a range of dealings with government and public bodies, in which their formal position gives them status or influence, and indeed more widely. It is a useful function: often, paradoxically, because of the distances and intricacies of actual governmental bureaucracy within a parliamen-

tary-democratic governmental system. Yet of course it has very little
to do with the central ideas of 'representative democracy', which
imply that the elected assembly is a means of representing the diverse
political views of all citizens. In practice, in Britain, if we have a local
or personal problem with some public body, we write to our elected
members and ask them to act on our behalf, but if we have a political
argument or cause, while we may seek to influence them (often
knowing in advance that their political views are quite different or
are indeed explicitly opposed to our own), we look for other
channels to represent ('make present') our views: members elsewhere, in another party, or more general public argument or action.

This familiar problem takes us to the heart of the general question
of 'representation'. The notion of responsibility to what members
call, with a fine modesty, 'my constituents', rests on the old territorial basis of parliament, in which members were gathered from
counties and boroughs, both before and after any electoral procedures. Originally these were 'representative' in a supposed fusion
of the two senses of 'represent'; they 'made present' a particular
locality at the centre of power, and they were able to do this because
they were taken to be symbolically 'representative' of that locality as
a whole. This latter is in the powerful second line of meaning, as
when people speak of a 'representative housewife' or 'representatives
of the younger generation'; meaning not 'elected' or 'delegated' or
'mandated' but simply *characteristic, typical*. It is then crucial to
maintain a distinction between the two meanings. It is sometimes
said, for example, that the House of Lords is in some ways 'more
representative' than the House of Commons, since it includes bodies
of experience – notably in industry and the professions, from current direct involvement – which the 'party politicians' of the Commons cannot rival. It is an interesting but deeply confused argument,
since the two meanings of 'representative' are made to slip in and out
of each other.

Thus if representation were made consciously to depend on
typicality – by locality, by gender, by occupation, by age-group –
we should have one kind of assembly (not then, in practice, at all like
the House of Lords), whereas if it were made consciously to depend
on representing a diversity of formed opinions we should have
another and very different kind. In practice most 'representative'
systems are confused medleys of these different basic principles. If

the latter has tended to predominate, through modern party systems which generalise and then usually in practice monopolise the 'diversity of formed opinions', it is significant that it is then almost always (following the main lines of power in whole actual social relations) very 'unrepresentative' in terms of locality, gender, occupation and age group. The real social composition of most elected assemblies, including the contemporary House of Commons, offers glaring examples of this, especially by gender and occupation. The principle used to defend this – the organised representation of formed opinions, overriding these other differences – is up to a certain point affirmed: the parliament is legitimate because it was elected on these formed and stated opinions. Yet beyond this point it is denied, since most representatives assert other ultimate principles: 'the good of the country as a whole'; 'general public opinion'; 'personal experience'; 'private conscience'.

Of course resolution of these sometimes conflicting points of reference is not easy. What matters is the false ease with which the genuine conflicts are evaded, by moving from one idea of representation to another, as fits occasion or convenience, or, very commonly, by first using and then qualifying the supposedly predominant idea of 'representation' as the representation of 'formed opinions'. The long argument between ideas of a 'representative' and a 'delegate' has to be seen in this light. Election through an organised party system has moved decisively away from the ideas of symbolic or typical representation; formed and stated opinions are presented and voted upon. Legitimacy then necessarily depends upon the continued representation – the active presentation – of these consciously elected positions. Unforeseen changes of circumstance, or real changes of mind, can lead to difficulties, but by the chosen principle of representation they require either further formal consultation or resignation and new election. Some representatives do this, but most do not, and they justify themselves by moving to another idea of 'representative'; an experienced and competent person who acts in his own best judgment: the 'representative', we might say, as a *professional* representative.

This idea now has considerable force. In broad terms, a class of 'representatives' has been formed, initially in close relation to bodies of formed opinion, who at a certain point enter personal careers of being representative, in what is really the old symbolic sense. They are persons of political experience and judgment. If they do not already (through some accident of career or election) have anyone or anywhere to 'represent', there is public discussion and private action about 'finding them a seat'. Thus it often happens that there are important political representatives who do not yet represent anybody, in the carefully retained formal sense. Defined in this way, so that being a representative amounts to a career, a position or a job, the actual process of representing formed opinions can be set aside or made subordinate, to the extent that 'failure' to select or reselect such a person can be described as 'sacking' or 'firing' him, turning him out of his 'job'. But this is ludicrous, while the legitimacy of the assembly is still formally derived from open election within the 'diversity of formed opinions'.

There are many problems within the actual procedures of representation and delegation, of mandate and recall, and of the selection of representatives of bodies of formed opinion. These need to be precisely discussed, not only in existing terms, but within the now rapidly changing social and material conditions of public information and communication (to be discussed in the chapter on 'Culture and Technology'). Yet little progress can be made in the argument until we have clarified the notion of what it is to represent and to be representative, and then chosen between the now confused and alternative versions.

5

The distinction between 'representative' as actively presenting a formed and agreed position and 'representative' as being more generally characteristic or typical takes us into a profound problem of modern democracy. The simplest version of 'charactrersitic' representation rests, historically and theoretically, on a view of the social order as constituted by 'estates', from which representatives are summoned. This presupposes an actual and symbolic 'unity in diversity' of the State. In modern conditions, formed bodies of opinion – 'parties' – can be made to resemble 'estates', or, more specifically, social classes. In Britain, however, another version of characteristic representation became dominant, based not on estates but on territorial localities. Yet, although these were naturally diverse, the same principle of 'unity in diversity' – as still in that potent ideological description 'the United Kingdom' (or, as it is now increasingly referred to in commercial and official talk, the U.K.) – was asserted as governing the character and function of 'representation'. Thus Burke's influential distinction between a 'representative' and a 'delegate' was explicitly based on an idea of national unity: 'parliament is a *deliberative* assembly of *one* nation, with *one* interest, that of the whole'. (This 'whole' includes, for Burke, not only the living but the dead and the unborn!) Equally, from the other end of the political spectrum, the new French constitution of 1791 stated that 'the representatives chosen in the departments shall not be representatives of a particular department, but of the entire nation, and no one may give them any *mandat*'. Yet we can distinguish between this desire to avoid mere localism and particularism, so as to address the general interest, and the Burkean presumption of '*one* nation, with *one* interest', which determines the mode of loose representation rather than specific delegation.

The rhetoric of such a pre-given 'national interest' of course powerfully survives. At its worst, by being presumed, it preempts all basic arguments about what the nation and its interest are and should be. Beyond that, it is clear that there is an immediate difficulty in the presumption of a unity of interest over and above classes. Much of the practice of politics, on all sides, is the conscious representation of specific social and economic class interests. The details of instruction or mandate may vary, but the consciousness of *interest* – including, very obviously now, the special interests of locality – is openly and obviously there. Moreover, in the modern practice of manifesto which on successful election becomes and is called a *mandate*, the idea of deliberation by loosely charactersitic representatives about a presumed and agreed national interest has in practice long been abandoned.

What then actually happens, at the level of ideas? On the one hand the Burkean idea is retained for use when there is some subsequent conflict between elected and electors, or elected and the party through which election has been deliberately, on a principle of mandate, been sought. On the other hand, there is a new radical challenge to characteristic or semi-autonomous representation, and an attempt to develop the alternative idea of making present, in continuing and interactive ways, the views and interests of those who are in this more specific sense represented.

It is significant that it has been mainly in socialist and social-democratic parties that these alternative ideas have come into open conflict. For the dividing line, very deep in the alternative theories, appears to be between the presumption of a pre-existing common interest and the presumption of radical *conflicts* of interest. In the former, characteristic and autonomous or semi-autonomous representatives meet to deliberate by their own judgment and conscience. In the latter, opposed representatives assemble to negotiate or to fight out the conflicts, the criterion then being the formed and stated views of the people and interests being represented, *made present*. Most actual assemblies theorise the former and typically practise the latter.

There is another level of the problem. In conditions of extended or full adult suffrage, representation of either kind is determined by numerical aggregates of individual votes. Even in proportional electoral systems, where all individual votes count (as distinct from 'first-past-the-post', where many individuals are counted and then disregarded; often, in contests with three or more candidates, when those thus disregarded are the majority), the basis of election and mandate is individual. This presumes the sovereign individual making his choice about the whole government of his country, and then all or some individuals being counted. This theoretical presumption of the 'sovereign individual' of course prefigures the sovereign individual 'representative', though then with some obvious confusions. In either case the whole range of social relations is reduced to two entities: the 'individual' and the 'nation'.

But there is then a theory of parliament as the choice of the 'whole people', through which majorities emerge and form governments. It is not wholly a false theory, but it is not wholly true either. For in practice, in other ways, people form active institutions to represent their interests: trade unions, employers' organisations, special-interest campaigns and so on. The theory of parliament indicates that all interests are gathered and represented there, and it is then not easy to say what these other representative forms really are. One answer is that they 'make representations' to the sovereign parliament, which then decides on the issues. In practice the situation is at once more indirect and more direct. The presumed mandate of a government rests on a majority in the elected assembly. But such a majority, like the original general election, typically rests on a general package of issues, which through the parliamentary-representative system have to be chosen *as packages*, thus leaving much room for actual and subsequent diversity and disagreement. What in practice usually happens is that a government, based on its general majority, actively consults and often negotiates with representative bodies outside parliament; indeed at times more actively than it consults and negotiates with parliament itself. Some such complexities are inevitable, but what they show in practice is that the claims of parliaments to monopolise and exhaust the representative process – on which their theory still depends – are in actual conditions unrealisable.

What has to be faced is the practical coexistence of two different forms of represented interest. At one level the counting of all or some individual votes – at intervals of some years, though the process is periodically mimicked by opinion polls – leads to a representative parliament of some duration, and a government generally dependent on it. It is then already true that representation is both indirect and partial. It is notorious that hardly any modern government, in Britain, has received the positive votes of half or more than half of the electorate, and it is unusual for a government to have received even half of the votes cast. Yet a further distance and attenuation then supervene. The leader of the majority or largest party 'is invited' to form a government: the constitutional interlock with the monarchy. From that point on, the powers of the Prime Minister are in effect the powers of the whole State. Other ministers are selected by the Prime Minister and not by the elected assembly. There are always some ministers who have been elected by no one. It is necessary for such a Prime Minister and Government to retain the general support of a majority of elected representatives, but in practice they almost at once achieve an effective autonomy. This system, described in *The Long Revolution* as the periodic 'election of a court', has since been described more harshly, from the Right, as an 'elective dictatorship'. The power of the Cabinet, and increasingly of minority committees with Cabinet authority, is thus of a sovereign kind, derived from the representative process and in the end answerable to the electoral process, but in the crucial space between these autonomous. Much of the detailed information on which decisions depend is disclosed neither to parliament nor to the public, and some key decisions, on major issues, are not even announced.

What has happened is the institution of a temporarily absolutist body within the carefully preserved contradictions of the electoral process and the monarchic state. It is defended by the (in itself fair) argument that this body is 'answerable' to Parliament and eventually to the electors. But the effective meaning of 'answerable' is systematically post-dated, transferring any substance of representation to the first and last phases of a complex process. All the intervening phases are effectively and deliberately controlled by what is quite properly called a 'cabinet', an inner body of royalist-style State officers (the original *cabinet* was the monarch's private room). In relation to this system, Parliament retains a considerable importance, but most observers agree that the dominant system is not parliamentary but cabinet government, within which represented interest has been effectively divided and distanced.

This situation was crucially evident in the recent Falklands/ Malvinas crisis, when the complex details of various stages of negotiations to prevent a war were not at the relevant times laid before the House of Commons, which had in part approved the sending of armed forces as a way of backing up these negotiations. There was then an extraordinary combination of military display – 'to support the negotiations' – and military secrecy. But there was also an effective secrecy about the precise negotiations, and this was justified, in a matter of obvious public importance, and one in which by definition the details were known to 'the other side', in terms of an effective sovereignty of cabinet government. Fuller information was laid only when the negotiations were ending and military operations were about to begin.

At another level, both as new issues come up and as general policies are made specific, there is an interplay of such government with other bodies of formed interest and stated views. Of course this is described, sometimes accurately, as 'consultation with those affected'. But much of it is a very different social process, which a certain mystique of parliament disguises. For beyond the theory of sovereign individuals being counted, there are major extra-parliamentary formations of political and economic power. The financial institutions, the great capitalist corporations (including the key multinationals) and of course the capitalist press – always the loudest version of 'public opinion' – play key roles, directly and indirectly, in the formation and viability of all major policies. It is usually trade unions and radical campaigns which are identified as seeking to exercise extra-parliamentary power. Yet they are doing no more than join in an already active, powerful and accepted process, in which, by their command of resources, the extra-parliamentary forces of the capitalist system, national and international, now play the dominant part.

If the argument is that parliament should be defended against these interests, two things must be said. First, that there are honest and dishonest versions of this, and the dishonest version is that which selects trade unions, radical campaigns and party committees as the prime agents of extra-parliamentary pressure. They are at times the most visible, because they usually do not have systematic and therefore often private access, but they are far from the most powerful. Second, and more radically, that it is time to look again at the real processes and institutions of decision-making in large-scale and complex modern societies, and so look beyond the received definitions of how the system works.

6

The central objection to existing systems of representative democracy, including 'parliamentary democracy as we know it', is that their claim to constitute the whole government of the society is manifestly false. Certain key political and economic decisions are of course made and contested through such systems, but always within conditions in which control (and therefore decision-making) of the major economic resources of the country remains firmly in 'private' hands: in fact the hands of national and international capitalist corporations. Thus major decisions affecting the lives and livelihood of a majority of (individual) citizens are quite legally made beyond the reach of the system of political 'representation'. Genuine programmes to extend and achieve economic democracy, as the necessary counterpart to political democracy, are necessarily centred on measures of public ownership and control. At the same time, such programmes vary in decisive ways. They can lead to public ownership, control or direction in the already constituted and generalised sense of 'the public' as the State which emerges from the interaction between established institutions and a government derived from political representation. But the lines of control and policy are then so indirect that to speak of them as analogous with political democracy is illusory or deceptive. Moreover, the immediate social relations of decision-making, within such enterprises, are usually in no way changed. Any authentic claim to economic democracy is very different, for it is centred on the control and management of enterprises by all those working in them, and on specific policies for relating such self-management to more general and more extended interests.

Until economic democracy in this full sense is established, it is necessary to describe existing representative political systems as what they are: bourgeois democracy. The description has been sloganised, but it has a precise meaning: it is the coexistence of political representation and participation with an economic system which admits no such rights, procedures or claims. Yet the growth of bourgeois democracy was accompanied and made possible, typically in long struggles, by what is often in practice taken as the true substance of democracy; free speech, free assembly, free candidature, free election. It is then one thing to point out that these are still incomplete in bourgeois democracy, and that the power of 'private' (corporate) money can limit or at times overwhelm them. It is quite another to make a false transfer from the genuinely distinguishing charactersitics of bourgeois democracy (the continuing capitalist monopoly of predominant economic power; the use of this power to influence and at times marginalise political democracy) and then try to argue that those historically established rights and procedures, which are necessary in any democracy, are merely 'bourgeois-democratic'. This line of argument, from a dominant tendency within the countries of 'actually existing socialism', is not only theoretically false. Its practical association with the positive denial or suppression of these rights – most evidently in matters of free speech but just as crucially in matters of free candidature and election – is both a threat and an obstacle to the development of socialist democracy. Moreover, and unforgiveably, it lets bourgeois democracy off the hook, allowing it to parade these undoubted if imperfect elements of its own system as a cover for its retention of economic and associated political power over its citizens.

But what then would a genuinely socialist democracy be like? Is there not ample evidence to support the now widespread belief that socialism and democracy are incompatible, or even that they are mutually hostile forces. It can be said that this belief is the result of propaganda, and there has certainly been plenty of that. But this kind of negative and displaced answer will no longer do. The principles of a socialist democracy have to be carefully explored and argued, and many serious problems are encountered almost at once.

7

Thus what is very striking, in an exceptionally active and militant European Left, is a reliance on two principles which, if not ultimately and necessarily contradictory, are at least not self-evidently compatible. These can be summarised, briefly, as (i) a Left Government in power, and (ii) self-management.

There is obvious need for a Left Government in power. Our social and economic crisis can be solved, or even mitigated, only by such a government or by one of a much harder Right. The problem is then urgent, and one set of democratic proposals is in practice tied to this urgency. Thus in Britain the Labour Left proposes a tightly organised mass party – the Labour Party – which arrives through majority decisions by a conference of delegates at 'formed and stated' policies. It then campaigns for these policies in a general election and carries them out in government, through representatives who are in a strong (but not the strongest) sense delegates: committed to these policies, subject to questioning on them and to eventual reselection, though not to positive recall. As a radical campaign against familiar evasions of the representative system and against claims to the loosest version of representation by those who have nevertheless ridden and chosen to ride the party machine, this pressure is welcome. But theoretically and then practically it is vulnerable in several respects.

First, the source of legitimacy, in conference, is itself open to most of the objections that can be made against representation in general. This is not only a matter of the version of representation in union block voting. The content of the block vote is variably arrived at but only in a minority of cases is it based on positive voting by all members who wish to participate, and in none does it preserve the actual distribution of such votes or of the more indirect votes of committees and delegates. It is also a matter of the relative indirectness of representation even by party delegates, which again is only occasionally based on positive votes by all members who wish to participate and again fails to preserve the actual distribution of any such votes or more indirect votes by committees and local representatives.

Secondly, what is intended to emerge from such a system is an elected assembly which retains its existing sovereignty and duration. No proposals are made – and indeed such proposals are often resisted – for representation in proportion to the actual distribution of votes. The residual non-democratic assembly – the House of Lords – is correctly identified for necessary abolition, but no proposals are made for any other form of second chamber, in spite of some obvious disadvantages and dangers in unicameral government.

Thirdly, and most fundamentally, connected with the first two points, the proposals can be seen as elements of a *command* programme. Some elements of this limited democratisation could be converted into elements of political monopoly, to function within the existing sovereignty of the state machine. Since the programme is avowedly socialist, there are then many important questions arising from our whole critique of bourgeois democracy. Indeed it is here, for what start as honest reasons, that the command element enters.

It is reasonable for socialists to believe that only a determined and powerful central government can beat back and overcome the inevitable capitalist resistance to socialist measures: resistance which would typically be made in extra-parliamentary ways, through the money markets and their international alliances and institutions. Clearly the hope is that an elected parliament with a temporary monopoly of political power could use the state machine to overcome this. There are persuasive historical reasons for the *need* for such an attempt, a need which has been the origin of all socialist command economies. Yet it is one thing to identify this need, and to interpret democracy through it, and quite another to use the need to justify – by historical presumption, by theories of a vanguard, or by the fact of *past* decisions or elections – a practical monopoly of political power.

It is then a matter of great urgency to distinguish, within this now active and hopeful movement, between the genuine democratic impulses which are intended to improve and extend parliamentary democracy, and the actual methods proposed. In their existing form – without shorter parliaments, without proportional representation, without reforms of conference, without primary democratic selection of all delegates and candidates, without procedures of positive recall, and unicameral – these methods could go as easily in the direction of a command-bureaucratic government as in the direction of socialist democracy. 'Actually existing socialist democracy' is of course much nearer the former than the latter.

It is at this point that the second principle is invoked, often by the same people and in the same apparent theoretical position. What will be achieved through the command programme, some say, is self-management: popular democracy, community socialism, workers' control. There are of course others who put their primary emphasis on these means to direct democracy as an *alternative* to representative democracy. Representatives are then only those who, for unavoidable physical reasons, make present and report back to the people who retain primary responsibility and can alone make decisions. This whole mode, now attempted and active in our newest social forms – in working cooperatives and collectives – is not likely to be reduced to the status of an intended result within a command-representative system. Yet this, in muddled and generous ways, is where the argument now often rests.

It is my belief that the only kind of socialism which now stands any chance of being established, in the old industrialised bourgeois-democratic societies, is one centrally based on new kinds of communal, cooperative and collective institutions. In these the full democratic practices of free speech, free assembly, free candidature for elections, and also open decision-making, of a reviewable kind, by all those concerned with the decision, would be both legally guaranteed and, in now technically possible ways, active. This is really the only road which socialists in these countries have left to travel. It is then necessary to begin a very open and practical discussion about the relations between such institutions and the undoubted need for larger-scale institutions, whether in the unavoidable struggle against major capitalist or external resistance, or in the actual working of a complex and numerous modern industrial society. The existing dominant formula, of the tight party government which will deliver self-management, seems to me at best a pious hope, at worst a pathetic delusion.

8

The attraction of self-management, as now commonly foreseen, is its whole and direct democratic character. It is a conscious stage beyond representative democracy, whether in its post-feudal or bourgeois or social-democratic forms. Yet it is clear that most of its projections and experiments assume small-scale enterprises and communities, where its principles are more evidently practicable. What is then left beyond these, on larger scales, is either some vague and general goodwill or . . . the socialist command economy.

Some new definitions and principles need consideration. First, the problem of scale is more complex than the customary contrast of small and large. Thus certain industrial processes are necessarily complex, within both vertical and horizontal divisions of labour, and decision-making in them cannot in all respects be assigned to elements of the enterprise. Similarly, there is a range of social policies from those which affect only the inhabitants of a definable locality to those which affect much wider populations and the relations between localities. Self-management then cannot be confined to isolable enterprises and communities, for which some models exist, but must be taken, as a principle, into what are necessarily more indirect, more extended and therefore more complex forms.

This can be defined as the need for many new kinds of *intermediate* institutions, though we must be careful not to accept, uncritically, the received language of the intermediate between the dominant large and the locally autonomous small, which is evident in such terms as 'devolution' and 'decentralisation'. The condition of socialist democracy is that it is built from direct social relations into all necessary indirect and extended relations. This is expressed in received language as 'power from the base' or 'starting from the grass roots': each better than 'devolution' or 'decentralisation', with their assumption of authentic power at some centre, but in some ways affected by the continuing assumption of a 'centre'. The real emphases are better expressed as 'power *in* the base', *at* 'the grass roots'. In any event the principle is, and the practice should be, that all decisions are taken by all those who are directly concerned with them.

Yet this returns us to the problem of scale. In fact, here, we can get some help from the present crisis of British local government. What is now being fought out there, and increasingly also thought out, is this precise problem of the definition of an area of concern and responsibility. It is a very difficult problem, since it necessarily includes the provision of resources as well as the often simpler provision of services. It is then a matter of urgency to discuss and identify the appropriate scales of decision-making, through a range of size of communities from the parish or ward to the county or city, on through the minority nation or region to presumed national levels, and beyond these again to any wider international community. In practice, in orthodox policies, these scales and levels are being continually negotiated and contested, and there is much available practical experience. The socialist intervention would introduce the distinctive principle of *maximum self-management*, paired only with considerations of economic viability and reasonable equity between communities, and decisively breaking with the now dominant criterion of administrative convenience to the centralised state. On a range of current issues, from transport policies to rating finance, such an intervention is already on the agenda, but the full definition must cover the whole ground.

It soon becomes apparent, in such an inquiry, that the scales of relevant community vary, often greatly, according to the interest or service in question. Such variation is additionally necessary in the organisation of economic self-management: by the variation of labour processes; by factors of relative monopoly or relative profitability or attractiveness of enterprises, and so on. Once these complex questions are no longer determined by the imperatives of capital or of the centrally-originated plan, new forms of self-management and of cooperative agreements between self-managed enterprises and communities have necessarily to be shaped. In the perspective of socialist democracy, this reality introduces the second redefinition: that we have to move beyond the *all-purpose* political unit and the *all-purpose* representative to a range of *specific and varying* political units and *specific and varying* representatives. This becomes the full democratic ground for any socialist critique of existing systems of political representation.

It is certain that, in any foreseeable situation, forms of general political representation, at the level of every kind of community, will be necessary, if only as a means of deliberating and negotiating the necessarily complex relations between different forms and areas of self-management. But in the perspective of socialist democracy such representatives cannot be seen as all-purpose representatives, who exhaust and dominate all the decision-making processes. Indeed it is a powerful factor against socialism that, even under monopoly capitalism, many economic decisions by non-capitalist citizens have at least some free play, and that it is this which is seen as likely to be reduced or extinguished by an all-purpose socialist representative system which had greatly extended its powers in the economic sphere.

Thus there is a both political and ideal need for new kinds of parallel representative institutions. For example, publicly-owned industries and services could be reformed by new modes of internal democracy and the election of managements and boards, and those thus democratically elected, through these specific institutions, could further associate and elect to form representative industrial councils, which could act and negotiate in parallel with general political representatives, rather than indirectly and divided in relation to ministries. State and other public departments would then become genuinely executive, under the control of the two broad kinds of decision-making, in industrial and political representation.

The emergence, through such processes, of alternative forms of general representation could in turn be related to the emergence of direct representatives of newly autonomous minority nations and regions. These two and other related sources in fact form a shape for a relevant second chamber, in which the democratic process would run equally strongly but along different lines of relationship. This would apply not only at existing 'national' levels, but at all appropriate levels, to be determined by local (which could then also be variable) decision.

The purpose of these redefinitions, which to be given full practical detail would require careful and widespread inquiry and discussion, is to indicate the shape of a practicable socialist democracy, as distinct both from the model of a centralised command economy and from the developing model of an increasingly fragmented self-management. It cannot be claimed that they do more than indicate a resolution of the tension and confusion between these models, but they are based on the belief that any foreseeable socialist society must have fully adequate general powers, and that at the same time such powers must depend on deeply organised and directly participating popular forces.

It is this kind of resolution which is now our central historical challenge. Inspiring modes of direct popular power – none of which, historically, has lasted for long – have to be taken through to new possibilities of endurance by the building of complex interlocking systems which can deal not only with emergency but with continuing everyday life. Breakdowns into monopoly (party or bureaucratic) power can be avoided only in this way, by a depth and variability of institutions. Equally, in the old capitalist societies, which have experienced and valued representative democracy, only those processes which increase real representation, and which make this practically open to full and informed participation, can generate the political will to attempt and achieve the profound transformations which are going to have to be made, in the coming decades of this long crisis, if any effective idea of socialism is to survive. The closer alternative, meanwhile, as the margins narrow, is an increasingly authoritarian social order, confining and if necessary getting rid of any substantial democracy.

CULTURE AND
TECHNOLOGY

I

High technology can distribute low culture: no problem. But high culture can persist at a low level of technology: that is how most of it was produced.

It is at plausible but hopeless conclusions of this kind that most current thinking about the relations between culture and technology arrives and stops.

In a period of what is certain to be major technical innovation in cultural production and distribution and in information systems of every kind, it will be essential to move beyond these old terms. Yet there is now an effective coalition, including not only cultural conservatives but many apparent radicals, who are agreed that the new technologies are a major threat. Cultural conservatives are saying, in that once elegant argot, that cable television will be the final opening of Pandora's Box, or that satellite broadcasting will top out the Tower of Babel. As for computers, since that flurry of argument about whether they could or could not write poems, most of the old cultural intellectuals, in a diversity of political positions, have decided that they are best ignored.

At the same time, however, on quite different bearings, a new class of intellectuals are already occupying and directing the sites of the new cultural and information technologies. They are talking confidently of their 'product' and its planned marketing, and are closely engaged with the major supplying corporations and the myriad of new specialist agencies in their interstices. They are oriented, within exposed and declining primary economies, to a new phase of expanded 'post-industrial' consumerism, with its models and vocabulary firmly based in the United States.

Observing all this, many radicals draw back to defensive positions: identifying the new technologies with the corporations which control them, and both with a new and disastrous phase of 'paranational hyper-capitalism'. The forces they are identifying are real, but all that follows from so undeveloped a position is a series of disparaging remarks and defensive campaigns, leading in many cases to tacit alliance with the defenders of old privileged and paternalist institutions, or, worse, with the fading ideas of the old cultural argument: a high culture to be preserved and by education and access extended to a whole people.

None of this is good ground. Even the best of earlier arguments need restating in new terms. For the rest, what we have is an unholy combination of technological determinism with cultural pessimism. It is this combination that we must now disentangle and explain.

2

In the early years of any genuinely new technology it is especially important to clear the mind of the habitual technological determinism that almost inevitably comes with it. 'The computers will take over.' 'The paperless office of the Nineties.' 'Tomorrow's World of cable and satellite.'

The basic assumption of technological determinism is that a new technology – a printing press or a communications satellite – 'emerges' from technical study and experiment. It then changes the society or the sector into which it has 'emerged'. 'We' adapt to it, because it is the new modern way.

Yet virtually all technical study and experiment are undertaken within already existing social relations and cultural forms, typically for purposes that are already in general foreseen. Moreover, a technical invention as such has comparatively little social significance. It is only when it is selected for investment towards production, and when it is consciously developed for particular social uses – that is, when it moves from being a technical invention to what can properly be called an available *technology* – that the general significance begins. These processes of selection, investment and development are obviously of a general social and economic kind, within existing social and economic relations, and in a specific social order are designed for particular uses and advantages.

We can look at two examples, which show this to be the case but which have interesting internal differences. Radio can be said to have begun with Hertz's scientific discovery of radio waves, itself based on what was already known about electrical induction. Many people began experimenting with their transmission, which within twenty years was shown to be possible over very long distances. What was in mind at this stage was a new ancillary or even substitute system for the wired telegraph or telephone, which could pass individual messages over long distances or to places which for physical reasons wires could not reach. As its practicability was proved, there was interest from the existing telephone and telegraph companies, and from military establishments needing better signalling forms. There were then significant developments in the terms of these existing interests, though the original sector of amateur and experimental radio persisted and is indeed still active. There was nothing in the technology as such which pointed it in any other direction.

But in a very much wider social and cultural dimension, at just this historical stage, there was active search and demand for new kinds of machine in the home, in this case for news and entertainment. There was then active research to produce a domestic radio receiver, and this proved relatively easy. Its active development was opposed by the old telegraph and telephone interests, whose signals could be interfered with, and by governments which did not want internal establishment channels overridden (and, it was said, trivialised) by general 'broadcasting'. Yet the decision was made, mainly by the existing communications companies, to market the receivers and to create a public demand for them. This proved very successful, and it was then necessary to think in new ways about both programming and financing.

Again nothing in the technology determined these plans. Programming ideas ranged from 'common carrier', as in telegraph and telephone systems, through 'sponsored' programmes, as in the North American system, to state-controlled or state-licensed programme-providing companies. The varied decisions for one or other of these, with all their specific cultural effects, were made on already existing political and economic dispositions in the societies concerned, since the technology, obviously, was compatible with any or all of them.

Thus it is not a case of a technical invention leading to social and cultural institutions. The invention itself was developed, within existing forms and possibilities, into two quite alternative systematic technologies: radio telephony and broadcasting. Broadcasting, in its turn, was developed into alternative and contrasting cultural systems, by choices quite beyond the technology itself. These facts are reasonably well known. In whose interest can it then be to reduce the real history, in all its complexity but also its openness at each stage, to the meaningless proposition that 'the invention of radio changed the lives of millions'?

The case of satellite broadcasting begins in part in the same way, but with one key difference. The general usefulness of communications satellites had been hypothesised before they were practical. What was foreseen was an improvement comparable to that of early radio signals: that they could improve the signals from existing earth-based transmitters – whether in telephony or eventually in broadcasting – and that they could take signals to many hitherto inaccessible places. There was to be a world of political significance, eventually, in that apparently neutral term 'inaccessible'.

The key factor, however, was that satellite technology in this field was at first wholly dependent on major research, development and investment in a quite different field: that of military rocketry and its associated communication and espionage systems. All the primary investment and production was in this military field. Continuing civil developments followed, in telegraphy and telephony, and there was then a critical stage in which the technology became available for interlock with the by now well-established television broadcasting systems. At this point, within the technology itself, the matter is relatively neutral. Satellites can be used to improve and extend signals, and for fast relay of distant signals. Both uses are advantageous, though the former has to be compared with other kinds of improvement and extension of signals, for example by new forms of cabling. That is as far as the technological argument takes us. But it is clearly not as far as the actual development is taking us: a development foolishly referred to the 'inevitable' technology.

For there are at least three general purposes, deriving not from the technology but from the whole social order. First, there is great pressure, from the manufacturing corporations and their allies in governments, to initiate a new marketing phase. At one level this is the development of whole satellite transmitting and receiving systems, which can be sold to governments and sold or leased to other corporations. At another level it is to initiate a large new domestic demand, either for domestic satellite-signal receivers, or for ground-station distribution through new and more elaborate cable systems (which might also prove advantageous without reference to satellites or indeed be preferred to them, using ordinary transmitters). All these developments, with their many technical complexities, are characteristically discussed as if they were only technical. Yet especially in the speed of development now being urged they relate primarily to industrial rather than cultural intentions, and closely follow the main lines of force in economic and political institutions.

The second purpose is even less technologically determined. There is a clear intention, in the strongest centres, to use this technology to override – literally, to fly over – existing national cultural and commercial boundaries. The satellite is seen as the perfect modern way of penetrating cultural and commercial areas hitherto controlled or regulated by 'local' national authorities: that is to say, societies with their own arrangements and governments. In the distribution plans of film, television and sports-producer corporations, and in the marketing and advertising strategies of multinational companies, satellites and satellites-with-cable are critical new modes of access.

The third purpose is partly connected with this: a penetration of *politically* closed areas, or of relative political monopolies, as has already happened with short-wave radio. In either of these purposes there are problems in the legal sovereignty of national air spaces, but against this there is the ideology of freedom of the skies, and there is also a range of conniving initiatives, through offshore siting and surrogate 'local' corporations. The determinations, in this whole range, are evidently economic and political, in a range quite beyond the technology.

3

Thus the real situation is not one of technological determinism, even in some refined version. The sense of some new technology as inevitable or unstoppable is a product of the overt and covert marketing of the relevant interests. Yet in practice it is powerfully assisted by a mode of cultural pessimism, among quite different and even apparently opposed people.

The roots of cultural pessimism are deep. The argument in terms of technologies and institutions is only a first level. Yet it must be directly engaged.

At first glance there are simply dire predictions based on easily aroused prejudices against unfamiliar machinery. Newspapers, cheap magazines, cinema, radio, television, paperbacks, cable and satellites: each phase has been announced as an imminent cultural disaster. Yet there are also phases of settlement in which formerly innovating technologies have been absorbed and only the currently new forms are a threat. At the same time it is usually not clear whether it is only the technologies that are being adduced. Past the shudder (which I have seen physically) at the very mention of cable and satellite there is a fuller position. 'Of course it isn't just the cables, it's the kind of rubbish that will be pumped along them.' To the mild question 'By whom, and by whose assent?' there is a range of answers, from the identifiable capitalist corporations – the radical version, but how radical is it to suppose that these are unstoppable? – to what is prudently called the modern world (what is meant is modern people): 'Think of it, thirty channels, a hundred channels. What else could that many carry but absolute rubbish?'

The formula underlying this type of objection is the contrast between 'minority culture' and 'mass communications' which was made and developed at each stage of the new cultural technologies. In any particular phase, it is entangled with objection to some currently new technology, but its base is always a social and political position. Thus in our own day printed books – the obvious first example of multiple mechanical reproduction and eventually 'mass' distribution – are typically placed, with some paperback and other exceptions, on the minority side of the formula. In the course of the twentieth century, radio and recorded music – those other once new technologies – have also in part been shifted to this side, together with some films, since there is the new many-headed technological beast – television – to contrast with them. There is then not only a selective shift of technologies. There is also a shift to defence of certain kinds of 'responsible public-service institutions'.

I respect some of this defence. I still in part relied on it in *The Long Revolution*, though attempting also to surpass it with some new and quite different principles. Developments since 1959 have both changed the situation and clarified the necessary argument. It is now clear that it is impossible to identify any 'public service' institution without at once relating it to the social order within which it is operating. This can be shown most clearly in the actual development of 'public service' institutions: for example, in Britain, the BBC. A certain kind of 'public service', through phases of paternalism to genuine attempts to make serious work of many kinds more generally available, was possible and important in a period of state-regulated protection from market competition. When this protection was removed, in television and then in radio, the 'public service' definitions did not disappear but in practice weakened and in some areas became wholly residual. It is a difficult, because mixed, record to analyse. There has been a combination of substantial and innovative work with both old and new forms of cultural monopoly and control. Periods of relative openness and diversity have alternated, within the same institutional forms, with periods of closure and privilege. Contrast with wholly commercial systems elsewhere shows these 'public service' forms favourably. Contrast with a modified indigenous commercial system is more complicated. The 'public service' system has some residual advantages but the commerical system offers important opportunities for work beyond a monopoly employer. It is then not only the cultural systems and institutions that we have to compare, but the changing forms of their interlock with a developing capitalist society.

There are very few absolute contrasts left between a 'minority culture' and 'mass communications'. This situation has to be traced, eventually, to the deep roots of 'minority culture' itself, but we can first consider it at a more accessible level. The privileged institutions of minority culture, bearers of so much serious and important work, have for many years been fighting a losing battle against the powerful pressures of a capitalist-sponsored culture. This is the most evident source of cultural pessimism. But its deeper source is a conviction that there is nothing but the past to be won. This is because, for other reasons, there is a determined refusal of any genuinely alternative social and cultural order. This is so in theory, in the determined objections to new forms of democracy or socialism. But it is even more so in practice, in the effective interlock – now so clearly visible – between the social conditions of the privileged institutions and the existing social order as a whole.

There are still some genuine asymmetries between the old privileged culture and the imported and indigenous commercial cultural market. It is from these that the most plausible defences are mounted. There are still authentic standards in serious art and opinion. Yet within all the available privileged institutions, from the BBC through the Arts Council and the British Council to the dominant universities, these standards are in majority inextricable from their received social conditions. They now positively emphasise their connections with state and state-theatrical forms, monarchic and military, and with the still residually preferred *rentier* and country-house styles. Some of their defenders see hope in the asymmetries, in certain sensitive areas, such as public morality, religion, orthodoxy of language, preservation of the traditional arts. But there is now too strong a functional link between a weakened privileged culture and the major economic forces by which its generally approved social order must, under pressures of its own, reproduce itself and survive, for there to be any genuinely independent cultural position of the old 'minority' kind. Indeed as one after another of the stylish old institutions, which had supposed themselves permanently protected, is cut into by the imperatives of a harsher phase of the capitalist economy, it is no surprise that there is only a bewildered and outraged pessimism. For there is nothing most of them want to win or defend but the past, and an alternative future is precisely and obviously the final loss of their privileges.

Thus, within the terms of the old formula – the 'minority' against the 'mass' – there is a losing battle which its most established participants cannot in any real terms want to win.

4

'It all comes down to the money', the sad voices now say. Yet money operates in so many forms. It was a condition of self-respect, in the old privileged culture, that the money was usually indirect. It came from enlightened patrons, responsible trusts, charitable bequests, and people of independent means. 'Independent means': that was the keystone of the arch. It was not necessary, it was indeed impolite, to look round the back of this independence of disposition to the evidence of its actual dependence on a general system of property, production and trade. As the need for money increased, there was a new and apparently unproblematic source, with which there were already close connections within the class: the enlightened State, steering some of the tax revenues in these admirable directions. But again, if anyone looked round the back, as some taxpayers began to do, there was the vulgar question of why taxes should be paid to support minority institutions and autonomous cultural purposes. Inertia kept some indirect money, of both kinds, coming, but as costs increased there was suddenly the new ideological threshold: direct money. But if they accepted direct money were they not also accepting a frankly *commercial* culture? Through the contradictory habits and signals, pessimism, in some, went down into despair.

Yet only in some. New figleaf terms were soon found. 'An enlightened partnership of the public and private sectors': that old friend, the 'mixed economy'. But then it was pressure to *reduce* the public sector, in a new phase of capitalist competition, which was producing the need for direct 'private' money anyway. Another figleaf, quickly: 'sponsorship'. That dear old word, for was not a sponsor once a godfather? Thus no vulgar hiring. Sponsorship. The making of promises. Promises of money.

This system is now developing most rapidly in the institutions of broadcasting. The problem of the electronic institutions, throughout, has been that unlike all previous capitalist trading relations – in books, newspapers, pictures, concerts – they have no direct points of sale. The receiving machines can be directly sold, but from the nature of broadcasting there is no point of sale for actual programmes. Thus funding for production was arranged in other ways: by direct state subsidy; by licence fees, in societies where the state element in the state/capitalist combination was relatively strong; or by general advertising money, either directly for specific productions or in systematically constructed 'natural' breaks.

The advertising option had already been seized by the 'popular' press (the new kinds of commercial high-circulation news-entertainment-and-sports sheets) as a way of reducing cover prices and thus extending circulation. The option was also, at a deeper level, a way of extending and organising a new kind of 'consumer' market, at critical stages of domestic manufacturing and of extension of the electoral franchise. The first purpose was seen as a mere 'support system' to a primary communicative function, but the second and deeper purpose was always stronger. What was earlier seen as a relative balance shifted heavily towards the 'consumer' and electoral market priorities. Deep inside their own forms, most newspapers changed their definitions of their manifest purposes. Certain necessary elements were retained, but there was increasingly open definition of the success or failure of a newspaper in terms of the condition required by its advertisers: the reliable delivery of an effective body of purchasers. There was then a rapid disappearance of newspapers, under these pressures. This is evident not only in the reduced number of titles but in the form of those publications which are still conventionally described as newspapers but in which the regular news content is typically less than ten per cent. Increasingly, now, these are tabloid entertainment and advertising sheets, with trailers of simplified news and aggressive opinionation. It can be said that there are only three surviving national daily newspapers in Britain, in any formerly recognisable sense. Yet even these depend closely on association with the delivery to advertisers of relatively well-off readers. In many of these cases, the tail wags the dog so vigorously that tail is rapidly becoming the definition of any useful dog.

In broadcasting, whether in directly commercial or state-protected systems, there has been a comparable shift of function. Productions are estimated in terms of the numbers of people who can be delivered, through some interest, to either system. As in newspapers, the figures for 'viable' production have been vastly inflated, by a specialised system of reckoning. What is called a 'vast throng' at a cup final or a coronation – a hundred thousand people – is described as an insignificant or failed broadcasting audience. Pressure to adapt to the conditions of competition for a predictable and packaged market of vast size is rationalised as if it were a matter of responsible relationships with actual people. The real primary pressures are either for direct advertising money or for a major share of the political and cultural market, on which all indirect systems finally depend.

It is here especially that the sponsors, the new godfathers, appear.

The cultural assimilation has been very rapid. Old institutions and competitions now have, as a matter of course, trade names attached as the first element of their description. These descriptions flow so easily from hired tongues that it seems reasonable to ask how long it will be before other forms of competition go the same way. Shall we see, soon, a 'British Chemicals General Election'? It would certainly save all that bureaucratic overtime money. Close by-elections would facilitate market penetration by corporations which had targeted certain U.K. sectors. Trade sponsorship could finance stylishly open elections of trade-union officials. If these examples sound (as they should) fantastic, they would still not be much more surprising than, to an earlier generation, the definition of English cricket competitions by the names of insurance and tobacco firms. The takeover powers of corporate advertising money are now so great that a wide range of familiar social activities, effectively funded in their own terms in early and much poorer periods, are becoming dependent for their survival on calculated favours from this new sector of patronage and dominance.

This process connects with much wider movements of the society: in an increasingly home-based culture; in electronic rather than physical assembly; in major rises in production costs, partly from the relative improvement in the wages of production workers but also heavily inflated by adaptation to the norms of an international cultural market, which have put rewards in the most favoured sectors at the level of speculative fortunes. It is the ideological interpretation, directly influencing political decisions, which then matters. The new forms of sponsorship are interpreted as 'free money', in contradiction even of the old capitalist principle that somebody, somewhere, has to pay, since 'money does not grow on trees'. Within this new blandishment, even liberal men and women, puzzling over accounts in committees, are persuaded to believe in manna: *mammon manna*, the new modern brand.

There is no free money. It is all spent for calculated and usually acknowledged purposes: in immediate trading, but also to substitute a healthy for an unhealthy association (as in tobacco sponsorship of sports), or to reassure what are called 'opinion-formers', or to enhance, as it is slyly put, a 'public image'. The specified manna is for this and that. The general manna is for the public reputation of capitalism. But it is paranational manna, from the true paranational godfathers, that has now to be most closely looked at.

The new technologies of cable and satellite, because they can be represented as socially new and therefore as creating a new political situation, are in their commonly foreseen forms essentially paranational. Existing societies will be urged, under the excuse of technical reasons, to relax or abolish virtually all their internal regulatory powers. If the price includes a few unproblematic legalities, or gestures to 'community' interests, it will be paid. 'Not only free but clean-mouthed and concerned'. The real costs, meanwhile, will be paid elsewhere. The social costs and consequences of the penetration of any society and its economy by the high-flying paranational system will be left to be paid or to be defaulted on by surviving national political entities. The costs will be paid in the relief of unemployment, as national industries are bypassed and reduced. The consequences will fall in marginalised and unprofitable regions, already bypassed industrially but increasingly unserved by the new profit-selected systems of distribution (commercial cable or commercial mail). Beyond these we can foresee the last-ditch defensive measures to preserve a penetrated and ravaged social identity and its failing social order.

Free money! The godfathers are taking us to a point where it will seem cheaper, everywhere, to be steadily ruined or simply to give up. The known alternative principle, of common provision of all necessary common services, will be made to appear a receding utopianism, though it remains our only realistic hope of varied and responsive communications systems.

5

If this is what has to be resisted, it is not enough to oppose this or that technology. Any such opportunism will fail and deserve to fail. Nor are there any other ready allies in place. The capitalist state, for these purposes, is unavailable; it is now part of the agencies of the offensive. The case is different with the surviving institutions of autonomous policy and selective patronage, such as, in Britain, the BBC and the Arts Council. In the decisive areas these are now being outflanked, and will either join the new forms or withdraw to narrower and more evidently residual interests, based in a few affordable minorities. Within the forms of cultural pessimism, many concerned people have already adapted to this narrowing future. But what has then to be emphasised is how this is affecting what is still called 'minority culture itself'.

It is already significant that many minority institutions and forms have adapted, even with enthusiasm, to modern corporate capitalist culture. This is so in everyday practice, where a graded market has some room for them. It is so in the fact that the metropolitan areas of serious drama and fiction have been willingly incorporated into the market operations of sponsorship and prizes. The basic institutions of publishing and dealing have in any case been adapted to the main lines of modern corporate selling. Many other kinds of artistic enterprise, confident in the seriousness and validity of their projects, have joined the queues outside the offices of the corporations, for sponsorship money.

None of this can go on for long – indeed in some ways none of it can even start – unless deeper adaptations have already been made. What is treated as mere 'support money' never stays like that. Production itself becomes steadily more homogeneous with the sponsoring and directing institutions. For some time this can be masked by real elements in the minority culture: work from the past, which seems still to survive and flourish in its own terms; or work in highly specialised areas, typically associated with scholarly organisations and interests. Each of these is important, but there can be no full and authentic minority culture in their limited terms. It is always contemporary practice and usage which makes these elements and specialisms a *culture*.

There is now varied and active contemporary practice and policy. But it is necessary to identify, within them, certain adaptive and submissive forms. Thus a relatively overt and adaptive nostalgia is now saturating the minority arts: in contemporary reproductions of the more graceful and elegant ways of selected periods of the past; in country houses and an old 'pastoral' order; in 'classical' literature and music; in biographies of the once dazzling and powerful; in the taste for playful or suggestive myth. This is flanked by an overt exoticism: of the imperial and colonial pasts; of the peripheral, often poverty-ridden picturesque; of versions of primitivism.

But these overt contents, which make so long an inventory of current minority art and literature, are mainly its compensatory forms. Its truly adaptive forms have a much harder and rougher surface. This is where we need to look at the two faces of 'modernism': at those innovative forms which destabilised the fixed forms of an earlier period of bourgeois society, but which were then in their turn stabilised as the most reductive versions of human existence in the whole of cultural history. The originally precarious and often desperate images – typically of fragmentation, loss of identity, loss of the very grounds of human communication – have been transferred from the dynamic compositions of artists who had been, in majority, literally exiles, having little or no common ground with the societies in which they were stranded, to become, at an effective surface, a 'modernist' and 'post-modernist' establishment. This, near the centres of corporate power, takes human inadequacy, self-deception, role-playing, the confusion and substitution of individuals in temporary relationships, and even the lying paradox of the communication of the fact of non-communication, as self-evident routine data.

Buttressed in these assumptions by popularised versions of cognate theories – psychological alienation; relationship as inherently self-seeking and destructive; natural competitive violence; the insignificance of history; the fictionality of all actions; the arbitrariness of language – these forms which still claim the status of minority art have become the routine diversions and confirmations of paranational commodity exchange, with which indeed they have many structural identities. They are also heavily traded, in directly monetary forms, by their intellectual agents and dealers, some of whom, for a residual self-esteem, allow themselves a gestural identity with the exposed artists and theorists of the original innovative phase. Even substantial and autonomous works, of this tendency, are quickly incorporated into this now dominant minority culture.

Yet what is much more decisive, altering the very terms through which the situation can be analysed, is the transfer of many of these deep structures into effectively popular forms, in film and television and heavily marketed books. Apparently simple kinds of adventure and mystery have been transformed and newly marketed in highly specific representations of crime, espionage, intrigue and dislocation, mediating the deep assumptions of habitual competitive violence, deception and role-playing, loss of identity, and relationships as temporary and destructive. Thus these debased forms of an anguished sense of human debasement, which had once shocked and challenged fixed and stable forms that were actually destroying people, have become a widely distributed 'popular' culture that is meant to confirm both its own and the world's destructive inevitabilities.

The reasons are not in some abstracted 'popular taste': the idea of the 'vulgar masses' which was the first condition of cultural pessimism. The true reasons are more specific and more interesting. The original innovations of modernism were themselves a response to the complex consequences of a dominant social order, in which forms of imperial-political and corporate-economic power were simultaneously destroying traditional communities and creating new concentrations of real and symbolic power and capital in a few metropolitan centres. Losing their relationships in depressed, declining and narrowing communities, the innovating artists of that period went to the new material bases and the negative freedoms of those centres, in which, ironically, the very reductions and dislocations were the material and the means for a new kind of art which the metropolis, but it alone, could recognise. The first social analyses of the newly centralised culture of the cities identified only its superficial features: typically 'commercialism' and 'democracy', forcibly yoked together from traditional perspectives. Yet as part of the same fundamental processes, new means of universal distribution, in cinema and then in broadcasting, were at just this point being discovered and developed, and control and production for them followed these same centralising and would-be universalising forms.

What was eventually projected as the 'global village' of modern communications was the fantastic projection of a few centres which had reduced human content to its simplest universally transmissible forms: some genuinely universal, at the simplest physical levels; others simple versions of negotiable and tradeable features. The dynamic charge of the first shocks of recognition of a reduced and dislocated humanity was eventually transformed into the routines of a newly displayed *normality*. Thus the very conditions which had provoked a genuine modernist art became the conditions which steadily homogenised even its startling images, and diluted its deep forms, until they could be made available as a universally distributed 'popular' culture.

The two faces of this 'modernism' could literally not recognise each other, until a very late stage. Their uneasy relation was falsely interpreted by a displacement. On the one hand what was seen was the energetic minority art of a time of reduction and dislocation; on the other hand the routines of a technologised 'mass' culture. It was then believed that the technologised mass culture was the enemy of the minority modernist art, when in fact each was the outcome of much deeper transforming forces, in the social order as a whole. It was here that the simplicities of technological determinism and cultural pessimism forged their unholy alliance. The technologies were falsely seen as necessarily carrying this kind of content, while in both action and reaction the minority art despaired both of itself and of an alien technological world.

The dominance of a few centres of 'universal' production, and the simultaneous dominance of artistic and intellectual life by a few metropolitan centres, have now to be seen as inherently related. The climax of the pretensions by which this situation was hidden was the widely accepted proposition of the 'global village'. What was being addressed was a real development of universal distribution and of unprecedented opportunities for genuine and diverse cultural exchange. What was ideologically inserted was a model of an homogenised humanity consciously served from two or three centres: the monopolising corporations and the elite metropolitan intellectuals. One practised the homogenisation, the other theorised it. Each found its false grounds in the technologies which had 'changed and opened up the world, and brought it together'. But nothing in the technologies led to this theory or practice. The real forces which produced both, not only in culture but in the widest areas of social, economic and political life, belonged to the dominant capitalist order in its paranational phase. But this was an enemy which could not be named because its money was being taken.

6

'If we got cable television, in the ways now proposed', a senior BBC official said recently, 'we should have no way of making *Brideshead Revisited* and *Smiley's People.*' He was appealing to what he took to be incontrovertible examples of excellence. No two examples can stand for a repertory, but these two go a long way. One is a nostalgic reconstruction of a destructive and literally decadent but still regretted elegance. The other is an owlish confirmation of deep inner betrayals through an almost indecipherable but politically 'inevitable' and violent code. Over an earlier representation, through 'Smiley', of the inner filth of espionage, the pure voice of a choirboy singing an anthem accompanied a reverent image of the old dreaming spires. This is where corporate production and official minority art now embrace, in the form of old displaced pieties and the resigned and accommodating versions of war, cold war, exploitation and arrogant wealth. Could cable television indeed be so marvellous that it could deliver us from all this?

In no way. That is not how things happen. But it seems that we cannot think about it at all until we have recognised our real as distinct from any idealised current situation. What we now mainly have is a huge sector of capitalist-sponsored art, displayed in the polished routines of crime, fraud, intrigue, betrayal and a glossy degradation of sexuality. Grace notes of diminishing audibility are played at its edges, and there is a certain vitality in mimicry, parody and pastiche. The sector is supported by light intellectual formulations of the ruling ideas: 'alienation' as violent competition and impersonal appetite; 'dislocation' as arbitrariness and human disability. There are sectors within the sector, but to anyone outside it their fundamental correspondences are evident. Beyond them, nevertheless, in what, though they are many, most know as extreme isolation, are other figures: autonomous artists and independent intellectuals, in a diversity of kinds of work. Their immediate problems are the monopolies which marginalise or exclude them, but many can then slip into the prepared ideological positions: the 'mass' culture; the 'technologised' world. Moreover, within the orthodox culture it is already 'known', from earlier periods, what autonomous artists do and what independent intellectuals think. Many such proxy figures, embellishing already incorporated forms, are busily at work and are allowed their gestures within the official culture. The more authentic figures, often doing and saying very different things, are in this situation barely visible at all, even to each other. Pessimism then spreads even where the vigour is most actual. A sobriety of real isolation darkens though it can never finally suppress the joy and vitality of innovating autonomous practice.

It used to be said that such innovating energies could only ever be fully released when they were connected to genuine communities.

This may be true but in its ordinary proposition it is vague. It is the available conditions of practice that count.

There are two areas of 'popular' culture which can be seen as relatively distinct from the dominant capitalist sector. The first is a deliberately rooted popular history and action. This has emerged strongly in Britain in some television and theatre plays, in some novels characteristically placed by the metropolitan culture as 'regional', and in certain innovative forms of oral history, video and film. In other countries, over a range from new forms of oppositional theatre and television, through varieties of street performance and community arts, to popular revolutionary art within political struggles, there is a vitality of cultural activity. Even in the oldest and most established cultures, the shapes of an alternative radical culture have been forming, repeatedly, during the last fifty years and with many earlier precedents. They have not so far been institutionally strong enough to come through as general, and this actual weakness has been exaggerated, from outside them but also from inside, to their characterisation as 'merely political', 'primarily political'. But their important practices and images are deeper than anything that is ordinarily meant by 'politics'. It is more general and more immediate human alternatives and challenges that the real forms now carry and inspire.

Yet there are problems of overlap, in parts of this tendency, with the dominant culture itself. Some work of this apparent kind has already been incorporated, taking its weakest elements: radical nostalgia, leading to the familiar acceptance and ratification of loss; or roughness and coarseness inside an imposed poverty, leading to slangy recognition and matiness inside bourgeois theatres which always enjoy 'low life'. There is also a pseudo-radical practice, in which the negative structures of post-modernist art are attached to a nominal revolutionary or liberationist radicalism, though all they can do in the end is undermine this, turning it back to the confusions of late-bourgeois subjectivism. It is not surprising that, seeing all this, the strongest alternative artists have started a long march to alternative institutions, which have to be raised from the resources of surviving and potential in-place communities.

Secondly, however, there is a resilient area of a very different popular culture, much of it now marketed but much of it, also, not originated by the market. This area is diametrically opposed to an incorporated 'modernism'. It is a simplicity, of every kind, which is quite differently sustained. It is there in the genuinely popular scepticism of some comedians, who keep human fallibility at its everyday and therefore reparable levels. It is there in the intense vitality of some kinds of popular music, always being reached for by the market and often grasped and tamed, but repeatedly renewing its impulses in new and vigorous forms. It is there also (against many of our preconceptions) in some kinds of popular 'domestic' drama and fiction, in that always edged-towards-sentimental embodiment of everyday lives and situations. These often amount to little more than composed gossip, but a gossip which has some substantial continuities with irrepressible interests in the diverse lives of other people, beyond the reduced and distorted shapes of the modernist and post-modernist representations. It is in this very general area of jokes and gossip, of everyday singing and dancing, of occasional dressing-up and extravagant outbursts of colour, that a popular culture most clearly persists. Its direct energies and enjoyments are still irrepressibly active, even after they have been incorporated as diversions or mimed as commercials or steered into conformist ideologies. They are irrepressible because in the generality of their impulses, and in their intransigent attachments to human diversity and recreation, they survive, under any pressures and through whatever forms, while life itself survives, and while so many people – real if not always connected majorities – keep living and looking to live beyond the routines which attempt to control and reduce them.

7

The moment of any new technology is a moment of choice. Within existing social and economic conditions, the new systems will be installed as forms of distribution without any real thought of corresponding forms of production. New cable or cable-and-satellite television will rely heavily on old entertainment stocks and a few cheap services. New information systems will be dominated by financial institutions, mail-order marketers, travel agencies and general advertisers. These kinds of content, predictable from the lines of force of the *economic* system, will be seen as the whole or necessary content of advanced electronic entertainment and information. More seriously, they will come to define such entertainment and information, and to form practical and self-fulfilling expectations.

Yet there are readily available alternative uses. New cable and cable-satellite television systems, and new teletext and cable-signal systems, could be wholly developed within public ownership, not for some old or new kind of monopoly provider, but as common-carrier systems which would be available, by lease and contract, to a wide range of producing and providing bodies.

In television there could be at least four new kinds of transmission service. First, an alternative film and video network, to be used by a variety of independent producers. Second, an exchange network, to be used between the existing television companies and independent producers of different countries. Third, a library or backlist network, serviced by an electronic catalogue from material now owned or stored by a wide range of producer companies. Fourth, a reference and archive network, drawing on material now stored in various forms of public trust.

The first three of these networks would be best financed, in all their early stages, by systems of pay-as-you-view. It is only in this way that revenue could be directly returned to producers. The free British public library service, with which such networks have analogies, is unsatisfactory in just this respect. It admirably distributes all kinds of books, without point-of-borrowing charge, but it fails, even after the belated introduction of Public Lending Right, to return fair revenue to their authors. An all-purpose free-using and subsidised-producing system would be a different matter, but it is damaging to have either element without the other. There is also much to be said, from the experience of centralised socialist cultural production, for the relative independence of individual and small-collective producers. They can be in more direct relations with audiences than can be achieved either through a system of hiring by capitalist and corporate programming institutions or through a supposedly 'public' system with its intermediate bureaucracy of programme controllers.

Nothing, either way, is determined by the technology, but it is an important feature of the new systems that they offer opportunities for new cultural relationships, which the older systems could not. Thus the multiplication of channels makes the programme organisers and controllers of scarce channels unnecessary. Similarly the range of channels allows self-selecting and self-timed viewing: an opportunity already welcomed in the use of video-recorders, though the imposition of these on unchanged production and distribution systems quickly becomes parasitic. More generally, the numbers games of advanced production are capable of being transformed. 'Negligible' or 'unviable' audiences for centralised network production are fully practicable in systems of continued availability and exchange, beyond the terms of the limited competition for peak network viewing and its associated advertising.

These are examples of the many ways in which the new technologies could be quite differently used, by starting from different basic social and cultural positions. The technologies themselves would be assessed, in this alternative perspective, as means to diverse and equitable provision, rather than selective profit-taking. Thus the development of cable television, within the now dominant order, will systematically exclude rural populations and the poorer towns and city areas. But it is only one of several available technologies, which in the right mix could offer general and equitable provision: telephone signal systems, satellite domestic receivers, community relays.

The new perspective should not be limited to the reproduction, by some altered means, of existing services. Cultural production of new kinds would positively depend on new local and specialist workshop facilities for the range of alternative producers who are already working or waiting at the edges of the existing centralised systems. The quality of this independent work is already impressive, and there are also some clear shifts of formal content and relationships. The same could be true of new information systems. The early systems of medical call, metering and security alarm could become general within a decade. This will especially be the case if they are seen, from the beginning, as social provision, rather than as extras to a commercial system. If adequate switch systems are installed with the new cables, there will be room for growth beyond the simple interactive systems in routine administration, moneyhandling, ordering of goods, booking of travel and other facilities, which could become general over the next decade. It is already important to move beyond these limited concepts of 'information', now funded by existing interests in finance and travel and hypermarketing, and supplemented by a relatively feeble range of 'general' interests, culturally very similar to the *TitBits* stage of journalism. As is already beginning to happen, encyclopaedias and library catalogues can be moved into the databases, for a greatly expanded system of public inquiry and reference. There is also a body of already stored but now largely inaccessible information, in public hands, about the real and comparative qualities of various goods and services; this is the public information system which could steadily replace adveritsing.

There is a further range beyond this. What are now called 'interactive' uses are for the most part very uneven, as between provider and user. Selected databases offer simple and determined choices. At the unprivileged end, all the rest of us do is press this or that button, as in the election booths we press buttons or make crosses. Real interaction would be very different, as can be illustrated in the case of the use of these technologies to register social and political opinions. It is easy to transfer the preformed questions of interview-polling to the technologies, and have buttons pressed in their terms. This is the format of the electoral market, which has to be distinguished from any more active democracy.

The crucial point is the relation between opinion and information. Recent research (Himmelweit et al: *How Voters Decide*, 1981) has shown that there are differences not only of degree but of kind in the range of what is called, and by simple polling registered as, 'opinion'. Some opinions are deeply grounded, with or without full information, but others, however confidently expressed at the time, are comparatively shallow and volatile, easily affected by the flow of current contexts and circumstances. This is one of many grounds for distinction between a participating democracy and a representative or apparently representative system. The aggregations without specific valuation, which now run through polling as through voting systems, flatten these real differences, stabilise the range of choices, and themselves become persuasive forms of apparent information, not only indicating but at some levels forming 'public opinion'.

More adequate and more respecting procedures are now at last technically possible. The mode of the opinion poll, by interview or by button, deploys its agenda of questions on the assumption of an existing competence to answer them in the selected terms. This is a form of the apparently flattering manipulation of a commercial or electoral market. In an alternative democratic form, it has already been shown in pilot studies that stages of questioning and of inquiry and information can be progressively correlated. Thus a first broad indication of opinion can lead into an encounter with opposing arguments and evidence, from any of the real range of points of view. Questions can then be amended and reformulated, or alternative propositions made, in a process of genuinely interactive learning and exchange. The opinions that would emerge from such processes – and they are, crucially, indefinitely repeatable and variable – would then have some real grounding in active social relations. Indeed this is a technical means of achieving, within a complex society, some of the processes of the formation of opinion in active and equitable small groups, in which grounded beliefs and the modes of direct democratic discussion and decision were traditionally based but then in larger societies lost.

Again, one of the major benefits of the new technologies could be a significant improvement in the practicability of every kind of voluntary association: the fibres of civil society as distinct from both the market and the state. Today, though the dominant lines of communication and organisation are powerfully and centrally funded and controlled, millions of people, continually and irrepressibly, set up their own organisations, either for purposes ignored or neglected by the established forms, or as means of positive support and influence. Typically they now work under serious difficulties, of resources and especially of distance. An association can have a hundred thousand members and yet not more than a few hundred, and often only one or two, in any particular place. The consequent problems of travel and funding are then devotedly addressed, but for many purposes the new interactive technologies could transform them by providing regular facilities for consultation and decision from people's own homes, workplaces and communities. In many formal organisations, such as parties and trade unions, such facilities would greatly assist the improvement of democratic communication and decisions. But there would also be a great strengthening of every kind of voluntary and informal association, from special interests and charities to alternative and oppositional political and cultural groups. This could be, in practice, the achievement of full social and cultural powers by civil society, as opposed to their appropriation or marginalisation by the corporations and by the state.

These uses touch even wider possibilities, in new forms of co-operation and consultation in work. In some processes they could effectively replace the now cumbrous and expensive daily transportation of people to physically centralised workplaces, passing and repassing each other on the roads and lines. Ecologically this will be desirable and perhaps imperative, before the end of the century, for many kinds of work and service. Its flexible forms, in further applications of the technologies, would be fully congruous with new working relationships in self-managing agencies. This should be one of the main shapes of a genuinely socialised economy, in which direct relations in placeable enterprises and communities can be efficiently extended to much wider and more varied organisations over a very much larger physical space.

In education, also, there are important new possibilities, already indicated by the success of the Open University. There can be a new range of formal learning systems, which people can use in their own time and at their own pace. This will be especially important in a period in which there are new needs for permanently available education. Yet what is now happening, in the existing institutions, is a steady pressure from a late-capitalist economy and its governments to reduce education both absolutely and in kind, steadily excluding learning which offers more than a preparation for employment and an already regulated civic life. The alibi word for this reduction and exclusion is 'academic', now used for most kinds of organised and sustained learning as a way of distancing and disparaging them. The formula of 'the academic child' is similarly used to specialise sustained learning and to find an excuse for excluding a majority from it. Yet this only exploits certain real features of relatively enclosed and distanced academies, within an unequal and privileged culture. Much can be done to extend and change the existing institutions, by the serious development of the comprehensive principle, and by its extension beyond the now wholly inadequate leaving age. But use of the new technologies can add diversity and permanent availability to the most comprehensive institutions, above all in making them outward-looking, taking their own best knowledge and skills to a wider and more active society.

These are some of the general directions in which we could choose to develop the new technologies, by chosing a different kind of economy and society. Taken together they offer the possibility of new kinds of active social and cultural relations in what is going to be in any case an exceptionally complex technological world. The crude and reductive interests now engaged in capturing and directing them are outrage enough. But it is really just as outrageous if, on the threshold of these possibilities, there is surrender to the old formulas of technological determinism and cultural pessimism, among the very people whose central responsibility is to inform and propose and act to realise them. For these uses, within the processes of much broader changes, are among the indispensable means of a new radical democracy and a new socialism, in numerous and complex societies. They are also among the authentically modern movements beyond the long and bitter impasse of a once liberating modernism.

CLASS, POLITICS, AND SOCIALISM

I

The labour movement has two wings: industrial and political. Or so it is said, in a dying metaphor. Wings? But then where is the body, where is the head?

The answers to these questions are very well known. The body is the whole working class. The head is the party which will lead it to socialism.

Happy days!

On the other hand, getting beyond these old ideological assumptions does not exempt us from some new ideology. Two forms, in this area, are now current. First, that there used to be a very close relation between class and politics, but that changes in the 'old working class' – changes which are also called 'the dissolution of the classical proletariat' – have permanently eroded this. Second, that recent changes have halted the long march of labour through and beyond the institutions of capitalist society.

Ideologies have to engage with some otherwise observable elements of reality, if they are to retain plausibility. The new current forms, no more and no less than the old socialist propositions, engage with some real situations and some real changes, though they then overstate and distort them. We can see these processes as we look into the evidence.

What is wrong with the first proposition – the political dissolution of the 'old working class' or 'the classical proletariat' – was sufficiently shown in *The Long Revolution*. The ideological element in its interpretation of recent changes is the wholly false assumption that the 'old working class' was predominantly socialist in persuasion, or at least, in the more habitual electoral perspective, voted Labour. It is worth looking back at the actual figures through this century.

	Labour vote '000s	% of Vote
1900	63	1.8
1906	330	5.9
1910 (a)	506	7.6
1910 (b)	372	7.1
1918	2385	22.2
1922	4241	29.5
1923	4439	30.5
1924	5489	33.0
1929	8390	37.1
1931	6650	30.6
1935	8325	37.9
1945	11995	47.8
1950	13267	46.1
1951	13949	48.8
1955	12405	46.4
1959	12216	43.8
1964	12206	44.1
1966	13065	47.9
1970	12178	43.0
1974 (a)	11646	37.1
1974 (b)	11457	39.2
1979	11532	36.9
1983	8461	27.6

It is obvious that there has been a steady decline, and in 1983 a very sharp fall, from what is not so much the 'peak' as the 'plateau' between 1945 and 1970. It is equally obvious that before reaching this plateau Labour did not poll a vast majority of what was then, proportionally, a much larger 'old working class'. Another factor has then to be assessed: that between the mid-1920s and the late 1960s, and especially between 1945 and 1966, British elections moved predominantly towards a two-party system, as distinct from the earlier three-party system (before the decline of the Liberals) and also the later three- and four-party system since the late 1960s. In the

1983 election, a fourth party, the Social Democrats, formed in a leadership breakaway from Labour, polled in alliance with the revived Liberals as follows:

1979	Labour 36.9	Liberal 13.8	Conservative 43.9
1983	Labour 27.6	Alliance 25.4	Conservative 42.4

It seems reasonable to suppose that many 'Labour votes', for the undivided party in a two-party system, went to the breakaway party in a three/four party system. This need not be interpreted as a decline in the 'socialist vote'; it seems, rather, to reveal the 'social-democrat' vote previously held within the Labour Party. In a multi-party system Labour is then back to the relative position of the early twenties: a very serious reverse for a broad radical party but not necessarily an indication of sudden political shifts. The two-party system had always simplified, polarised and thus disguised the actual spread of political opinion.

It is in any case obvious that the 'old working class' or 'the classical proletariat', at whatever dates these are supposed to have existed, did not vote 'socialist' in the way that many interpretations presume or infer. The 'long march' perspective makes much more sense on this point, accepting that a new political formation (as in the working class of the beginning of the century) takes time to make its way through the old structures. It emphasises, correctly, an *increasing* correlation between class and electoral politics, broadly from after 1918, to the 'peak' of 1951. But then this ideological assumption of the 'long march' theoretically extrapolates a continuing rising line. When the line fails to rise, and goes instead into a substantial fall, the assumption is not abandoned but short-term reasons are sought, in particular conjunctures, policies or leaders. However, it seems more probable that what really failed was the concept of an all-purpose radical party, nominally but always ambiguously socialist, which temporarily succeeded within a two-party system but then fell back within a multi-party system. This does not invalidate an underlying concept of a long march. It means only that the march was much longer than was supposed under the spell of this apparent 'short cut to socialism'.

We can look briefly at another relevant index. The membership of trade unions rose from just under 2 million in 1900 to more than 8 million in 1921: from some 12 per cent to some 43 per cent of the employed population. It declined sharply through the 1920s and most of the 1930s; in 1935, at 4½ million, it was down to 23 per cent. It then rose to more than 9 million by 1951, at 45 per cent, and to more than 12 million by the late 1970s, at 46 per cent. In the years of the 'plateau' union membership was maintained at a stable percentage of the employed population, with a significant growth in actual numbers as the employed population increased (though even now only just over a third of employed women are in unions). Beyond the simple incidence of general unemployment, union membership has not declined in the period of decline of the Labour vote. Yet, given the changing proportions of types of work, and increased clerical and professional unionisation, trade-union membership is no simple and uniform indicator of class membership or class affiliation.

The shape of the relations between class and politics, as expressed by these general indices, is already more complex and more interesting than the ideological interpretations allow. In any fuller view, both the Labour vote and trade-union membership are uncertain indices of the real relations between class and politics. We can then look more realistically at some figures from recent elections, of which so much has been made. Thus the votes of union members divided in 1979 and 1983 as follows:

1979	Labour 50	Liberal 12	Conservative 35
1983	Labour 39	Alliance 28	Conservative 32

This is a shift within an already imperfect correlation, but it does not mean that 'union members have shifted to the Conservatives'; on the contrary, though declining, there is still a clear Labour lead. This is also true of the unemployed: in 1983 Labour 45 per cent, Conservative 30 per cent, Alliance 26 per cent. More generally, we can look at the conventional socio-economic class divisions which are used in advertising and marketing: very practical divisions, despite what is said by some of the same people about the 'disappearance of classes':

	AB	C1	C2	D
% 1983 voters				
Labour	12	21	35	44
Alliance	27	24	27	28
Conservative	62	55	39	29

In the distribution of both Labour and Conservative votes there are very clear class profiles, though that of Labour has been blurred by declines in C2 (skilled manual) and D (semi-skilled and unskilled manual), while remaining stable in C1 (office and clerical). The problem of class and politics is often discussed as if it related only to the Left, and it is then worth emphasising that the strongest class correlation is in the best-off group, AB (managerial and professional), where three out of five voted for the most right-wing party. At the same time nearly half of the worst-off voted for the most left-wing party. It would be impossible to conclude from these figures that there are not still powerful (but not determining) links between voting and 'socio-economic position'. On the other hand the remarkably even distribution of the Alliance vote, between all four groups, indicates a sector which sees itself, in the Alliance's offered terms, as 'getting beyond class politics'.

The main point of including this kind of evidence, from what are at best relatively mechanical and external indices, is not to propose some general interpretation in their terms but mainly to get the ordinary ideological interpretations out of the way. That there have been very significant changes since the 1960s is not in doubt, but it is not possible to think about them, politically, if we retain the false assumption of the 'socialism of the classical proletariat or old working class' or if, overriding other factors such as the number of parties in the system or the social composition of trade-union membership, we treat 'the Labour vote' or 'the trade-union vote' as if they were simple and uniform properties. The most interesting visible shifts, of a general kind, are in the especially indeterminate areas of new types of community and new forms of employment which have been developing quite rapidly since the 1950s. There are many signs of political lags and uncertainties in relation to these, as was already observed in 1959, but equally the changes in the social order which produced them can no longer be seen to rest on the 'permanent' affluence and expansion then assumed by the main parties. Here, as elsewhere, we must move beyond simple categories of determination to more complex ideas and to a still changing reality.

2

The key category is that of 'class' itself, and especially, in this context, of 'working class'. There are two underlying problems: first, that of the criteria by which particular classes are distinguished and defined; second, that of historical changes in kinds of work and in more general economic position, which alter not only the proportional distribution between classes but also the distinguishing criteria. A great deal of work has been done to try to clarify these matters. I am here concerned only with the most general results.

Among the criteria, we have a received definition of the 'working class' as manual-working wage-labourers. In some nineteenth-century estimates this category excluded the small and declining number of farm labourers, but even so a good estimate in 1867 put the working class in this sense at just under seventy per cent. By this criterion there has been a straight decline in the proportion of working-class people in Britain. Comparable current figures would put the proportion at something over a third of the employed population. There are then two further common criteria: the definition of those who are wage-earners, whether doing 'manual' labour or not; and the old Marxist definition of 'productive workers' (those from whom surplus value is extracted within capitalist relations of production). A further criterion is often introduced, to distinguish between supervisory and supervised kinds of work, with a possible class line between them.

The point is not so much to choose the 'correct' definition but at first just to be aware of the radical differences according to the category chosen. A recent analysis of the 'economically active' population of the United States in 1969 (E. O. Wright, *New Left Review* 98, 1976) found 'the working class' definable over a range from 88 per cent to just under 20 per cent (among men from 84 per cent to 23 per cent; among women from 95 per cent to 15 per cent). The high figures are for all wage-earners; the low for productive non-supervisory manual workers – the old 'classical' definition. All wage-earners who were not supervisors were at 52 per cent; 'blue collar' wage-earners, including supervisors, 47 per cent; blue-collar non-supervisory wage-earners 31 per cent. Broadly similar figures would be found in Britain, and in the intervening years there would be a still further decline in the low-percentage category, as 'productive' industry, in the old sense, has continued (irrespective of recession) to reduce its workforce.

There is no way of solving or even of discussing the political problems at this level. What in any case all such categories exclude is the whole diverse body of people who are not, in such terms, 'economically active'. This matters very much for electoral politics, since the quarter or more of people of working age who are not employed, together with the increasing number of those who are reckoned as too old or who have retired from work, are all voters. Thus the archetypal working-class man, on whom so much traditional socialist analysis was based – the wage-earning manual male productive labourer – would now be fewer than one in ten of all citizens. Even the broader figure, without the confusing 'productive' differentiation, would be not higher than one in four or five. In the cruder older analyses, the wives of working-class men were often included as dependent figures in this category, to arrive at an estimate of the working class as a whole. Yet, at the level of electoral politics, there have until recently been significant differentials by gender. In 1955 50 per cent of men voted Labour, 45.5 per cent Conservative; 54 per cent of women voted Conservative, 42 per cent Labour. In 1983 30 per cent of men voted Labour, 46 per cent Conservative; 43 per cent of women voted Conservative, 28 per cent Labour. The old obvious differential seems to have disappeared yet it is still clear that 'class', either in a broad social sense, or in the narrow electoral sense, as on 'issues', can never be made to override gender differences, however these may in turn be interpreted.

It is crucial to remember these problems when we go on to look at class changes through time. For it then matters very much which criteria we are working with. Thus, if it is the simple wage-earning criterion, there are now more wage-earners, both absolutely and as a proportion of the population of working age, than in any earlier 'more proletarian' period. Indeed the classical 'bourgeoisie', of employers and proprietors, has correspondingly declined, from some 7 per cent at the beginning of the century to less than 4 per cent. But it would obviously not be sensible to conclude, from these trends, that Britain has become a more proletarian and less bourgeois society. If the 'manual' or 'productive manual' categories are chosen, there is a rapid and significant decline in the working class. On the other hand, if we look for the proportion of employed people who lack any significant control over the purposes, methods and conditions of their work – an important kind of contrast with the independent worker – we find a large majority the other way.

It is then crucial not only for analysis but for politics to think through what the significant objective criteria now are. It is not likely that manual work, in the older sense, would in any way decline as a socially significant marker. There is still a radical difference between that kind of labour and all others. This is not to say that it can on its own, or in association with definitions of 'productive' labour, draw the decisive line in any complex modern economy. Indeed it may be a guarantee of the continuing day-by-day, life-by-life exploitation of such workers, to offer to isolate them, politically, by continuing social and political definitions in these terms. Nor is much to be gained by the rhetorical extension to the formula of 'workers by hand and brain', since this either merely assimilates the objective differences or, in its characteristic political uses, actually masks the problems of working and social relations which have to be clarified and assessed if they are ever in practice to be solved.

Thus the received definitions of class, as they bear on politics in the widest or simply in the electoral sense, have at best some general indicative value, of a complex kind, and at worst the effect of confusion and displacement, especially when they are used to support received general theories, whether of a socialist or anti-socialist kind. For where these matters really bear on politics is at the level of the whole social order, and then specifically on questions related to capitalism and socialism and to the forms of both.

3

We can take one of the hardest questions first. What are the real relations between the labour movement and socialism? We can pause first on that description of a *movement*. Many of us know why our forebears called it and served it as a movement. It was a coming together of people, under hard conditions, to help each other, to connect immediate struggles, to try to move through and beyond them to a different kind of society. It was thus also, in that other significant word, a *cause*, and it is historically and culturally very important that it shared a vocabulary with religious associations and campaigns, centred on conversion and change. At the same time, throughout its development, another description was adopted: the labour *interest*. Most of the early electoral politics was in terms of representation of the labour interest.

It is apparent that two underlying intentions were present: to change the social order, and/or to be better represented in a modified social order. These were often translated as choices between 'revolution' and 'evolution', though in that transfer of attention to the means or pace of change there is a masking of the more fundamental distinction between a new kind of society and the existing social order reformed. In practice even this distinction becomes a matter of degree, at many actual points, though the underlying distinction, as it relates to alternative descriptions of a *movement*, a *cause* or an *interest*, remains.

In contemporary political discussion, these problems of choice and perspective are usually blurred. Leaders still speak of 'the movement' on festive occasions, while actually seeking to direct their organisations to institutions of interest. That now daily phrase, 'industrial action', shows this most clearly, and throws some retrospective light on the image of 'industrial' and 'political' wings. For the term makes sense only within the idea of a movement which is looking for advance on two fronts: either in industrial forms – wages and conditions – or in political forms – representation, legislation and government – or both. It is the linkage within a movement that finally matters. If the idea of a movement is replaced by the idea of separate or mutually consulting institutions, with the political party defined as an alternative government in the 'national interest' and the trade unions defined as industrial bargaining units, the phrase 'industrial action' becomes residual, and deserves the mockery it now so often gets. For if it is only a routine description of any kind of strike or working-to-rule, even with fully justifiable reference to the interests of that particular group of workers, it has lost, or at least does not necessarily carry, significant connection with the essentially general aims of a movement.

This is now the specific crisis of what is still called the labour movement: at a first level justifiably so called, since for all the faults of parties or unions they are still the historical creation and the most organised embodiment of the working people. But under the stresses of major social and economic change, and given the fact that they have at no time received the active endorsement of all working people, the rhetorical connection between their interests and a true general interest can no longer be assumed. Indeed the assertion of this rhetorical connection may be one of the practical obstacles to making it real. What has to be proved, rather than asserted, is that the defence and advancement of selected particular interests, properly brought together, are in the general interest, and are capable of being its highest form.

In any society that is far from easy. There is now a tendency to assert militancy as a value, but militancy is nothing special to the working class. To see this we have only to look at the militancy of stockbrokers or country landowners or public-school headmasters, in defence of their particular interests.

The traditional claim that the labour movement was more than a congeries of certain particular interests was made on two different grounds. First, within the culture of poverty, where the movement began, the claim that these particular interests amounted to a general interest had a certain absolute cast. It could not be right for so many human beings to have to live like that. Indeed this is what has still to be said about the absolute poverty of hundreds of millions of people in the 'Third World'. It is what has also still to be said about specific sectors of extreme poverty within the rich countries. The very success of the labour movement itself, in the old industrial countries, has at least qualified that kind of claim. The organised workers have moved well above absolute poverty. Meanwhile the significant extension of trade-unionism to relatively comfortable, even relatively privileged white-collar and even professional occupations has had the effect that there is no longer any reliable basis for the claim to a general interest in absolute human need. Where that claim has really to be made is among the millions of marginal and beyond-the-margin poor who are outside the well-organised bargaining procedures, or who are in poor societies on international terms of trade within which internal wage bargaining, in the rich societies, is fundamentally privileged.

The second argument for the labour movement as an inherent general interest was different. It was said that the capitalist system, by expropriating the common means of production, and by the private appropriation of the surplus value of labour, is inherently hostile to the general interest, and thus incompatible with it. This is indeed my own belief. I am one of the small minority, within capitalist societies, who continue to see this as a relatively obvious fact. The familiar next stage of the argument is that the organised labour movement is the only force which can end capitalism. Thus *any* action against it, however local and particularist in form, connects with this underlying general interest. It is a persuasive argument, among minorities who have in fact been losing ground. The reason for this loss of credibility is that in its most popular form the argument is uncertain and negative. For it cannot be assumed that any action against a particular capitalist enterprise is by definition an action against the capitalist system. It may, for example, simply force the transfer of capital elsewhere, often to capitalist advantage. Even more, it cannot be assumed that an action against a particular 'public corporation' which within a capitalist social order has reproduced capitalist wage-relations but is also, by the specific policies of the labour movement, state-owned and directed, is an action against the capitalist system. It is often in practice seen as an action against the 'general public' and taken as evidence of the failure of *socialism*!

As these problems become evident, what actually happens is a weakening or forgetting of the original founding position: that the capitalist system is against the general interest, and that by industrial and political action it can be ended and replaced by a system which is in the general interest: socialism. Everything then depends on the practical and visible connection of any particular action with that clear and serious intention; moreover, if it is to persuade others, on evidence that the foreseen alternative system is both practicable and in the general interest. It is at this point that there have been repeated failures. Many leaders and spokesmen fall back on more limited and particularist actions and arguments. The word 'socialism' may still be on tap. But if it is claimed that the general direction even of particularist struggles is against capitalism and towards socialism, credibility is bound to depend on more than a verbal affiliation. The point at which particular interests, properly brought together, can be seen to be a general interest is the moment of socialism. But this moment comes not once and for all. It comes many times; is lost and is found again; has to be affirmed and developed, continually and practically, if it is to stay real. Without this development, there is the devastating loss and damage of our own period.

Most labour struggles begin as particularist. People recognise some condition and problem that they have in common, and make the effort to work together to change or to solve it. Within the culture of poverty any such effort had a certain absolute cast. No matter what those very poor and hard-driven men and women were actually thinking, even if they had nothing in mind but some temporary easement, the concept of a general interest was still valid. In fact, even in the hardest times, some of them were thinking much further. It is still often so today. It has been true, in recent struggles, of the nurses (connecting with the true general interest of a health service), of the miners (connecting with the true general interest of a domestic energy policy) and of many others.

But it cannot be taken for granted that such links are there by the mere fact that it is a trade-union action. It is often much more a case of the busy competitive bargaining of interest groups. It is seen like that, most of the time, from inside, and is almost always seen like that from outside, including by many of the other interest groups. It is in prevailing conditions a necessary process. In its definition as free (collective) bargaining it is part of the mechanism of a modern capitalist society. Even most modern capitalists want only to regulate it, and to steer it away from more dangerous ideas like direct action or changing the social order. Other much more powerful interest groups, in the State, in the City, in the big corporations, are still there, combining and bargaining for advantage, and the rest of us can settle to saying: 'while they do it, we do it'. There is then no accessible general interest; only the competition of particular interests.

This is the practical triumph of *capitalist* thinking. It is only the bourgeoisie which has ever tried to believe that pursuing special interests ensures the general interest, by a hidden hand. Enough of us have now seen that hand to know who it belongs to: the capitalist social order. It was that whole mean, false and privileged view of society that first the labour movement, and then more consciously and more effectively the socialist movement, set out openly and coherently to challenge, to limit, and eventually to surpass and replace. An implacable hostility, from all the old interests, was to be expected and has still to be expected and outfaced. Of course the rich and the employers, and their agents and friends, believe and say that we are all only interested in selfish advantage. But the most shattering fact in our culture is that a *majority* believe and say this, including a large and growing number of those on whose behalf, as a general interest, the actions are supposed to be based. This is so among many of the bargaining employed, but it is especially so among the less organised workers, the unemployed and the really poor.

What has then really failed, inside the labour movement and in the whole society, is any accepted concept of the general interest. That is why appeals to it, in standard political currency, are so often resisted or rejected. What makes this worse is that the forms in which we have been offered the general interest – the undifferentiated 'nation', the 'needs' of 'the economy' – are demonstrably false. For these are labels stuck over a systematically and radically unequal society, and over a necessarily privileged and exploiting financial and economic order. Paradoxically, by keeping so firmly to particular interests, the falsehood of these versions of the general interest has been thoroughly demonstrated. Yet not consciously; not at the level of argument and alternatives; only really at the level of mood. There is a common sense of scepticism about all propositions of the general interest, especially in everyday practice, where they not only don't hold but are visibly not believed. At the same time everybody, on demand, can intone the false versions, until they are disadvantageously applied to themselves; or can intone any version, against the interests and demands of other people.

There is only one good way out of all this. A practical and possible general interest, which really does include all reasonable particular interests, has to be inquired into, found, negotiated, agreed, constructed. Under any conditions, but especially in contemporary conditions, this is at once a heavy job and seems to have to be started from scratch. Yet it is not really that hopeless. There are more positive resources than we usually assume, and the central problem of the labour and socialist movements is that they have neglected or lost touch with so many of them.

4

The central theoretical difficulty in relations between the labour movement and socialism is that they have been closely associated historically and that at least one major element of this association appears to be universal. At the same time, in any close analysis, there are marked variations of degree, both in the association itself and in its persistence, in different cultures, nations, regions, localities and industries.

It is very striking that the institution of modern industry, especially in the most aggregated forms of factory, mill, mine, docks, shipyard, has produced, in otherwise diverse cultures and societies, the characteristic forms of unionisation and some regular minority association of these with socialism. Even the variable extent and success of these processes, under identifiable pressures ranging from legal obstacles to savage repression, cannot cancel this element of universality – a response based on a common sense *as workers*, beyond other social and cultural differences. Yet it is not possible simply to project this structural universality into a whole social and political process: the projection which occurred in the most influential theories of the 'international proletariat'. Not only between countries and nations, where the working-class organisations, in overwhelming majority, continued to insist that they had their own fatherlands, but also between religious and ethnic groups, and between men and women, the realisable forms of the underlying universality fell far short of the theoretical projection.

We can understand this better, as a historical process, if we begin by recognising that an organised labour movement, even before the process of its association with socialism, has to insert itself in societies which are already strongly bonded in other ways. I mean by *bonding* the institution and exercise of those relationships which are capable of maintaining the effective practice of social life as a whole. In the simplest societies there are basic bonds of kin and of locality, and these are not cancelled, though their forms may greatly change, in more complex societies. Particular forms of kin relations – 'family' – are shaped and reshaped by types of landholding and by different forms of the organisation of work. Bonds of direct, placeable locality are complicated by the extended regimes of larger societies, offering a whole 'country' as a native place. In the form of the nation-state, defined by a particular regime and its laws, and in formal concepts of nationality or even race, new and less direct but typically effective bonds are forged. These offer to include the persistent direct forms but in practice change them.

It was within and into these complex forms of bonding that the labour movement had to make its way, offering a new category within social bonding itself. Its impulses were very powerful, under the dislocating pressures of new kinds of work and wage-labour. One effective form of this new bonding was the perception of at least some of the other forms as *bondage*. Already for the majority of men, and for an even larger majority of women, what can be abstractly described as positive bonding was experienced, in some degree, as bondage: imposed determining relations in social life as a whole. It was in these terms that there had been so many earlier forms of revolt, protest and passive resistance. The qualitatively new element of the labour movement was a form of regular combination, which took some of its elements from the new regularities and interdependences of industrial work. Long-established forms of the regulation of a trade developed, through great uncertainty and with much unevenness, into the self-organisation of a class. Yet at every point, forms of the older kinds of bonding – by kin, by locality, by country, by religion, and, to an often powerful degree, still by trade – persisted. The exposed common condition of the landless and unpropertied, of the hired and fired but now newly aggregated and interdependent wage-labourers, was the basis for a new bond against new forms of bondage. There was a new sense of *wage-slavery*; a condition in which, Marx and others argued, the workers had nothing to lose but their *chains*. Running ahead of its actual and difficult social development, theoreticians of this real process projected a dissolution of all other major bonds: there was 'a world to win', a foreseeable 'brotherhood of man', a general future condition of 'socialism' or 'communism'.

The basic idea of socialism was inherent in the new movements. It was an emphasis of mutual and cooperative, *social* practice, as distinct from the dominant bourgeois idea of *individual* practice, reference and advantage. In some definitions socialism was simply this growing movement of mutuality, cooperation and collective organisation: the social movement which would become a whole positive society. In more ideal projections, socialism was at once a cancellation of the forms of bondage, centrally in property and in rank, and then, in two connecting but distinguishable tendencies, either the reinstatement of the simpler forms of original bonding, by kin and locality ('primitive communism') or the development of new and higher forms of complex interdependence and equality. Yet the decisive agency of the movement was seen as this one critical relationship, of wage-labour. Other factors and agencies were not denied, though they were often in practice neglected (the forms of family under wage-labour; the positions of women and children; locality and nationality; cultural forms of custom and belief). What was seized as determining was perceived as dominant, to the point where many theories of socialism, but also and more specifically the forms of trade-unionism itself, which were centred not only on the working man but on the man *at work*, often amounted in practice to the *isolation* of this one powerful form.

Two points have then to be made. First, that the highest development of trade-unionism, and even more its association with socialism, have been in practice most active in situations of much more complex bonding. Second, that at a certain stage of its development the isolation of economic bonding, already open to the pull of other existing and persistent social bonds, permits its incorporation within non-socialist or anti-socialist economic forms, which can meet it, at least temporarily, on isolated economic grounds.

It is true that the major centres of trade-unionism, in many different societies, are primarily correlated with the major centres of aggregated industry, by contrast with lower stages of development in more dispersed or more mixed forms of work. But it seems also to be true that in its most active and militant forms, and in its bonding association with socialism, other social factors are vividly present. It may be useful to compare different kinds of community in which there are still practical majorities of wage-earners. In one kind of community – the South Wales mining settlements, or the Clydeside shipyard communities – there is a predominantly common working situation and workplace but also a relative simultaneity of other major social bonds. Through their still significant individual differences, the people of such communities are simultaneously fellow-workers, husbands and wives of fellow-workers, neighbours, interlinked extended families. Other kinds of bond, as of being consciously Welsh or Scots against a dominant 'English' system, or (though here in more complex and at times in divisive as well as uniting ways) of religion, provide positive and in some cases supporting resources. Though always incomplete and internally contentious, such communities have taken the active practices of the labour movement and of popular socialism to the highest points that, within Britain, they have yet reached. On the other hand, in the most contrasting kinds of community – for example in the resorts, one of which Tressell described in *The Ragged-Trousered Philanthropists*, or in the mixed suburbs or the old country towns – there is less common practical experience of shared work and workplace. But there is also a more mixed and varied neighbourhood, and the older positive bonds of the interests of the place as a whole, together with the absence of distancing 'national' or 'ethnic' factors, often actually work against the offered new bond of a united working class which is learning to commit itself to socialism.

There are many complexities within this perspective. The most closely-bonded 'traditional' working class can be arrested, by its own positivities, at 'Labourism' rather than socialism; may indeed typically mistake one for the other. In more fragmented and diverse communities, which are in any case through historical change becoming more typical, the real problems of the general processes may be more clearly seen, though then only by small minorities. It is significant that the first socialist working-class novel in English, *The Ragged-Trousered Philanthropists*, was written not in the close labour communities but by a travelled immigrant, in one of the most fragmented. Significantly, also, the novel does not celebrate but questions and seeks to inform the working people who are not yet a class, and who in majority oppose the idea of a class.

At many levels, from degrees of union organisation and militancy through percentages of Labour voting to centres of active socialist education and campaigning, this correlation by type of community appears to be confirmed (including the less welcome correlations as the older types change internally, as recently in South Wales). It would need extensive research and analysis, over many types of community and in relation to other industrial societies, to test this initial strong impression. But the kind of thinking it represents is more relevant, and in changing conditions increasingly more significant, than the abstract undifferentiated counting of wage-earners as if they were, or were only, a single class. This position is underlined by the experiences of revolutionary socialism in the world of the middle and late twentieth century, where the most significant bonding has included strong national commitments against a foreign imperialist or colonial power, and where links with an organised industrial working class have not been dominant.

In the old industrial countries themselves, the problems of bonding, and specifically the problem of the weakening of the theoretically assumed dominant bond, are of central importance for socialists. In some societies with unique problems of bonding (for example, the United States) certain tendencies have proposed that the organised labour movement is irrelevant or only marginally relevant to socialism. There is no general reason to conclude this. It is impossible, for example, in Western Europe, to conceive any important socialist movement which is not largely based on the industrial working class, including its most traditional formations.

Yet we have certainly to move beyond conceptions of this class which are centred on the male wage-earner at work. This not only neglects the internally subordinate position of employed women, but the radically different and more general subordination of women (including above all the 'non-employed') within wider social relations. Moreover, in its isolation of the citizen as the worker, it regularly tends to exclude, or to include only as marginal 'benefits', the primary processes and needs of social life as a whole, on which the production of both work and worker radically depends.

There is a common form of trade-unionism which is expressed in the image of a man or woman holding up a payslip, on which only the bottom line – after tax, insurance and contributions – is emphasised. It is true that this is called 'take-home pay': a form of conscious re-entry into other social relations, specifically the individual family. But the more general social contributions are increasingly written off as mere losses, 'stoppages'. This is a deep tendency which is not really hidden, though it is frequently masked, by more local arguments about the uses to which the social contributions are put. These arguments are often convincing in themselves but much more often they merely reproduce the bourgeois perception of 'my money', which society is 'taking from me'.

It is at this point that trade-unionism can be effectively incorporated. The recent electoral shift of 'young male semi-skilled workers', choosing tax reduction before social services and public development, is the most obvious example. There are other forms of incorporation: the prosperity of 'my firm'; the attachment to employment as such, regardless of its social purposes (as in the armaments industries); the priority of competition against the industries of other nations, rich or poor. All these exert powerful pressures on individuals and organisations who in any case have little effective space for choice, within societies and economies still centrally controlled by capitalism.

What then most needs to be emphasised is that it is capitalism which proposes and tries to enforce the isolation of economic bonding: 'the cash-nexus between man and man'. To reproduce this as a principle or model of socialism is to move, step by step, into the capitalist consciousness which is now a majority force in the old industrial societies, determining the thinking and practice even of majorities of wage-earners. That there is fierce competition within such an ethos does not alter this fact. Wage-bargaining groups compete with their employers, but their employers also, by necessity, compete with each other. The sources of a different ethos are then primarily in those other social bonds, those ultimately deeper attachments and purposes, which capitalism tries to push into a lower importance, or where necessary to cancel. It is then in what happens or can happen in these other practices and relationships that the resources of a wider socialism have to be developed. It is a matter of what happens in the primary care of people, in families and neighbourhoods and communities. It is a matter of what happens in the organised services of health and education; in protection and enhancement of our physical environment; in the quality of our public information and entertainment.

In each of these matters, there are either capitalist or socialist solutions. The capitalist solution, now rapidly gaining ground, proposes forms of provision which start from the primacy of economic relations, on the money from which people buy varying degrees of care, medical treatment, education, information. The physical environment is made subject to calculations of short-term profit, as in the many kinds of industrial and agricultural pollution, which are for the most part foreseen when the processes start and which are minimised only if the cost is not too high. All relations with others, within and between nations, are governed by the calculation of competitive advantage. Human society becomes a network of aggressive marketing, and other human needs are admitted only *after* this priority, when by its presumed success they can at last be afforded.

The alternative, socialist solution? This is where we are now in trouble. The movement of so many trade unions and of so many wage-earners towards the principles of economic competition has radically weakened the idea of an alternative. This is especially the case when they impose such thinking on socialist political parties, turning them back into 'interest' parties. The 'demand' for wider social provision, which can usually also be heard from such unions and parties, is fundamentally unconvincing, since it is typically an argument in terms of consumption, with production left as it is. Historically this is a mark of the cultural and political subordination of the labour movement. It is basically asking for – indeed rhetorically 'demanding' – all these conditions and services *from an employer or from an abstracted State*. The test comes when, as in any real accounting, the costs of such conditions and services – monetary but also as priorities of energy and resources – have to be integrated with the isolated calculations of production and of wages. It is only at the point of contribution, by taxes and the like, or at the higher point of a willingness to become responsible for the *whole* process, reshaping production to these social ends, that the hard questions are asked. That they have not yet been answered, by enough people in any socialist way, is obvious. That they have been displaced to rhetoric or to fantasy, making other people even tired of the questions, is also very clear. So a hardening capitalism now carries everything before it, in politics, while the broader realities of social life continue to show it as demeaning, reckless and trivial.

5

All significant social *movements* of the last thirty years have started outside the organised class interests and institutions. The peace movement, the ecology movement, the women's movement, solidarity with the third world, human rights agencies, campaigns against poverty and homelessness, campaigns against cultural poverty and distortion: all have this character, that they sprang from needs and perceptions which the interest-based organisations had no room or time for, or which they had simply failed to notice. This is the reality which is often misinterpreted as 'getting beyond class politics'. The local judgment on the narrowness of the major interest groups is just. But there is not one of these issues which, followed through, fails to lead us into the central systems of the industrial-capitalist mode of production and among others into its system of classes. These movements and the needs and feelings which nourish them are now our major positive resources, but their whole problem is how they relate or can relate to the apparently more important institutions which derive from the isolation of employment and wage-labour. At the margins of those institutions, in fact, there have been significant developments which make new kinds of linkage possible. The movement for workers' control, in its strongest form, is an answer to the question about the willingness to take responsibility for the whole social process. The detailed proposals by some groups of trade unionists for new kinds of social production bear in the same direction. So also, in crisis, do the proposals for new kinds of industrial cooperatives, for alternative financial institutions and for an alternative press. None of these proposals has yet come to command the substantial support of the labour movement as a whole, yet they show that the possible resources are there.

It is then still true, as was argued in *The Long Revolution*, that the institutions of the labour movement 'can go either way, and that their crisis is not yet permanently resolved'. Yet the pressures on them are now very much heavier: not only from their traditional enemies but from developments and failures to develop within themselves. The old solid working-class communities are being broken up by industrial change. The old room for manoeuvre by steady bargaining is being drastically restricted by the crises of capitalist profitability and of the international relocation of industry. What will now happen is either the final incorporation of the labour movement into a capitalist bargaining mechanism, with socialism left stranded as a theory and a sect, or the wide remaking of a social movement which begins from primary human needs. These needs are for peace, security, a caring society and a careful economy. They are needs which the capitalist social order cannot adapt itself to, but which equally the narrowed interests of maximum wage-earning in any kind of employment (the now dominant definition of what was once a whole labour movement) cannot define or support.

These are very hard things to say: especially hard for someone who grew up in and was formed by the old labour institutions and perspectives; a contemporary of the present leaders of the industrial labour movement, from a working-class family like their own; a contemporary also of the present political leaders, whose class-formation, significantly, is usually very different. But it is better to say them than to go on acquiescing in the limited perspectives and the outdated assumptions which now govern the movement, and above all in its now sickening self-congratulatory sense of a taken-for-granted tradition and constituency. The real struggle has broadened so much, the decisive issues have been so radically changed, that only a new kind of socialist movement, fully contemporary in its ideas and methods, bringing a wide range of needs and interests together in a new definition of the general interest, has any real future.

IV

THE ANALYSIS EXTENDED

THE CULTURE OF
NATIONS

I

There was this Englishman who worked in the London office of a multinational corporation based in the United States. He drove home one evening in his Japanese car. His wife, who worked in a firm which imported German kitchen equipment, was already at home. Her small Italian car was often quicker through the traffic. After a meal which included New Zealand lamb, Californian carrots, Mexican honey, French cheese and Spanish wine, they settled down to watch a programme on their television set, which had been made in Finland. The programme was a retrospective celebration of the war to recapture the Falkland Islands. As they watched it they felt warmly patriotic, and very proud to be British.

2

The contradictions in what is meant by nationality, and even more by patriotism, are now very acute. If they are more noticed and thought about by some people than by others, they are still not of a kind to be projected only to those who are most evidently and practically confused. There is a strongly effective continuation of relatively old ideas of nationality, and beyond these of race, while at the same time there is an extraordinary and yet widely accepted penetration and coexistence of powerful international and paranational forms. These are to be found not only in the obvious cases of world markets in food and in manufactured commodities, but also in active membership of a political and military alliance and of a paranational economic community. Each of these has radically altered the nature of sovereignty, yet that idea is still quite centrally retained. Our couple may well not have noticed the American aircraft, armed with nuclear weapons, flying high above their house from an English base, or the new heavier lorries on the bypass, whose weight has been determined by an EEC regulation, yet regularly, systematically, these are there.

'Contradiction' is a curious analytic term. It can be applied quite easily to cases where people actually say contradictory things, or act on contradictory beliefs. If somebody says that his country means everything to him, but that as a consumer he must buy what he wants at the most suitable price and quality, whatever its national origin, the element of contradiction is obvious. But the term has been extended to much more difficult cases, when it is not so much what people say and believe that is contradictory but when actual forces in a society are pulling in opposite or at least different directions and thus creating tensions and instabilities. The former cases, of verbal or everyday practical contradiction, can be met by arguments. They are what most of us come to notice, at various points in our lives, when we have to decide what we really (most) believe. The other kinds of 'contradiction' are not so readily dealt with. Indeed it is already assuming a lot to say that they are simple contradictions. The mental model by which we test coherence or compatibility may be simply what we are putting into the situation, and what looks contradictory, in its selected terms, may in fact be no more than an unfamiliar system, which in its own terms is coherent enough. There is then still a problem of the things we say about it, which may be muddled or locally contradictory. But the system itself, not only creating but also containing and managing tensions and instabilities, is not something that can be refuted by argument alone.

This is now the case, I believe, in these central problems that are indicated by talk of 'nationality', 'patriotism' and – for it is part of the same complex – 'internationalism'. There are innumerable muddles and stupidities, and there is some very powerful political and cultural exploitation both of these and of the genuine difficulties.

But in general these are problems of the surface of politics and culture. They would be relatively easily solved if the underlying and obscured problems of contemporary societies, on which they feed, were not so great.

3

It is human nature to belong to a society, and to find value in belonging to it. We are born into relationships, and we live and grow through relationships. There is a whole range of such forms, variable in different places and times, but any actual forms are close and specific to those who are living in and through them. Intellectual analysis, of an historical or comparative kind, can show very quickly how 'limited' or 'local' any such form may be. But while in times of pressure and change this wider perspective is encouraging, showing us that it is possible for people to find meaning and value in many different kinds of relationship and society, it can also be an effective evasion of the actual problems which, with such meanings and values as they have, people are trying to resolve.

Thus in several modern intellectual systems there has been rapid progress to forms of universality – what is believed to be true of all people everywhere – which are then used to define what most people are still trying to live by as mere local illusions and prejudices. Genuine progress towards establishing the universality of social situation by class is offered as a way of dissolving stubborn self-definitions by nationality or religion. A presumed universality of situation by primary relationships, as in psychoanalysis, is offered as a way of enlightening and questioning forms of relationship which are, nevertheless, being continually reproduced. Each of these systems, with other similar systems, clearly affects the ways in which many people have learned to think about their relationships, but, except in certain very specific groups, they have nowhere come near to realising their own apparent logic, by which the offered universalities would prevail over more local forms.

Yet this is only half the story. The real 'universalities' – large forms which do succeed in prevailing over more local forms – are not to be found in intellectual systems but in actual and organised relationships which achieve, over the relevant areas, effective power. This is the way to look at the urgent modern problem of the 'nation'.

It is ineffective and even trivial to come back from a demonstration of the universality of the human species and expect people, from that fact alone, to reorganise their lives by treating all their immediate and actual groupings and relationships as secondary. For the species meaning, and the valuation of human life which it carries, is in practice only realised, indeed perhaps in theory only realisable, through significant relationships in which other human beings are present. No abstraction on its own will carry this most specific of all senses. To extend it and to generalise it, in sufficiently practical ways, involves the making of new relationships which are in significant continuity – and not in contradiction – with the more limited relationships through which people do and must live.

Thus there is little point in jumping from 'the nation' to a projected 'internationalism'. Instead we have to move first in the other direction, to see what in practice this widely accepted 'universality' now amounts to. 'All modern peoples have organised themselves as nations'. Have they? The artificialities of many forms of modern 'nationality' and 'patriotism' have often been noticed. Some relatively detached or mobile people see them as merely 'backward' or 'primitive', and have a good laugh about them, until some war makes them weep. But the real point of entry for analysis is that the artificialities are functional. That is to say, they are neither backward nor primitive but contemporarily effective and deliberate forms. That they are now increasingly artificial, with very serious effects on what is also residually quite real, is then the central point.

4

'Nation', as a term, is radically connected with 'native'. We are *born* into relationships, which are typically settled in a place. This form of primary and 'placeable' bonding is of quite fundamental human and natural importance. Yet the jump from that to anything like the modern nation-state is entirely artificial. What begins as a significant and necessary way of saying 'we' and 'our' (as so much more than 'I' and 'mine') slides by teaching or habit into bland or obscuring generalities of identity. The strongest forms of placeable bonding are always much more local: a village or town or city; particular valleys or mountains. Still today in societies as different as Wales and Italy people say where they come from, where they were formed or belong, in these insistently local ways. It is of course possible to extend these real feelings into wider areas: what are often spoken of now as 'regional' identities and loyalties. But that term, 'region', illuminates a very different process. A 'region' was once a realm, a distinct society. In its modern sense, by contrast, it is from the beginning a subordinate part of a larger unity, typically now a part of a 'nation'. What has then happened is that the real and powerful feelings of a native place and a native formation have been pressed and incorporated into an essentially political and administrative organisation, which has grown from quite different roots. 'Local' and 'regional' identities and loyalties are still allowed, even at a certain level encouraged, but they are presumed to exist within, and where necessary to be overridden by, the identities and the loyalties of this much larger society.

It is of course true that some of these wider identities and loyalties have been effectively achieved through real relationships. Even where, as in the great majority of cases, the larger society was originally formed by violent conquest, by repression, by economic domination or by arbitrary alliances between ruling families, there are usually generations of experience of living within these imposed forms, and then of becoming used or even attached to them. What is still in question, however, is the projection of those original 'native' and 'placeable' feelings to the forms of a modern state. Nothing is now more striking, for example, than the images of 'England' which are culturally predominant. Many urban children, when asked what is really 'England', reply with images of the monarchy, of the flag, of the Palace of Westminster and, most interestingly, of 'the country-side', the 'green and pleasant land'. It is here that the element of artifice is most obvious, when the terms of identity flow downwards from a political centre, and yet when the very different feelings of being 'native' and being 'loyal' are invoked and in this way combined.

In nations with long and complex histories the procedures of invocation and combination are deeply embedded in the whole social process. Yet it is an evident historical fact that the processes of political combination and definition are initiated by a ruling class: indeed to say so is virtually tautologous. The building of states, at whatever level, is intrinsically a ruling-class operation. The powerful processes that then ensue, in the complex transitions from conquest and subjection to more embedded formations, necessarily take place, however, over much wider social areas. War stands out as one of the fundamentally unifying and generalising experiences: the identification of an alien enemy, and with it of what is often real danger, powerfully promotes and often in effect completes a 'national' identity. It is not accidental that talk of patriotism so quickly involves, and can even be limited to, memories and symbols of war. Meanwhile the assembly of armies, from diverse actual communities into this single and overriding organisation, is one of the most notable processes of actual generalisation and unification.

In modern societies, engaged in the transition from a subject people to a civil society, education of every kind, in churches and then mainly in schools, exerts more regular pressures. When children start going to school they often learn for the first time that they are English or British or what may be. The pleasure of learning is attached to the song of a monarch or a flag. The sense of friends and neighbours is attached to a distant and commanding organisation: in Britain, now, that which ought to be spelled as it so barbarously sounds – the United Kingdom, the 'Yookay'. Selective versions of the history underlying this impressed identity are regularly presented, at every level from simple images and anecdotes to apparently serious textbook histories. The powerful feelings of wanting to belong to a society are then in a majority of cases bonded to these large definitions.

It is often the case that this bonding moves at once from the smallest social entity, within the family, to the available largest, in the nation-state. These are offered as non-contradictory. Indeed they are rationalised as levels, the personal and the social. Many other kinds of bonding may then occur: distinction by streets or by parts of a town or village; distinction by gender and age-group; distinction by city or region. Many kinds of active 'local' or 'regional' groups, and of more passive groups of fans or supporters, grow up around these and carry powerful feelings. But typically they are unproblematically contained within the initial bonding between 'family-individual' and 'nation', which in all important and central cases is felt either to be an extension from them (as in particularised army regiments) or to override them.

It is a matter of great political significance that in the old nation-states, and especially the imperial states, scepticism and criticism of such bonding has come almost exclusively from radicals. They have seen, correctly, that this form of bonding operates to mobilise people for wars or to embellish and disguise forms of social and political control and obedience. It is true that opposition comes also from incompletely assimilated or still actively hostile minority peoples who have been incorporated within the nation-state, but this characteristically takes the form of an alternative (Irish or Scots or Welsh or Breton or Basque) nationalism, relying on the same apparent bonding though within a political subordination. The complex interactions between such nationalisms and more general radicalisms have been evident and remarkable, though in general it is true that unique forms of national-radical bonding, unavailable by definition in the larger nation-state, come through and have powerful effects. It is sadly also true that not only the majority people, with 'their own' nation-state, but also many among the minority peoples, regard *this kind* of nationalism as disruptive or backward-looking, and are even confident enough to urge 'internationalism' against it, as a superior political ideal. It is as if a really secure nationalism, already in possession of its nation-state, can fail to see itself as 'nationalist' at all. Its own distinctive bonding is perceived as natural and obvious by contrast with the mere projections of any nationalism which is still in active progress and thus incomplete. At this point radicals and minority nationalists emphasise the artificialities of the settled 'commonsense' nation-state and to their own satisfaction shoot them to pieces from history and from social theory.

The political significance is then that radicalism becomes associated, even in principle, with opposition to 'the nation'. In the old nation-states this has been profoundly damaging, yet it can be understood only by reference to the history and formation of actual social orders. For what has been most remarkable in the twentieth century has been the successful fusion of nationalism and political revolution, including armed struggles, in many other parts of the world, from Cuba to Vietnam. The conditions of such fusion evidently derive from a pre-existing colonial or semi-colonial status, in which relatively direct and powerful bonds of identity and aspiration are formed as against both foreigners and exploiters. There are then usually major problems, at a later stage, in relations with other national-revolutionary states, and the elements fused in the struggle enter a new stage in which the bonding can no longer be taken for granted. Meanwhile the political problem, for radicals back in the old nation-states, who are quick to identify with the national-liberation struggles of the ex-colonial peoples, lies in their fundamental attitudes to their own nation. For again and again, hurling themselves at the mystification of social reality by the ruling definitions of the nation and patriotism, they have found themselves opposed not only by the existing rulers and guardians but by actual majorities of the people in whose more fundamental needs and interests they are offering to speak.

There are many false ways out of this basic problem. All of them depend on subjection to the existing terms of the definitions. Contemporary social democrats, in particular, do their calculations and emerge with an amazing and implausible mix of patriotism, internationalism and social justice, drawing on each principle as occasion serves, or rhetorically proclaiming their compatibility or even identity. All this shows is their profound subordination to the forms of existing interests. The increasing irrelevance of social-democratic politics, in the old nation-states – indeed the transformation of social democracy itself, under a merely confusing retention of an old name, which in different conditions had more significance and coherence – is a direct result of this basic subordination.

For what they will not challenge, except in selected marginal ways, is capitalism itself. Yet it is capitalism, especially in its most developed stages, which is the main source of all the contemporary confusions about peoples and nations and their necessary loyalties and bonds. Moreover it is, in the modern epoch, capitalism which has disrupted and overriden natural communities, and imposed artificial orders. It is then a savage irony that capitalist states have again and again succeeded in mobilising patriotic feelings in their own forms and interests. The artificialities of modern nationalism and patriotism, in states of this kind, have then to be referred not to some intellectually dissolving universality, but to the precise and powerful functions which, necessarily in the form of artifice, they are now required to perform.

5

Both in its initial creation of a domestic market, and in its later organisation of a global market, the capitalist mode of production has always moved in on resources and then, necessarily, on people, without respect for the forms and boundaries of existing social organisations. Whole communities with settled domestic forms of production, from farming to brewing and clothmaking, and from small manufacturing to local services, were simply overridden by more developed and more centralised and concentrated capitalist and capitalist-industrial forms. Communities which at simpler levels had relatively balanced forms of livelihood found themselves, often without notice, penetrated or made marginal, to the point where many of their own people became 'redundant' and were available for transfer to new centres of production. Capitalist textile-production, ironmaking, mining, grain production and a host of other industrial processes set in train immigrations and emigrations, aggregations and depopulations, on a vast scale. Typically, moreover, people were moved in and out on short-run calculations of profit and convenience, to be left stranded later, in worked-out mining valleys or abandoned textile towns, in old dockyard and shipbuilding areas, in the inner cities themselves, as trade and production moved on in their own interests.

Through these large and prolonged dislocations and relocations, which are still in progress in every part of the world, the older traditional forms of identity and community were dislocated and relocated, within enforced mobilities and necessary new settlements. It is significant that William Cobbett, observing just these processes in one of their most decisive stages, is in effect the last authentic English radical: a man in whom love of birthplace, love of country, and root-and-branch opposition to the whole social order could be authentically integrated. Even in him there were tensions, underlying his radical change of political direction as his idea of the old England encountered the reality of the new. In all later periods, the kind of continuity which Cobbett still saw as ideal, from home and birthplace to county to country – none in tension with or cancelling the other – was increasingly unavailable. What took its place was an artificial construction, which had increasingly to be defined in generalising and centralised images because the only effective political identity still apparently compatible with the dislocating and relocating processes of industry was now at that deliberately distanced level.

But this was still only an early stage. What was done within the first industrial societies was soon also being done, at an accelerating pace, in every accessible part of the world. Whole tracts of land, where people had been living in their own ways, were ripped for minerals, ores, gems, fertilisers. Whole forests, in which people and animals had been living, were felled and exported. Simple subsistence farming communities were dispossessed and reorganised for plantations of rubber and cotton and sugar and coffee and tea, or for any and every kind of export-oriented monoculture which the physical conditions of the land, irrespective of the needs and preferences of its inhabitants, indicated for profit. The long forced trade in human beings, moving them as slaves into new kinds of work, was succeeded by various kinds of economic forcing, in which whole communities and peoples, or by selection their young men and women, had to emigrate to the new centres of work and subsistence.

Some of these developments struck back into the old economies, depressing or ruining other traditional kinds of production, and forcing new internal emigrations from what had been made into 'marginal areas'. Flows of people following these externally induced flows of trade and wealth broke up, at either end, the older types of settlement and community in which identity had been directly engaged. Moreover, as in the first industrial societies, it was never a movement once and for all into a new adjustment. As production and trading advantages shifted, vast numbers had to move yet again, or be left stranded in the debris of a worked-out economy. Massive movements of this kind are still occurring, in thousands of authorised and unauthorised emigrations and immigrations, and in the desperate trails from land dispossessed by agribusiness to the shanty towns on the edges of the already densely populated cities.

What is really astonishing is that it is the inheritors and active promoters, the ideologists and the agents, of this continuing worldwide process who speak to the rest of us, at least from one side of their mouths, about the traditional values of settlement, community and loyalty. These, the great disrupters, not only of other people's settlements but of many of those of their own nominal people, have annexed and appropriated, often without challenge, many of the basic human feelings about a necessary and desirable society. They retain this appropriation even while their hands are endlessly busy with old and new schemes in which the priorities are wholly different: schemes through which actual people and communities are depressed or disappear, under the calculations of cost-benefit, profit and advantageous production.

It is an outrage that this has happened and been allowed to happen. Yet while we can protest and fight in these terms, we can only analyse and understand if we bring in another dimension, which is now probably decisive. Instead of looking only at the promoters and agents of this vast dislocation and relocation, we have to look also at the changes that have happened and are still happening in the minds of those to whom, in effect, all this has been done.

6

Most human beings adjust, because they must, to altered, even radically altered conditions. This is already marked in the first generations of such shifts. By the second and third generations the initially enforced conditions are likely to have become if not the new social norms – for at many levels of intensity the conditions may still be resented – at least the new social perspective, its everday common sense. Moreover, because so many of the shifts are enforced by a willed exploitation of new means of production and new products, sometimes ending in failure but much more often increasing goods of every kind, there are major if always unequal material advantages in the new conditions. Capitalism as a system, just because of its inherent one-dimensional mobility, can move on very rapidly from its failures and worked-out areas, leaving only local peoples stuck with them. By its very single-mindedness it can direct new and advantageous production in at least the short-term interests of effective working majorities. In any of its periodic crises it can make from one in ten to one in three of a numbered people redundant, but while it still has the other nine or the other two it can usually gain sufficient support or tolerance to continue its operations. Moreover, identified almost inextricably with positive advantages in improved products and services, it not only claims but is acclaimed as progress.

Thus while on an historical or comparative scale its forced operations are bound to be seen as arbitrary and often brutal, on any local and temporarily settled scale it flies with the wings of the dove. It brings factories and supermarkets, employment and affluence, and everything else is a local and temporary difficulty – out of sight, out of time, out of mind – or is the evident fault, even the malign fault, of those who are suffering. In any general examination, the system is transparent, and ugly. But in many, and so far always enough, local perspectives it is not only the tolerated but the consciously preferred order of real majorities.

For now from the other side of its mouth it speaks of the consumer: the satisfied, even stuffed consumer; the sovereign consumer. Sovereign? That raises a problem, but while the production lines flow and the shopping trolleys are ready to carry the goods away, there is this new, powerful social identity, which is readily and even eagerly adopted. It is at best a radically reduced identity, at worst mean and greedy. But of course 'consumer' is only a general-purpose word, on the lines of 'citizen' or 'subject'. It is accepted only as describing that level of life: the bustling level of the supermarket. When the goods from the trolley have been stowed in the car, and the car is back home, a fuller and more human identity is ready at the turn of a key: a family, a marriage, children, relatives, friends. The economic behaviour of the consumer is something you move out to, so as to bring the good things back.

There is then a unique modern condition, which I defined in an earlier book (*Television: Technology and Cultural Form*, 1974) as 'mobile privatisation'. It is an ugly phrase for an unprecedented condition. What it means is that at most active social levels people are increasingly living as private small-family units, or, disrupting even that, as private and deliberately self-enclosed individuals, while at the same time there is a quite unprecedented mobility of such restricted privacies. In my novel *Second Generation* (1964) I developed the image of modern car traffic to describe this now dominant set of social relations in the old industrial societies. Looked at from right outside, the traffic flows and their regulation are clearly a social order of a determined kind, yet what is experienced inside them – in the conditioned atmosphere and internal music of this windowed shell – is movement, choice of direction, the pursuit of self-determined private purposes. All the other shells are moving, in comparable ways but for their own different private ends. They are not so much other people, in any full sense, but other units which signal and are signalled to, so that private mobilities can proceed safely and relatively unhindered. And if all this is seen from outside as in deep ways determined, or in some sweeping glance as dehumanised, that is not at all how it feels like inside the shell, with people you want to be with, going where you want to go.

Thus at a now dominant level of social relations, systems quite other than settlement, or in any of its older senses community, are both active and continually reproduced. The only disturbance is when movements from quite outside them – movements which are the real workings of the effective but taken-for-granted public system – slow the flow, change the prices, depreciate or disrupt the employee-consumer connection: forcing a truly public world back into a chosen and intensely valued privacy.

The international market in every kind of commodity receives its deep assent from this system of mobile-privatised social relations. From the shell, whether house or car or employment, the only relevant calculations are the terms of continuing or improving its own conditions. If buying what such calculations indicate, from another nominal 'nation', leads directly or indirectly to the breaking or weakening of other people's shells, 'too bad' do we say? But the connections are not often as direct as that. They work their way through an immensely complicated and often unreadable market system. The results emerge as statistics, or as general remarks in television. Mainly what is wrong, we usually conclude, is what all those other shells are doing.

The fiercest drives of the modern international capitalist market are to extend and speed up these flows across nominal frontiers, these mutual if uneven penetrations that are properly called (including by some of the most surprising people) 'aggressive marketing'. If there is a fen of tended strawberries or an orchard valley of apples, each coming to fruit, it is of positive advantage, we are told, that at the crucial moment an entrepreneur who might be your neighbour ships in foreign strawberries or apples at a lower price, leaving your produce to be ploughed in or to rot. What is visible and wretched (and an annual occurrence) in grown natural produce is as wretched but less visible when it happens to every other kind of production. Thus a planned penetration or disruption of other people's economies, by the strongest national economies and by the multinational companies which are already operating without respect to frontiers, is offered as unambiguously in the general good. If you or you suffer from it, many more others benefit. All you have to do or can do is cut your costs and improve your product. If you cannot sufficiently do either, you must become redundant; go bankrupt; get out of the way of the leaner and fitter; join the real world.

It is an evil system, by all fully human standards. But what has then to be asked is why 'it' still has need of nations, of loyalty and patriotism, of an exaltation of flags and frontiers when the frontiers are only there to be economically dismantled and the flags, if the calculations come out that way, are quickly exchanged for flags of convenience? Why, in sum, in a modern free-trade capitalist international economy, have 'nations' at all?

7

The most dedicated consumer can only ingest so much. For other human needs, beyond consumption, other relationships and conceptions of other people are necessary. Similarly the market, great god as it is, can only exchange so much. It can produce and sell weapons, but it cannot, in any generally effective way, protect people. It can move and regulate producers and consumers, but it cannot meet all the essentially non-profitable human needs of nurture and care, support and comfort, love and fidelity, membership and belonging.

Where then will these needs be met? The current orthodoxy rules off many of them as private, not public matters at all. Yet it is surely a public matter that there are now in materially rich societies so many neglected, deprived, emotionally dissatisfied and emotionally disabled people; so many problems of loneliness and of unbearable while undrugged depressions, tensions, despairs. Leave all that to the market? But the decision-makers know, even if some of them keep working to forget, that this would be unacceptable and dangerous. It is a matter then of where the lines are drawn. A welfare state, a health service, an education system: the mainstream political parties move through these with differences of degree. It is where something national – 'national assistance' – is still necessary but at levels to be negotiated, subject always to the needs of 'the economy'. Protection? Now that is another matter. Even the market itself, to say nothing of its luckiest beneficiaries, cannot stand unprotected among so many random and unpredictable individual wills. Thus 'law and order'; armed forces called a 'defence force' even when some of their weapons are obviously aggressive: these, unambiguously, are the real functions of a state. And then the basis of a state is a nation, and the circle is squared.

It can be seen either way: as a cynical retention of just those nation-state powers which defend the existing social and economic order and head off, at minimum cost, movements of discontent which its enemies might exploit; or as a more generous if still limited recognition that there are social purposes which must still be sustained, if necessary by protection from the market. It matters very much which of these interpretations is at any particular time more true – for indeed, as purposes and methods, they vary and fluctuate. But it matters even more to see that on either interpretation there is a nation-state which does not even claim to be a full society. What it actually is, whether cynically or generously, is a deliberately partial system: not a whole lived order but a willed and selected superstructure.

This is the functional significance of its artifices. It is significant that the aggressive radical Right who are now in power in so many countries combine a pro-State rhetoric and practice, in military forces and a heavily policed law-and-order, with an anti-State rhetoric and practice in social welfare and the domestic economy, and in international monetary and trading exchange. This can be said, in a comforting way, to be a 'contradiction', but it is better seen as an open and class-based division of powers which is a genuine adjustment to an intensely competitive and profoundly unstable late capitalist world.

The national statism is to preserve a coherent domestic social order, both for general purposes and as a way of meeting the consequences of its commitment to open 'international' competition. It permits the ruin of certain 'national' industries by exposure to full transnational competition, but it does this as a way of enforcing transnational efficiency in what remains: the efficiency, indeed, of 'the Yookay', no longer a society but a market sector. At the same time it permits and even encourages the outflow of socially gathered capital (in pension funds and insurance and in the more general money market) to investment in whatever area of the global economy brings the highest money returns. So far as it can, against the established interests of communities and workers who are still its political electorate, it withdraws what it sees as distorting or enervating support for its own 'national' enterprises.

Thus an ideal condition is relentlessly pursued. First, the economic efficiency of a global system of production and trade, to include a reorganised and efficient 'national' sector within an open and inter-penetrating market flow. But at the same time a socially organised and socially disciplined population, one from which effort can be mobilised and taxes collected along the residual but still effective national lines; there are still no effective political competitors in that. It is to this model of 'a people' that the rhetoric of an increasingly superficial and frenetic nationalism is applied, as a way of over-riding all the real and increasing divisions and conflicts of in-terest within what might be the true nation, the actual and diverse people.

I repeat that this is a genuine adjustment to late twentieth-century conditions. It is a conscious programme to regulate and contain what would otherwise be intolerable divisions and confusions. Moreover, there is no way back from it to some simple and coherent national-ism. Some alternative programmes are now being offered, combin-ing a recovery of full political and military sovereignty with a national economic recovery plan, including heavy domestic invest-ment and controls on the export of capital and on selected imports. It is at first sight very surprising that this fails to strike any resonant 'national' chord. But this is the real complication, that this kind of emphasis on the nation-state taking control of a national political and economic life contradicts very openly the practices and ideals of market mobility and free consumer choice. To substantiate 'nationality' at the necessary depth, for alternative policies, means drawing on resources in active social relations which both mobile privatisation and consumerism and the most superficial and alienated versions of nationalism and patriotism have seriously weakened.

Thus 'nationalisation' is not perceived as connected to 'national-ism'. It is widely seen as an alien intrusion, from the other side of the statist coin. Meanwhile 'patriotism' has been so displaced to its functional images – the monarchy, the heritage, the armed forces, the flag – that alternative policies not only do not connect with them but by talking about other emphases and priorities often literally contradict them. Thus a 'nationalising' programme can be perceived as 'unpatriotic' – 'unBritish', 'unAmerican' – while a transnational strategy, pursued even to the point where a national economy loses heavily within unrestricted competition, is by its structural retention of the most artificial national images perceived as the 'patriotic' course.

8

What headway can be made against such intolerable confusions? Little or none, I judge, by the familiar intellectual jump to this or that universality. It is not in the mere negation of existing social perceptions that different forces can be generated. It is in two positive and connected initiatives: first, the cultural struggle for actual social identities; and second, the political definition of effective self-governing societies. I will first consider these separately.

What is most intolerable and unreal in existing projections of 'England' or 'Britain' is their historical and cultural ignorance. 'The Yookay', of course, is neither historical nor cultural; it is a jargon term of commercial and military planning. I remember a leader of the Labour Party, opposing British entry to the European Community, asserting that it would be the end of 'a thousand years of history'. Why a thousand, I wondered. The only meaningful date by that reckoning would be somewhere around 1066, when a Norman–French replaced a Norse–Saxon monarchy. What then of the English? That would be some fifteen hundred years. The British? Some two thousand five hundred. But the real history of the peoples of these islands goes back very much further than that: at least six thousand years to the remarkable societies of the Neolithic shepherds and farmers, and back beyond them to the hunting peoples who did not simply disappear but are also among our ancestors. Thus the leader of a nominally popular party could not in practice think about the realities of his own people. He could not think about their history except in the alienated forms of a centralised nation-state. And that he deployed these petty projections as a self-evident argument against attempts at a wider European identity would be incomprehensible, in all its actual and approved former-European re-organisations, if the cultural and historical realities had not been so systematically repressed by a functional and domineering selective 'patriotism'.

All the varied peoples who have lived on this island are in a substantial physical sense still here. What is from time to time projected as an 'island race' is in reality a long process of successive conquests and repressions but also of successive supersessions and relative integrations. All the real processes have been cultural and historical, and all the artificial processes have been political, in one after another dominative proclamation of a state and an identity. It is obvious that there can now be no simple return to any of what may be seen as layers of this long social and physical process. But it should be equally obvious that this long and unfinished process cannot reasonably be repressed by versions of a national history and a patriotic heritage which deliberately exlude its complexities and in doing so reject its many surviving and diverse identities. Thus the real inheritance of these hundreds of diverse and unevenly connecting generations cannot be reduced to a recent and originally alien monarchy or to a flag which in its very form records their enforced political unification. The consequences of the long attempts to suppress or override a surviving and remade Irish identity ought to show, clearly enough, the bloody stupidity of the prevailing versions of patriotism. Yet characteristically the consequences are functionally projected to the Irish themselves, butts of hatred or of complacent jokes. Again, it is a common ruling-class cultural habit, carefully extended by most schools, to identify with the Roman imperial invaders of Britain against what are called the mere 'native tribes'. Can such people monopolise 'patriotism'? In practice yes, since many of those whose actual ancestors were slaughtered and enslaved have reconstructed them in the images dispensed by their conquerors: savages in skins; even, in comic-strip culture, cavemen.

I do not know how far any real knowledge of the physical and cultural history of the peoples of this island might prevail against the stupidities of this narrow orthodox perspective. I cannot believe that it would make *no* difference, and I am encouraged by the growing positive interest in these misrepresented and obscured pasts. But at any time what has also to be faced is the effective stage of their current integration. It is here that there is now a major problem in the most recent immigrations of more visibly different peoples. When these interact with the most recent selective forms of identity – 'the true-born Englishman' who apart from an occasional afterthought is made to stand for the whole complex of settled native and earlier-immigrant peoples; or the imperial 'British', who in a new common identity used economic and military advantages to rule a hundred peoples across the world and to assume an inborn superiority to them – the angry confusions and prejudices are obvious.

At the same time many generations of formerly diverse peoples have experienced and adapted to a differently rooted though overlapping social identity, and as at all earlier stages of relative integration are at best deeply uncertain of, at worst openly hostile to, newcoming other peoples. This is the phenomenon now crudely interpreted as 'racism'. It is not that there is no actual racism: it flows without difficulty from the most recent selective forms, as it flowed also, in modern times, against the Irish and the Jews. But it is a profound misunderstanding to refer all the social and cultural tensions of the arrival of new peoples to these ideological forms. The real working of ideology, both ways, can be seen in that most significant of current exchanges, when an English working man (English in the terms of the sustained modern integration) protests at the arrival or presence of 'foreigners' or 'aliens', and now goes on to specify them as 'blacks', to be met by the standard liberal reply that 'they are as British as you are'. Many people notice the ideological components of the protest: the rapid movement, where no other terms are available, from resentment of unfamiliar neighbours to the ideological specifications of 'race' and 'superiority'.

But what of the ideology of the reply? It is employing, very plainly, a merely legal definition of what it is to be 'British'. At this strict level it is necessary and important, correctly asserting the need for equality and protection within the laws. Similarly, the most active legal (and communal) defence of dislocated and exposed groups and minorities is essential. But it is a serious misunderstanding, when full social relations are in question, to suppose that the problems of social identity are resolved by formal definitions. For unevenly and at times precariously, but always through long experience substantially, an effective awareness of social identity depends on actual and sustained social relationships. To reduce social identity to formal legal definitions, at the level of the state, is to collude with the alienated superficialities of 'the nation' which are the limited functional terms of the modern ruling class.

That even some socialists should reply in such terms – socialists who should entirely depend on deeply grounded and active social identities – is another sign of the prepotence of market and exchange relations. One reason is that many minority liberals and socialists, and especially those who by the nature of their work or formation are themselves nationally and internationally mobile, have little experience of those rooted settlements from which, though now under exceptionally severe complications and pressures, most people still derive their communal identities. Many socialists are influenced by universalist propositions of an ideal kind, such as the international proletariat overcoming its national divisions. Many liberals are influenced by North American thought, where for historical reasons a massively diverse mobility was primarily integrated at legal and functional levels. There can then be a rapid intellectual supersession of all the complex actualities of settled but then dislocated and relocated communities, to the point where some vanguard has a clear set of general 'social' positions only to find that the majority of its nominally connected people have declined to follow it. When this turns, as sometimes, to abusing them, there is a certain finality of defeat.

A socialist position on social identity certainly rejects, absolutely, the divisive ideologies of 'race' and 'nation', as a ruling class functionally employs them. But it rejects them in favour of lived and formed identities either of a settled kind, if available, or of a possible kind, where dislocation and relocation require new formation. It happens that I grew up in an old frontier area, the Welsh border country, where for centuries there was bitter fighting and raiding and repression and discrimination, and where, within twenty miles of where I was born, there were in those turbulent centuries as many as four different everyday spoken languages. It is with this history in mind that I believe in the practical formation of social identity – it is now very marked there – and know that necessarily it has to be lived. Not far away there are the Welsh mining valleys, into which in the nineteenth century there was massive and diverse immigration, but in which, after two generations, there were some of the most remarkably solid and mutually loyal communities of which we have record. These are the real grounds of hope. It is by working and living together, with some real place and common interest to identify with, and as free as may be from external ideological definitions, whether divisive or universalist, that real social identities are formed. What would have seemed impossible, at the most difficult stages, either in that border country or in those mining valleys, has indeed been achieved, though this does not mean that it happens naturally; there are other cases, as in the north of Ireland, where history and external ideologies still divide people and tear them apart.

This connects with the second emphasis: on the redefinition of effective self-governing societies. It is now very apparent, in the development of modern industrial societies, that the nation-state, in its classical European forms, is at once too large and too small for the range of real social purposes. It is too large, even in the old nation-states such as Britain, to develop full social identities in their real diversity. This is not only a problem of the minority peoples – Scots or Welsh or Irish or West Indian – but of the still significantly different cultures which are arbitrarily relegated to 'regions'. In this situation, imposed artificial definitions of 'Britishness', of 'the United Kingdom' and 'The Yookay', of the 'national interest' and of 'nationwide' lines of communication, are in practice ways of ratifying or overriding unequal social and economic development, and of containing the protests and resentments of neglected and marginalised regions and minorities within an imposed general 'patriotism'. The major economic and political divergence of the North and the South-East of even the supposedly unified and clamorous 'England' is an obvious current example.

It is clear that if people are to defend and promote their real interests, on the basis of lived and worked and placeable social identities, a large part of the now alienated and centralised powers and resources must be actively regained, by new actual societies which in their own terms, and nobody else's, define themselves. All effective socialist policies, over the coming generations, must be directed towards this practice, for it is only in the re-emphasis or formation of these full active social identities that socialism itself – which depends absolutely on authentic ideas of a society – can develop. In particular, it is only in these ways, as identifiable communities and regions are broken by movements of the national or international market, that there is the possibility of overcoming those reductive identities as mobile consumers which positively depend on advantage and affluence.

At the same time it is obvious that for many purposes not only these more real societies but also the existing nation-states are too small. The trading, monetary and military problems which now show this to be true, and which have so heavily encroached on the supposed 'sovereignty' of the nation-states, would not disappear in any movement to placeable communal self-management. It is not necessarily true that they would become more difficult. Many of the toughest trading and monetary problems flow directly from the system of international capitalist competition, and quite new forms of planned external trade would be possible in societies which genuinely began from the interests of their own people rather than from the interests of a 'national' ruling class integrated in and serving the international economy. The military problems are also very difficult, but it can now be seen that it is the arbitrary formation of generalised hostile blocs, overriding the diversities of real popular interests, which increasingly endangers rather than assures our necessary defence and security.

We cannot say, at any level, that these placeable self-managing societies could be 'sovereign'. Even to say that they could be 'autonomous' is taking a very limited sense. What has really to be said is different: that we have to explore new forms of *variable* societies, in which over the whole range of social purposes different sizes of society are defined for different kinds of issue and decision. In practice some of this now happens, as in the supposed 'division of powers' between local, regional, national and international bodies. But this is a false kind of division. The local and regional are in practice, as their names indicate, essentially subordinate to and dependent on the national. What goes through to an international level is first centralised or simply substituted by this national system ('it is felt *in London*'; '*Britain* has refused to ratify the Law of the Sea'). Meanwhile many of the most effective international forms – not only the multinational corporations but also the World Bank and the International Monetary Fund – are in effect wholly irresponsible to any full actual societies; indeed it is often their specific business to override them.

A variable socialism – the making of many socialisms – could be very different. There would be an absolute refusal of overriding national and international bodies which do not derive their specified powers directly from the participation and negotiation of actual self-governing societies. At a different level, there would be a necessary openness to all the indispensable means of mutual support and encouragement, directly and often diversely (bilaterally as well as in variable multilateral groupings) negotiated from real bases. Moreover, much of this negotiation would be at least in part direct, rather than through the necessarily alienating procedures of 'all-purpose representatives'. The true advantages of equal exchange, and of rooted contacts and mobilities, would be more fully realised in this variable socialism than in the current arbitrary mobilities, or in any merely defensive reversion to smaller societies and sovereignties.

To bring together these two emphases – on the cultural struggle for actual social identities, and on the political redefinition of effective self-governing societies – is, I believe, to indicate a new and substantial kind of socialism which is capable both of dealing with the complexities of modern societies and also of re-engaging effective and practical popular interests.

Very much remains to be done by way of detailed discussions and proposals, but we cannot in any case live much longer under the confusions of the existing 'international' economy and the existing 'nation-state'. If we cannot find and communicate social forms of more substance than these, we shall be condemned to endure the accelerating pace of false and frenetic nationalisms and of reckless and uncontrollable global transnationalism. Moreover, even endurance is then an optimistic estimate. These are political forms that now limit, subordinate and destroy people. We have to begin again with people and build new political forms.

EAST–WEST,
NORTH–SOUTH

I

It is strange to try to interpret a political world through cardinal points. Yet for many people the struggle between 'East' and 'West' is now at the centre of their understanding of contemporary world politics. Meanwhile, as shorthand for another kind of interpretation, of the relations between 'developed' and 'underdeveloped' or 'developing' societies, a contrast has been proposed between 'North' and 'South'. There are many problems in trying to relate these two axes, but it is necessary first to define them more precisely by considering the significance of the familiar cardinal points.

The contrast between 'East' and 'West' is very old, but it has repeatedly changed its content. Its earliest European form comes from the division of the Roman Empire, from the third century. This was followed by the division of the Christian churches, from the eleventh century. Yet these internal divisions were superseded by contrasts between 'the West' as a Christian civilisation and an 'East' defined either as Islam or as the civilisations beyond it from India to China. Western and Eastern (or 'Oriental') worlds were commonly defined in this way from the sixteenth century. Internal divisions within Europe then arose in new ways, as in the Western and Eastern fronts of the wars against Germany. In the second world war there were Western allies who had also, in the Soviet Union, an Eastern ally. In the subsequent division and polarisation, after 1945, 'West' and 'East' were given their current political content. This first rested on the evident political divisions between Western and Eastern Europe but was soon generalised to what was offered as a universal contrast, between political and economic systems of different types. In the course of this generalisation the limited geographical bases of the earlier contrast were often superseded. Japan and Australia, for example, were seen as parts of 'the West' or more cautiously as 'Western-style' societies. At the same time the presumed unity of 'the West' became, by deliberate repetition, an apparently substantial entity. Some people could then talk, loosely, about 'Western values', 'Western interests', and even, in an ideological move, of the President of the United States (who of course had also his own 'West') as the 'acknowledged' leader of 'the West as a whole'.

It is important to try to translate such descriptions into their real political terms, for which many people still see them as mere shorthand. Yet as soon as we try to do this, the ideological efficacy of the cardinal points is obvious. For there can be a translation either to 'liberal democracies' or to 'capitalist economies', and though there is substantial overlap between these there is nothing like identity, in the actual societies grouped as 'the West'. In practice, under the dominance of the military-strategic bearings which are primary in the definition, it is a capitalist economy that ranks first as a 'Western' qualification, however awkward this may be for those who also believe that liberal democracy and even Christianity are the true 'Western' values. Any consequent definition of 'Western values', or of their defence, is thus from the beginning imprecise and in ordinary political discussion profoundly confusing.

The 'East', meanwhile, is perceived mainly negatively, as the polar opposite of this generalised 'West'. This reminds us that all these cardinal definitions have come from 'the West': they are a culturally identifiable way of seeing others. This is especially important in the next persuasive form, in which, from an unstressed identification of 'the West' as the 'First World' and of 'the East', in its post-1945 sense, as the 'Second World', all other countries were grouped as 'the Third World'. Many uses of this description have been benevolent, but there is an unexamined dependence of any such identification on the initial East–West ideological contrast. This is also true of the description 'non-aligned', positively adopted by certain countries as a mode of distance from the East–West polarisation, but effectively conceding the priority of that form of division of the world. Subsequent disputes among the 'non-aligned', about the relation of their real needs to the contrasted strategies and interests of the aligned powers, have shown very clearly the negative and dependent element of the initial definition. The same has been true of most continued uses of 'Third World'.

It was on these uncertainties that the new North–South contrast was imposed. In some uses it was intended to emphasise a division of the world seen as more fundamental than the older East–West division: a basic division between the rich and the poor countries. There were the typical geographical incongruities: Australia, New Zealand, Argentina in the North; China in the South. But the broad contrast seemed to hold, except that this was still primarily a Western definition, typically between industrially developed and developing or underdeveloping economies, which was not accepted by 'the East' because there the same facts were interpreted by a division between imperialist and colonial or ex-colonial societies. The inequalities of development were seen as the consequences of a capitalist world trading system, in which 'the East' was not involved. Thus the North–South contrast is either: (a) an absolute contrast between industrially developed (rich) and underdeveloped (poor) economies; or (b) an extension of this to the terms of the East–West polarisation, as this primary competition extends itself to the 'South', which can go either way; or (c) an ideological form of relations between 'the West' (the capitalist world) and the exploited 'South', with 'the East' (the socialist world) as the 'South's' natural ally.

As we perceive these difficulties, which follow from basically diverse and eventually alternative or mutually hostile interpretations of an exceptionally complex world situation, we must at least conclude that the terms are not some universal shorthand. Yet the problems which they emphasise, as well as interpret, are so serious that we cannot rest on that kind of negative conclusion. This is especially the case in the uses of 'Third World'. Whatever its assumptions and origins, it has been a dramatic way of focusing attention on the appalling facts of contemporary poverty. Three quarters of the world's population, it is commonly estimated, live on one fifth of the world's income. Or, to bring it nearer home, one quarter of the world's population, including almost all of us involved in this argument, have four-fifths of the world's income. These facts have to be faced, and even the dramatic simplifications have been, for many good people, a way of beginning to face them. Yet, inevitably, when it comes to trying to change and improve this (for some) intolerable situation, the problems of the definitions at once return. Whether we are thinking of 'the Third World' or of 'the South', it matters very much whether we are seeing a blocked and generalised poverty, or a more complex system. Within the 'Third World' there is a variation of national per-capita income on a scale from 1 to 27, by comparison with a 'First World' variation from 1 to 3. Evidently the massive variation in degrees of 'national' poverty has to be emphasised, within any generalisation. There are not only radical but operative differences between the 'newly industrialising countries' (from South Korea to Brazil), the OPEC oil-producing countries, the strategic-mineral and cash-crop economies, and, through a whole series of variations of deprivation, the most desperately poor and disadvantaged peoples. But they are all taken as 'parts' of the 'Third World'.

Moreover, to these often decisive degrees of 'national' variation we have to add, if we are ever to understand the politics of the problem, the major *internal* variations of income and power within many of the very poorest as well as the relatively poor societies. Every kind of internal 'elite' (yet elites, typically, is what they are not; they are either classes or functional sectors of paranational classes) is evident in such societies. There are local economic groups functionally linked, through manufacturing and trade and banking, to the richest sectors of the First World. There are locally privileged and dominant military groups, linked to the profitable international arms trade and to the military and geopolitical strategies of the East–West confrontation. There are local political ruling groups, typically dependent both on internal property relations and on forms of patronage from elsewhere, which emerge and interlock internally as domination of their own peoples. The fact that some of these groups, the political and even at times the military, have broken through to their own forms of a genuinely national or even popular interest has to be set beside the heavier fact that most of them, and especially the economic groups, have not.

It is then a decisive question, when we listen to spokesmen of the 'Third World', to ask to what extent they are speaking and acting in the general interest of their peoples, including most evidently those millions of the absolute poor who find so few spokesmen, or in the functional and often contradictory interests of their own privileged sectors. These are very hard questions to resolve within the terms of undifferentiated cardinal blocs.

2

One way of facing these complexities and difficulties is to reconsider the familiar definitions and contrasts by way of the actual economic and political processes which have created these differentiated forms of the modern world. This is an area of major controversy as well as of some remarkable recent scholarship, but certain general points can be made.

It is necessary, first, to examine the underlying model on which, in their most common forms, both the East–West and the North–South projections have been based. The keyword here is *development*. This is based, literally, on an idea of the unfolding, the unrolling, indeed the evolution, of an inherent process. The eighteenth-century idea of a unilinear process of civilisation, through all the stages from savagery to barbarism to societies of the type in which the process itself was defined, was strengthened by nineteenth-century evolutionary ideas: 'nations proceed in a course of *development*, their later manifestations being potentially present in the earliest elements'. This could still mean different kinds of development, as for example into different species in the biological model, but steadily, in the twentieth century, under the practical dominance of industrial capitalism, a unilinear sense was assumed and was even seen as 'natural'. Thus the Brandt Report (*North–South*, 1980; 172) states:

The successive industrial revolutions of the past two hundred years in Europe and North America are now being followed by industrialisation in Latin America, Asia and Africa, a natural and indeed inevitable development which is already beginning to change the pattern of comparative advantage in the world economy.

Thus all societies other than the old industrial societies were 'naturally' seen as either 'undeveloped' or 'developing', and their futures were theoretically assumed to be governed by this pre-existent model.

In practice this model was only applied, or used for interpretation, in a world which was moving out of the older forms of political colonialism. It was then a path for the future implied by the old industrial (several of them also imperial) societies, and often eagerly adopted by the leaders of the new politically independent states, who for obvious reasons wanted to break out of the old kinds of colonial inferiority, dependence and poverty. This idea of a 'natural development', applied on both sides of this formerly antagonistic and dependent relationship, came to mask key questions about the purposes and methods of development itself. For at the centre of the world view of the old industrial societies was the quite different principle of the 'international division of labour'. That is to say, there was a specialisation of different economies to those forms of production for which, on the basis of their natural resources but also on the basis of all other forces and relations of production, they were 'best suited'. Thus within an economic system basically seen as 'global', a combination of existing resources and market relations determined specific roles for specific economies. So 'development', in practice, meant on one side of the fence development in terms of the global system: exploitation of raw materials, specialised food export crops, available migrant labour, in the 'developing' societies; finished manufactures, advanced technology, employment of immigrant labour in the 'developed'. On the other side of the fence, it was just this inherently unequal 'division of labour', leading to new kinds of economic advantage and disadvantage, which it was the purpose of any full sense of development to overcome and surpass.

Thus 'development' became an inherently ideological term. The processes instituted in its name, which should need precise assessment in terms of the advantages accruing to each 'developing' society, were bundled together as if any or all of them were unproblematically advantageous and 'natural'. This has in practice been very far from the case. Take a simple common example. A society may be effectively feeding itself by traditional forms of herding and agriculture: to be sure at what are often low levels of comparative productivity or of comparative nutritional value and variety. To introduce into that society new food-production technologies, typically involving new machines, new fertilisers, new strains, and as a condition of all these new capital and then, by that injection, new property relations in land, is not unproblematic development. Gross production will usually increase, though often by an increasing specialisation of products. The changes in technology and landholding will also, however, dispossess (as in the old 'industrial revolutions') the majority of traditional landworking families. They then 'migrate' to the already overcrowded and only partially employed cities.

In the model of 'development', and in part in practice, these families are available for transferred labour in new forms of production. That many millions of them remain 'available' but are not in fact employed is not allowed to disturb the simple original accounting. There has been agricultural development; food production (if of fewer kinds or at higher cost) has increased; the society is 'in the course of development'. But the well-being of the people of that society has not necessarily increased, even if overall figures show a higher national product, since the specific processes of development have altered social and productive relations and changed the forms of distribution of the necessities of life. This is the artificial and limited accounting of 'development'. It isolates and then measures specific processes of production, while leaving all other effects to a 'social' margin beyond its terms.

What matters is the origin and impetus of any particular developmental process. What the metaphor falsely implies, in its suggestions of natural unfolding or inherent self-realisation, has to be compared and usually contrasted with the actual determinations which set specific processes in train. It will then only occasionally be found that these spring from the decisions of the people immediately concerned and affected. Most actual forms, in mining and extraction, and in cash crops of specialised foods and materials, are introduced from outside the societies: indeed the demand for their products can, by definition, come only from elsewhere. At a certain stage local ruling groups, or in more radical cases wider popular movements, may adopt these processes and seek to or occasionally (as with oil) succeed in improving the related terms of trade. But even when this has been done, the inherent patterns of production, within the determinations of the 'global' economy, are very powerful, and typically enforce certain continuities and priorities. The problem for most such societies – for the poorest societies of all, with comparatively little to exploit in these terms, are below both the problem and the opportunities – is to combine a continuing reliance on patterns of development determined elsewhere with genuine policies for development in their own chosen terms. The pressures for continuing adaptation to externally conceived development are immense. It is usually on the basis of some relative adaptation that new or adapting groups achieve power in their own societies.

Except in the case of oil, where the basic conflicts of adaptation are still active, the conditions of most societies which have become dependent on the export of commodities to the global economic system have been very difficult not only to improve but even to sustain, let alone to modify in any radical way. The kinds of development that could substantially improve their conditions, above all the development of their own processing and manufacture of their indigenous materials, are very difficult to achieve. A typical share of the final price of such products, to the producers themselves, is now less than 25 per cent. It is at this level – where there is no longer any simple common interest but a complex of competitive and antagonistic interests in the relative returns from primary production, manufacture and selling – that the simple idea of development is again deceptive. For the finishing industries and the marketing organisations of the old industrial economies are of course unwilling to encourage or even to permit actual developments which would weaken their own positions. Thus in oil refining, timber manufacture, vegetable oil processing, food manufactures, fertiliser preparation and a hundred such cases there is pressure to obstruct the full local development of indigenous resources.

It is characteristic that this should be so while at the same time other kinds of manufacturing and assembly, together with forms of tourist and property development and, centrally, of military expansion, are increasingly encouraged. These are opportunities to unload certain industrial processes to societies in which, often as the result of previous 'development', there is what is called 'surplus cheap labour', at low or no levels of trade-union organisation. Or else they are developments of an externally defined market, directed mainly at the indigenous elites and in the case of advanced weapons exports supplying them with the means of their internal dominance and continuing external dependence.

In recent decades there has been a further twist to these already distorted versions of 'development'. Serious attempts by the poorer societies to determine their own lines of development have been met by a system which can appear mainly technical but is in fact the central condition of capitalism itself. There has been a sustained and often reckless development of an 'international credit economy', with both governmental and commercial banks lining up to supply capital for externally approved schemes. This kind of transfer of capital is also the central recommendation of the Brandt report, which is widely accepted in the orthodox perspective as the most liberal and enlightened policy now possible, indeed going beyond the terms of the normal capital market on the basis of an assumed and 'natural' mutual interest. Yet the results of the massive transfers already undertaken have become very clear during the current world recession. Several of the countries hitherto cited as examples of successful 'development' are facing virtually insoluble problems of debt, indeed are forced to raise new loans simply to pay the interest on the old. Many other countries, within the persistent conditions of economic inequality, are loaded with heavy debt without even any development. This 'natural' enforcement of the international capitalist system – especially when as during the current recession it threatens to turn back on itself and weaken or even destroy it – is not in any real sense development, in the neutral or generous ways which are so widely assumed. It is both a critical and a crisis-producing phase in the operations of the dominant 'global economy'.

3

It is within these real terms that the North–South formula, and in turn also the East–West formula, have to be reexamined. So many people have been moved by the appalling facts of poverty, hunger and disease in what is called the 'Third World' that they seek to transcend the terms of ordinary economic and political argument and assert a more general moral position. This is the substantial advocacy of what is called 'aid'. But here again there are necessary distinctions.

There are all too many cases when simple aid is all that is immediately necessary. Natural disasters, from earthquakes and cyclones to floods and droughts, and man-made disasters, in the suffering and dislocations of wars and repressions, call unequivocally for such general assistance: supplies of food, shelter, medical care, refuge. The devoted work and giving of very many people, moved by these needs in others, still requires emphasis and support. Yet it is often very difficult to distinguish between necessary first aid, in these critical conditions, and the different measures which would give sustained protection and welfare. The initial movement is one of charity, in its traditionally powerful and limited sense. But almost all later movements involve wider social relations and interests. Some of the very best of the initially charitable organisations have for this reason moved to different definitions, beyond or even within emergencies: definitions which shift attention to the provision and self-provision of people's own means of livelihood.

There is always an area which is relatively exempt from the determinations of the international economy, but its boundaries with an area which is by no means so exempt are often difficult to perceive. Medical aid of a necessary kind can be transformed, without obvious emphasis, into a market for the drug companies, at times recklessly developed and supplied. Emergency food aid can disrupt normal productive relations. Even general financial aid, making its way through the real institutions of the receiving society, can fail in whole or in part even to reach its intended beneficiaries or, worse, can further distort the existing inequalities of monetary relations. The hard task is to understand these unlooked-for results of an initially simple and generous impulse, in ways which prevent them from being used as excuses either for evasion of the moral concern or, more generally, for evasion of the underlying social and economic relationships within which many of the actual problems are generated.

'Aid', like 'development', has always to be understood in its real processes. When we have distinguished what is genuinely emergency aid – the bringing of relief in disasters or in extreme deprivation – three areas must be examined. These are: (i) aid for trade; (ii) the overlap of aid with the East–West confrontation; (iii) the relations between aid and existing class interests in the old industrial economies.

The first area becomes clearer as we review the variable meanings of 'development'. It is relevant that much that is called aid is simply the procuring, through credit, of markets for specific technologies or supplier-advantage. Moreover, aid of this kind is typically conditional on the continuation or expansion of exsiting market and political relations, within which there is systematically unequal exchange. If the flows of 'foreign aid' are isolated, within 'Western' societies – both as seeking to exemplify generosity and often in practice provoking internal hostility – there is a familiar false accounting, since the total flow of funds between 'developed' and 'developing' economies, through trade, aid and profits on investments, is heavily in favour of the 'developed' economies: in the most 'successful' cases by a factor of two or three.

It is then not surprising that the 1974 Coyoyoc Declaration and the 1979 Non-Aligned Conference saw the central problem as the market system itself. Proposals for a 'new international economic order', which have often united 'the South', are in practice variable at just this point. One typical set (as also in the Brandt report) aims at reasonable improvements in the market system, by the stabilisation and indexing of commodity prices and the regulation of capital flows. A more radical set includes many of these proposals but aims also at superseding the market system, including its representation by dominant groups within the poor economies. It is important to notice that even the more modest version is heavily resisted by the 'developed' societies, who insist on retaining their existing advantages and who are only rarely challenged, on this selfish resistance, by their own peoples and especially by their labour movements.

At a certain point, these problems overlap with the second area, of East–West confrontation. Geopolitical and military calculations are often decisive in flows of aid, and direct arms supplies and military training, now on a massive scale, move at times, in immediate terms, beyond the market system. On the other hand, in the 'West' arms exports are a significant element of normal trade, and discriminated military exports and training are seen as elements of 'defence' of the existing political and economic system, with the economic calculation (as in supplies to military and political dictatorships) dominant. In such supplies from the 'East', again discriminately to favoured regimes, the military and geopolitical calculations are of course evident, and several forms of genuine economic assistance are also subject to the same calculations. Yet it is in general true that there is another kind of alliance between the 'East', in its broad political sense, and regimes in the post-colonial societies which are seeking to alter internal social and economic relations – by nationalisations, redistributions of land, socialist development programmes – or in any case to detach themselves from dependence on the international capitalist market.

The theoretical distinctions here are clear, but there is a great deal of practical overlap between the two types of aid. There is some skewing of principled assistance by geopolitical calculations, and especially in the matter of capital investment there is a large degree of interrelation between what can be described in abstraction as discrete – 'East' and 'West' – world systems. The case of Poland, heavily indebted to Western banks for a classical – and failed – export development programme, is only the most striking recent example of the latter. Even the Soviet Union, to say nothing of its related and dependent economies, has been unable in any full sense to detach itself from the dominant international capitalist market, though variable degrees of distance have been achieved.

Meanwhile, alongside its military-strategic confrontation with the 'East', the 'West' has an active programme of market penetration directed positively towards the socialist and proto-socialist economies, which it is hoped in this way to alter and eventually reclaim. These tense and complex international relations are dominated by but cannot be simplified to alliance and superpower confrontations. Thus there is almost equal sensitivity between areas of military importance, such as the Near East, and areas of successful or attempted political and economic transformation, such as Angola. The complex issues are quickly translated (and often in part deformed) into the terms of the general confrontation. They are typically seen in 'the West' as areas of 'Soviet expansion'. Thus the extreme pressures of the existing international economic order, overlapping with the military-strategic confrontation, are heavy constraints on almost all forms of genuinely autonomous development.

These complexities feed back into the third area, of internal relations within the old industrial societies. The dominant factors there are at once national and class interests, which not only do not always correspond but are at times so contradictory that the whole mode of analysis derived from the blocking formulas of East–West and North–South is radically misleading. In each of these blocks the internal variation and at times conflict of interest can approach in importance, or even exceed, the more publicised contrasts. The problem is now especially acute in what is variably the 'North' or 'West'. Both in manufacturing trade and in the capital market there are structural factors which are shifting certain kinds of manufacturing employment and investment beyond the old 'national' frontiers. Typically this has direct results in unemployment and underinvestment in those parts of the economy on which the existing working class is most dependent. There is then a strange and misleading combination of highly differential motives and arguments.

Pressure to admit cheap imports of manufactured goods from the newly industrialising economies – most of them in practice still predominantly controlled by 'Western' capital – gets confused with the argument for an increasing share of trade by the 'developing' economies. It can be said that either process leads to new forms of 'mutual benefit', as the old industrial economies shed their simpler processes and move to more advanced technology. But while this may be a practicable shift in gross terms, it is very unequally experienced and paid for. The more advanced industries offer less employment than those that are being displaced. The returns on investment abroad, though presented as 'national' earnings, are very unequally distributed. They accrue primarily to the holders of private capital or, indirectly, to the agents of social capital. Moreover, the ideological shift to ideas of mutual benefit or even moral obligation, as reasons for helping the poorer economies, provoke in the residual national working class and in residual domestic capitalists urgent demands for kinds of protection which are genuinely incompatible with the dominant market and capital system.

The basis of such demands is fully understandable, but in their limited presentation they can lead to new forms of chauvinism, which are exploited by the residual political nation-states. They can lead also, in current market terms, to actual and damaging restrictions in world trade. More seriously, in their simplest form, they actually obstruct understanding of the international market and capital system which now dominates almost all economies. They then delay the necessary challenges to it, challenges which can be connected with internal opposition to the capitalist system but must necessarily go beyond it, to the world system.

These full challenges can only be made if 'the South', as already indicated, is itself seen in real economic terms, making possible (though still extremely difficult) new kinds of alliance, or political support, or at the very least political understanding and toleration, between the old working-class movements and the more urgent and desperate struggles of the real poor of 'the South'. For traditional socialist programmes of planned production can then be steadily extended to programmes of planned and equitable foreign trade and investment, which are the only alternatives to the world capitalist system. It is highly probable that any such extensions will occur first through regional groupings which can gather sufficient strength to be able, step by step, to find conditions for autonomous development, as distinct from exposure to a system which sees virtually all lands, peoples and resources as the mere raw materials of its own profitable operations.

4

A final ideological term has then to be examined: 'growth'. In the dominant economic system, but also in most actual and proposed alternatives to it, the idea of 'growth', both as a definition of the nature of 'development', and as the sovereign remedy for all existing economic inequalities, is taken for granted. To produce more is to be on the way to economic salvation, and all other good things will then follow.

This confidence is unshaken by the evident contemporary over-production of many of the most widely traded commodities: steel, ships, cars, oil. The idea of more production is neatly specialised – at the level of propaganda – to improved competitive national shares of this over-supplied market. This is called 'living in the real world'. The same abstract confidence is equally unshaken by the fact that more production, within a society, in no way on its own eliminates poverty. All the old industrial societies have vastly increased production, in historical terms, yet there are still serious and intractable areas of poverty inside them. Moreover many things that were formerly afforded are said now to be too expensive (an expanding educational system, a general health service). It is then wrong to equate 'more production' with 'growth'. The idea of growth, with all its natural and human precedents, must necessarily involve much wider considerations. The full effects of certain kinds of production and consumption; the relative human value of different kinds of production; the relations between certain forms of production and consequent forms of distribution: all these real considerations have

been overridden by an appropriation of the idea of growth as indiscriminate expanded production.

It cannot be the case that there is 'current world over-production'
when more than eight hundred million people are living in absolute
poverty, and many hundreds of millions more in relative deprivation. It is what is being discriminately produced and in available
terms marketed that has really to be examined. For the apparent
indiscrimination of production is actually the determined discrimination of the market: production, as we must still say, for profit
rather than primarily for use. Much can then be done if we revalue
our ideas of production in those terms of real and equitable use which
confirm the association with human growth.

Yet there are problems even in this. In the imperatives of the
market, in its endless drives for expansion and accumulation, an
effective infinity of production is in practice assumed. More local
forms of such infinities are reproduced in various national campaigns
and plans. Even in those economies which claim to have superseded
market imperatives – the economies of 'actually existing socialism' – the drives to indefinitely expanded production are faithfully
reproduced. We have then only to bring these very powerful tendencies together (though in practice they are carefully kept apart in
separate national or regional compartments) to confront the central
problem of this whole mode and version of production: an effective
infinity of expansion in a physically finite world.

What is now known as the ecological argument should not be
reduced to its important minor forms: the dangerously rising scale of
industrial and chemical pollution; the destruction of some natural
habitats and species. The core of the argument is very much harder.
Every local effect, however damaging, can be seen as a marginal
cost, an unavoidable by-product, of the still centrally necessary
productive process, until the reality of this process itself, in its
current forms, is at last faced.

What is really at issue is a version of the earth and its life forms as
extractable and consumable wealth. What is seen is not the sources
and resources of many forms of life but everything, including
people, as available raw material, to be appropriated and transformed. Against this, the ecological argument has shown, in case
after case, and then as a different way of seeing the whole, that a
complex physical world and its intricate and interacting biological

processes cannot for long be treated in such ways, without grave and unforeseen kinds of damage. It is not necessary to accept, though it is obviously necessary to consider, the warnings of certain absolute kinds of damage, to the atmosphere, to the climatic system, to sustainable populations, to recognise the intellectual inevitability of this new kind of examination of the real nature and effects of our dominant common activities. Particular estimates of absolute shortages of currently necessary resources, of absolutely unacceptable levels of pollution and environmental damage, of imbalances of population and food which would bring widespread famine, do not have to be accepted in their precise (and in practice always revisable) terms to persuade any reasonable person that the orthodox abstraction of indefinitely expanded production – its version of 'growth' – has to be considered again, from the beginning. The current ideological implication that these are sentimental or idealistic or simply 'anti-industrial' arguments could not be further from the truth. What is actually being faced is the full physical and material situation, by contrast with the received mental habits of the most recent versions of human livelihood.

It is important to take this argument into the area now governed by the formulas of East–West and North–South. It is obviously from the East–West confrontation, and its reckless strategic extensions into all parts of the world, that the gravest immediate risks derive, in the overproduction and proliferation of nuclear, chemical and bacteriological weapons. There are related heavy risks in what is presented as simply the technical export of nuclear power systems. Beyond this increasingly visible area, there is the more widely accepted process of the indefinite exploitation of raw materials, linked with the production of quickly consumed commodities. This is the central process of what are abstracted as North–South relations, but it has to be seen in its full terms.

It would be very wrong to extend the ecological analysis into an argument that the poorest societies should not enter, for their own purposes, all necessary stages of industrialisation. It is probable – many would say certain – that the earth will not be able to support its early-twenty-first-century population, 7,500,000,000 and rising, at even the most moderate levels of food and energy use of the old industrial societies. It is quite impossible that this vast human population could be supported at the currently wasteful levels of food and energy use, of the proliferation of short-duration and throwaway commodities, and of high artificial-input food production, now registered and even planned to rise in the most aggressive market economies. Yet this is not a problem that can be projected to the rise of population in the poorest countries, urgent though measures to control this, by changes within these countries, are. The population-resources equations have always to be related to the systematic inequality within which a quarter of this population have four-fifths of the world's income. It is then clear that both the technological directions and the processes of economic pressure have to be radically revised in every part of the world, and, first, that the penetration of other societies by these currently advantageous directions and pressures has to be halted and driven back.

As part of this change, alternative technologies, of an autonomous and locally resource-based kind, will have to take over as new diverse lines of genuine development. There can be real aid in this, from the most technically advanced societies, but only if their lines of research, now commonly subject to profit-marketing imperatives, are consciously redirected. Moreover, the deepest changes will have to come in the old industrial economies themselves: not only in major shifts towards conservation and more durable and economical production but also in their deep assumption that the rest of the world is an effectively vacant lot from which they extract raw materials. There will probably be even more scope than now for alternative technologies, including high technologies, in such societies, if they are to solve or even mitigate the problems of adjustment as this destructive assumption is abandoned or breaks down.

It is in this perspective that the North–South relation, but also the East–West relation, has to be seen and changed. The real change is a redefinition of socialism, which is the only liberating way beyond the East–West confrontation: a positive redemption of the central socialist idea of production for equitable use rather than for either profit or power. The only way beyond the command economies of 'actually existing socialism', now engaged in and limited by competitive accumulation, is in this broader socialist direction. This is also the only desirable future for the old capitalist societies. The different social processes which would emerge from this change, redefining 'production' as the sources and resources of life, would in themselves ease the pressures on the poorest societies, now locked into the old central drives. There would then be a basis for a genuinely new international economic order, beyond the attempted adjustment of its market terms.

The changes involved are so substantial, and resistance from existing interests so certain and powerful, that nobody can suppose that this will be anything but a very long and complex struggle. The issues have then to be restated in their hardest terms. It is already a distinct possibility that the most aggressive marketing and militarist societies will destroy the world simply by continuing their own current policies. It is also already clear that the rest of the world will not simply sit back and let this happen to them. Disadvantaged and pressured though they are, complicated and confused by many of their own internal political and economic structures, the poorer peoples have already passed the point at which they were for so long restrained and repressed: to be at the disposition of the interests of others. The struggles already in progress, the further struggles that are certain to follow, absolutely deny the possibility of any peaceful continuation of the present world order, on the bland and blinkered lines now proposed by the dominant powers. At the same time, such struggles cannot succeed, in positive ways, without the support and understanding of progressive movements in the old industrial societies. Indeed it is necessary to defeat the current mobilisation of active and ignorant opposition to such struggles. For in scattered, complex but finally inevitable ways, the choice within the whole economic as well as the whole political process will be between new and radically alternative kinds of relationship or chronic disorder and war.

WAR: THE LAST ENEMY

I

Neither war nor massacre is a twentieth-century invention. All the recorded centuries are stained with their incidence. Yet it does not then follow that an abstracted 'war' is a permanent element of an abstracted 'human nature'. Such a conclusion has been much too common. It is indeed the standard displaced response, cynical and manipulative as often as concerned and tragic, to the violence and cruelties of this century. In the actual human record, the termination and ending of wars, the making of significant kinds and periods of peace, are in fact more frequent. In any count of this kind, the balance lies with the peacemakers.

What has really changed, in the modern period, is the significance of this kind of reckoning: years of peace as against years of war. Deep and extending changes in the whole social and economic order have transformed, though unevenly, the nature of war itself. For war has been industrialised, as part of the general process of the change to industrial production. High explosives, phosphorus bombs and napalm, poison and nerve gases, have been part of the general development of the chemical industry. Machine guns, tanks, bombing planes, submarines, even nuclear weapons themselves, have been part of the general development of metal production and power engineering. In the latest phase, automation has been added to this developed industrialisation, in the guidance systems of both high-explosive and nuclear missiles. In their combined effects these industrialised and automatic processes have qualitatively changed the nature of war; have indeed transformed it, at its highest technical levels, into massacre.

Nor is such massacre to be understood by reference back to any earlier historical examples, bloody and cruel though those so often are. The general massacre of majority populations over the area of one or more continents is now technically possible, especially by nuclear missiles but also by the deliberate spread of lethal bacteria or of nerve-gas. War at this level, but also at several lower levels, including high-explosives and fire-bombing on cities, is from the beginning massacre, and should be called by its true name.

These changes have registered in many though not yet in enough minds. The major warning signals they indicate are inescapable, yet they are again and again overridden by a stupid or wilful assimilation of such indiscriminate destruction to old military and patriotic ideologies, doubtful enough in themselves but entirely irrelevant to the problems of avoiding or refusing massacre. Moreover, even when the signals have got through, there can be displaced and inadequate responses. There is now a brittle and fashionable kind of fatalism, which dissipates shock into knowall small-talk; whistling amusingly sad tunes as the *Titanic* – in that now regular image – steams towards the iceberg. Among more serious people the danger can settle as mute terror, depressing and disorienting but above all disabling: 'the Bomb' as a static and terrible entity, within but also just beyond our lives. Alternatively, the clearest recognition of the systematic character of these weapons of massacre – including the recognition that they are among the products of more general processes of industrialisation and automation – can lead to its own kinds of fatalism: a desperate recognition of overwhelming danger, and then the leap to prophetic warning or to impassioned protest.

This leap is at last to a fully human scale, but it is characteristically hard to sustain. Every description of the dangers has its systematic response, including the hitherto persuasive response from the controllers and manufacturers of the weapons of massacre that yet more must be produced, to save us or some of us from the dangers of others using them. The horror then agitates but cannot indicate. Militarist politicians and their chiefs of staff join in the chorus of warning, to get us to increase their appropriations. Practical philosophers tell us that this knowledge of doing evil can never be cancelled and so has to be 'lived with', as if knowing how to act in evil ways made evil action inevitable. Or again, among some of the most concerned and best informed, the systematic character of the weapons systems and their political institutions is seen as inherently overpowering and determining. A countdown to disaster is seen as having, in effect, already begun.

Some of these urgent warnings may be true. There is no certain way of knowing. But within some of the cries of warning, which are otherwise wholly reasonable, we can detect one especially disabling form of thought, which actually alters the character of the warning, and shifts it towards despair. This is derived from a special form of technological determinism. The technology of nuclear weapons is held to determine the nature of the contemporary societies which possess them, and further to determine their international relations. A deadly system, first of weapons and then of institutions and ideas, steadily assumes total and ultimately destructive control. It is this system which has been called 'Exterminism'.

2

It is necessary to look again, briefly, at technological determinism itself. (A fuller analysis was given in the chapter on 'Culture and Technology'.)

It is obvious that certain major technical inventions – steam power, electricity, internal combustion engines, nuclear energy – create the conditions for radical changes in social life. But it does not follow that the inventions caused the changes or inevitably led to them. What any such conclusion omits is the fact that the inventions occurred within an already existing social order, which was in many cases actively looking for them and which had invariably to select and invest in them if they were to become significant. It is then a reduction of reason to represent the invention as the prime cause of its effects, which have always to be traced to its development and use within the social order as a whole. Thus technological determinism – the new machine making the new society – excludes general human interests and intentions in favour of a selected and reified image of their causes and results. Further, it systematically postdates history and excludes all other versions of cause.

This is serious everywhere, but in the case of nuclear weapons it is especially disabling. It steers us away from originating and continuing causes, and promotes (ironically, in the same mode as the ideologies which the weapons systems now support) a sense of helplessness beneath a vast, impersonal and uncontrollable force. For there is then nothing left but the subordinated responses of passivity or protest, cynical resignation or prophecy. That the latter response in each pairing is infinitely better, morally and politically, should go without saying. But that the character of resistance to the threat of massacre can be radically affected by the initial assumption of so absolute and overpowering a system is already evident, mixed incongruously as it also is with the vigorous organisation and reaching out to others which follow from different initial bearings.

In the case of nuclear weapons, nothing is more evident than that they were consciously sought and developed, and have continued to be consciously sought and developed. It is true that as so often in modern technological innovation much of the basic research had been done for quite other reasons, without foreseeing this particular result. But the crucial moment of passage from scientific knowledge to technical invention, and then from technical invention to a systematic technology, depended on conscious selection and investment by an existing social order, for known and foreseen purposes. Thus the atomic bomb was developed within a situation of total war, under the familiar threat that the enemy might also be developing it, by states which were *already* practising the saturation-bombing and fire-bombing of cities and civilian populations. The atomic bomb gave them very much greater destructive power to do the same things more thoroughly, more terribly, and (in the new genetic effects of radiation) more lastingly. All the later developments, from fission to fusion bombs, from bombs to missiles, and from propulsion to self-regulated launch and guidance, were equally consciously sought, involving a major part of all contemporary industrial research and development.

Thus 'the Bomb' is not a Great Satan, stalking an otherwise innocent world. It is a specific climax of a specific social order – its industry and its politics. Yet there are then still questions to ask about the relations between this specific climax of modern weapons-systems and other parts of the social order. Military technology has often, perhaps always, been a significant factor in the constitution of a social order. The question that has now to be asked, about the full range of nuclear and related weapons, is what specific *variations* they have introduced into the relations between a military technology and a social order. Two types of variation are evident: international and internal.

3

It was commonly said, when the atomic bomb had just been invented, that there were now only two or three states capable of waging major war. Indeed this perspective, learned with much else from James Burnham, was the basis for Orwell's projection of *Nineteen Eighty-Four*, in which three super-states, in shifting alliance and counter-alliance, with absolute repressive and propagandist control of their internal populations, were in a state of effectively permanent war. It is essentially this Orwellian nightmare ('1984' as 'Exterminism') which is now being revived. The mere fact of revival does not affect its truth, either way. But it is worth comparing the prophecy with the history. The emergence of superpowers was correctly foreseen. As it happens this was not primarily a function of the atomic bomb or even of the hydrogen bomb, though these had conferred some decisive military advantages. For there were definite stages within the new technology. The crucial stage, we can now see, was, from the mid-1950s, the combination of nuclear weapons with advanced missile technology. This combination, at a continually rising level, still keeps the United States and the Soviet Union as superpowers in a period in which other states have acquired nuclear weapons but less effective or more vulnerable means of delivery.

All the other projections are more arguable. There has been a very powerful and dangerous grouping of secondary states in direct alliances with the superpowers. In the dimension of nuclear weapons and related military strategy these alliances have taken on something of the character of super-states, though at other levels this development is much less complete and is subject to other, often major, political interests and processes. At the same time, the rest of the world has been both object and subject in this dominating and dangerous history. It is ironic that one of the principal (mainly Chinese) arguments against agreement on the non-proliferation of nuclear weapons has been the evident danger of being dominated by the superpowers: the danger of 'hegemonism'. It is this initially reasonable impulse to political independence which, combined with certain regional rivalries, is in fact multiplying the nuclear arsenals.

In direct military ways, in the search for bases in the global strategy which has accompanied missile-nuclear and related technology, there has been constant pressure to reduce independent or ex-dependent states to objects in the superpower military competition. While much of this has followed from the imperatives of military technology, and has even been continued, in blind thrusts, when changes in the technology made it no longer so necessary in military terms, it is also true that the central thrust of this deadly competition has been, in the broadest sense, political. This fundamentally political character of the competition in its turn modifies the directly military competition. It is necessary for the superpowers not only to pretend but actually to be concerned with those broader interests which originate in the rest of the world.

Thus political and economic struggles which a simple military hegemonism would have *a priori* excluded have in fact continuously and powerfully occurred, and have included the substantial if still incomplete liberation of many peoples who are nowhere near having nuclear-weapons capability. At the same time not only the superpowers but many secondary states have exported other forms of armament with a recklessness, often distinct from the terms of the primary competition, which has led to twenty-five million (and rising) war deaths in a period in which nuclear weapons had been supposed to be determining and in which none had been actually used.

Nothing in this argument reduces the central danger of direct nuclear war between the superpowers and their locked-in nuclear alliances. But, as we shall see again in analysing the ideology of deterrence, the apparent technologically-determined process has been at most imperfectly realised and in many significant cases has been inoperative, within the complexities of a necessarily broader world history.

4

The other half of the Orwellian projection – the repressive state – has also to be taken seriously. First in the Cold War competition for the development of nuclear weapons, then in their continuing technical elaboration, there have been significant increases in the levels of surveillance and control, and of espionage and counter-espionage, in 'Western' capitalist societies. Whether there has been a similar increase in Soviet-controlled societies, and especially in the Soviet Union which before nuclear weapons already had an immense apparatus of this kind, is more arguable. But there can be no denying that, taken as a whole, as not only direct surveillance and control but as an increasingly powerful propaganda for war preparations, secrecy, xenophobia and distrust, these internal developments have been contemporary with nuclear weapons. Yet there is again a major qualification. Precisely because the central competition is not only military-technological but is also, in the broadest sense, political, it is an underestimate of the dangers to suppose that they relate to nuclear weapons alone. On the contrary, what is now most dangerous in capitalist societies is the attempt to achieve a symmetry between the external (military) threat – directly identified as the Soviet Union – and the internal threat to the capitalist social order which is primarily constituted by an indigenous working-class and its organisations and allies. We should be in a much better situation than we now are if surveillance and secrecy were directed only against actual and probable Soviet agents, or for national military security. There is at least as much use of these controls, now aided by major technological developments of their own, against home-grown working-class and related political organisations. If this threatening symmetry of an external and an internal enemy is ever fully politically achieved, we shall indeed be in extreme danger.

The projection of an organised repressive, propagandist, secrecy-and-security State – Orwell's '1984' – is not the most significant possibility in the range of internal effects of nuclear weapons. In those received terms it belongs to a pre-nuclear period, and above all to the experience of inter-war fascism and of Stalinism. Although Orwell's superstates are perpetually at war, the actual military element is barely evident in his account. The more persuasive contemporary version of an absolutist system is the idea of a 'military-industrial complex': an organised grouping of arms-production, military, research and state-security interests which has, in effect, moved beyond the control of civil society and is the true contemporary form of the State itself.

This is a crucial observation of certain major tendencies within contemporary advanced-capitalist societies. There is a fundamental interlock between State procurement of advanced weapons systems and the major capitalist aeronautic and arms-production corporations, and a further interlock of both with the best-funded organised scientific research. Moreover, in these areas, the most rigid secrecy-and-security controls, against both political and industrial espionage, are actively employed. It is the spread back of such controls into civil society and into the central political processes that is now the most significant threat to general liberty and knowledge. The local rationalities of the protection of national security have been extended, beyond their strict relevance, into areas in which any more general concept of national security positively requires public information and discussion (technical studies of the effects of nuclear war are only one of many such examples).

From this experience it has been argued that the military-industrial complex is now, in effect, the ruling class. It has been said that it operates beyond the controls of normal politics and that it is part of the virtually automatic system, based on the technical charactersitics of nuclear weapons, which is propelling us, beyond or against the general will, to mutual destruction.

Relations between a military technology and a social order are inevitably close. It is of the essence of a ruling class that it possesses a monopoly or a predominance of overt or threatening violence. Yet this is in no way a consequence of nuclear-weapons systems, and indeed it has been mainly in non-nuclear societies that the specific military-state-security formation has acquired absolute or determining power. The realities of more general productive development have created, in more advanced and complex economies, other effective major formations within the ruling class. The true political process, at this level, is much more a matter of the shifting relations between these formations than of any inevitable dominance by one of them.

The military-security formation has major advantages, and these are increased in conditions of international conflict. But just because what it produces is at once so deadly and so negative, it can only temporarily achieve that command of resources and policies which would ensure its stable dominance. It is then true that the present nuclear arms race is producing conditions in which the possibilities of dominance form a rising tendency. Yet the ruling class as a whole still has other interests, most obviously economic, both in its own immediate terms and in relation to assuring its continued dominance over the whole life of the society, which must include satisfying the increasing non-military economic needs and demands of its people. It has also political interests, in its need to present its central objectives in those broader terms which can command a necessary consent. Different versions of ruling-class interests, different combinations of these with the interests of other classes, are bitterly and relatively openly fought out in competitive elections, which in their results observably affect levels of military spending. Therefore, no ruling class, and a *fortiori* no whole social formation, can be reduced to the military-security element. If it is true that the military-security complex, just because of its negativity, moves on its own towards certain ultimate irrationalities, in which the whole social order exists to serve and supply it, it is also true that other ruling-class formations, to say nothing of other classes, exert constant and powerful practical pressures of a different kind, which are then the materials of real politics. The observable fluctuations of military spending programmes and of broad political strategies are the indices of these continuing internal and externally affected struggles.

The idea of the military-industrial complex was developed in relation to advanced capitalist societies, but it has been extended to analysis of other social orders, notably the Soviet Union and China. Yet it is almost certainly wrong, first, to fuse these very different formations as a single entity, and, second, to override their functional differences within different kinds of economy.

Within capitalist societies, the military and related industries may not, for all their command of research, be a genuine leading sector. Their crude counter-cyclical role, and their privileged rate of profit, can distort the programmes and the interests of the capitalist class as a whole, while their massive levies of public revenue can disrupt investment programmes and produce unintended crisis and socio-economic discontent. The present crisis of ordinary manufacturing industry, with its consequences in major unemployment, is perhaps just such a case, and it is significant that it is often from within the ruling class that campaigns against the 'military-industrial complex' have been mounted.

Meanwhile in the centralised socialist systems it is evident that the scale of military expenditure is economically crippling, and has virtually no advantages for any productive sector. There the linkage is different, between the bureaucratic formation of the ruling class itself and the necessary support of military and state-security formations. The contradiction between an objectively weakening high-military economy and the dependence of a political leadership on an exceptional monopoly of power and force is indeed very dangerous, but is itself reciprocally affected by external developments within the contradictions of the opposing system.

Thus we need not conclude that there is any genuine inevitability in the formation and tendency to dominate of these powerful internal sectors. Any full analysis must include a recognition of the dysfunctional – internally destabilising or destructive – aspects of the arms race for both social systems.

So the determinist proposition, that the development of nuclear weapons systems has produced international and national political systems which now in effect run by themselves, and which being beyond our control are certain or almost certain to end in total destruction, must be firmly rejected. It is as false as it is disabling. Moreover it masks, in its total rhetoric, the one actual technically-determined element of the systems which is now most dangerous. This is not the possession of nuclear weapons as such, but their combination with automated missile technology. What has happened is that there has been a dramatic shortening of time for effective military and, more crucially, political decisions. The greatly increased accuracy of recent guidance systems, in the period of microprocessors, and the related shift from counter-city to counter-force strategy, have again reduced this margin. It is then not only that secondary states have ceded their powers of ultimate political decision while they remain in nuclear alliances, but that within such a technology this ceding and centralisation of powers is, in its own terms, rational. While much might be done in the more normal political areas of approaches to such a crisis, the fact remains that to assent to missile-nuclear technology is to assent to the loss of independence in ultimate decisions, and, spreading back from that, to a steady loss of independence and openness in a much wider political area. It is this dangerous reality which now confronts the peoples of Europe, East and West. Combined, as it now is, with the siting of medium-range missiles, controlled from the same foreign centres, in the developing strategy of a 'theatre' (European) or 'limited' nuclear war, it compels, while we still have time, the most far-reaching political struggles.

5

It is a condition of the success of these struggles that they should both engage with and develop precise arguments and objectives. The first argument we must meet is that of 'deterrence'. The terrible weapons, we are told, are not meant to be used, but to deter others from using them.

In fact 'deterrence' is both a strategy and an ideology. We should be wrong if we failed to acknowledge some limited validity of deterrence as a strategy. Just because there is no effective general defence against nuclear weapons, or more strictly against nuclear missiles, there is some initial rationality in the argument that if an enemy possesses them, the only policy, short of pacifism, is to acquire and maintain a deterrent capability of the same kind. We have only to look at the international politics of the mid-late 1940s, when the United States but not the Soviet Union possessed atomic weapons. Proposals for use of this monopoly to destroy the world centre of communism while there was still time acquired significant support, including from some liberal intellectuals who were later supporters of nuclear disarmament. We then see that in this as in so much else a monopoly of such terrible power, in any hands, is profoundly dangerous. It was also argued (as by Burnham in *The Struggle for the World*, 1947) that as soon as two hostile nations possessed atomic weapons nuclear war would follow almost immediately, and predictions of this kind – that possession implied inevitable use – have been made ever since, with a recurring confidence (in fact a recurring despair) unshaken by the passage of several predicted crucial stages.

It has not only been military deterrence which has so far falsified these predictions. Other powerful factors have combined to hold back nuclear war. These have included the widespread public revulsion from any *first* use of nuclear weapons, and further those characteristics of nuclear weapons themselves, which in the unpredictable effects of fallout introduced a new qualitative and, in some respects, qualifying element in calculations of aggression. Centrally, also, there have been powerful and repeated campaigns for peace.

Yet in its limited direct context deterrence has not been ineffective. However, when we place the fact of 'mutually assured destruction' – in itself so insane a basis for any lasting polity – within actual world-political relations since 1945, we find that it was just because deterrence became operative in direct relations between the United States and the Soviet Union that steadily, and very dangerously, it had to be masked as a real strategic concept and replaced, confusingly under the same name, by deterrence as an ideology.

The crucial dividing line is between deterrence from direct military attack, which is still widely and properly supported, and the deterrence of communism as such. In practice the strategy and the ideology are intricately connected, but at the level of public argument they are deliberately confused. If it is evidence of Soviet aggression that an Asian or African country makes a socialist or communist revolution, then the simplicities of deterrence against a direct military attack are left far behind. The natural desire of all peoples to be secure against direct attack, which ought never for a moment to be denied or even questioned by those of us who are against nuclear weapons and the arms race, is systematically exploited for these other and only ever partly disclosed objectives. It is then a necessary element of any effective campaign to so clarify the differences between the strategy and the ideology that it will be possible to isolate all those who can, without hyperbole, be called warmongers. It is only on the powerfully organised Right of West European and North American politics that the ideology becomes again a strategy: to destroy communism everywhere. Yet it has in practice been far too easy for this grouping to enrol natural desires for security and independence into their quite different objectives. Moreover, the rest of us make it easier for them if we do not ourselves start, genuinely, from these desires, and go on to show their ultimate (if not always immediate) incompatibility with nuclear weapons and the arms race.

We can best do this if we can show that it is from the limited success of deterrence against direct nuclear attack that the most dangerous recent strategies have been developed. It has been in periods of significant political and economic change beyond the terms of direct US–USSR relations that an intensification of what is still called 'deterrent' nuclear-weapons development has occurred. This has been especially so in periods of intensified national liberation struggles, with peaks around Cuba in the early 1960s and after Angola in the 1970s. At these points the distinction between strategy and ideology is particularly evident, and it has been evident again, though in confused ways, in the complex actions in Iran and Afghanistan.

It is clear that direct two-way deterrence had been achieved by the late 1950s, at a minimum level, and by the late 1960s at a fully effective level. We have then to allow something – perhaps much – for the internal improvement and modernisation of these systems, at these levels and within this strategy. But it then becomes clear that the vast development of overkill capacity, now continuing at a rising rate, belongs strictly to the ideology. It has to be referred not to matters of national security but to both an overt and a covert world-political struggle. Moreover it is within the limited success of direct ('homeland') US–USSR deterrence that the particular and now exceptional danger for Europe has developed. It is from the facts of that stand-off that Europe has been nominated as a 'theatre' for another 'scenario', in which it is believed (on the military evidence, quite irrationally) that a limited nuclear war could be fought, as a controlled part of the global struggle.

Here, decisively, for the peoples of Western Europe – and especially in these years in which the nuclear weapons for just such a war are being actively deployed – the strategy and the ideology can be seen as distinct. From deterrent subjects, which we could still, however unreasonably, imagine ourselves to be, we have become objects in an ideology of deterrence determined by interests wholly beyond us as nations or as peoples, though significantly not beyond our frontiers as the interests of existing ruling classes. Whatever the scenario might be for others, for us as peoples it is from the opening scene the final tragedy. Global deterrence would have achieved a Europe in which there was nobody left to deter or be deterred.

6

'Multilateralism', as a concept, is often paired with 'deterrence'. This is the consistent orthodox argument which has so far commanded majority support. We can begin to break the pairing when we have distinguished between deterrence as strategy and as ideology. It is not impossible that from deterrence as military strategy, at a certain phase of its development, staged mutual disarmament might be negotiated. But within the *ideology* of deterrence, in which vast political forces, at their extremes of an absolute kind, are at once and necessarily engaged, there can and will be no disarmament. The long-sustained promise, that from this necessary strength disarmament can be negotiated, has been thoroughly falsified, and it is extraordinary that it can still be so brazenly asserted, as cover for yet one more stage of military escalation.

At the same time, however, multilateral disarmament is the only way to security. The World Disarmament Campaign is on very strong ground when it argues not only for this but for the urgent inclusion of other than nuclear weapons. Nuclear war is the worst possibility, though chemical and bacteriological war are only minimally less appalling. But even what is called conventional war, with the combined use of advanced high explosives (as the attack on Beirut terribly demonstrated) and the present capacities of missile technology, could now destroy urban civilization. Thus only multilateral disarmament can be accepted as an adequate objective.

It is then important to distinguish between multilateralism as a political strategy and multilateralism as an ideology. To a very large extent, in current debates, 'multilateralism' is a codeword for continued acquiescence in the policy of military alliances and the arms race. In deceptive or self-deceptive ways, the longing for disarmament is ideologically captured as the cover for yet another stage of rearmament. It is an essential objective of any campaign to break this false pairing, but this can only be done if the reasonableness of genuine multilateralism is fully acknowledged. One important way of doing this is to break the multilateralist code at its weakest point, which while speaking of 'multilateralism' really entails an exclusive *bilateralism*. It is not, for example, the governments of Europe which will attempt negotiation on the possible reduction of nuclear bases and missiles within their territories. Within the unstressed logic of the alliances this primary and indeed multilateral responsibility is surrendered and displaced to bilateral negotiations between the United States and the Soviet Union.

'Multilateralism' of that orthodox kind is then only a codeword for accepting the current polarization, and for the consequent submission to the loss of national independence. It is against this dangerous and habitual obscuration that an impulse to genuine multilateralism, and precise proposals for it, have much to contribute.

7

The most relevant and precise proposals now are:

(a) the United Nations resolution calling on the USA and USSR to freeze nuclear-weapons stocks, production, development and testing for at least five years; this is supported by the USSR, gaining political approval in the USA, and deserves wide general support, since what happens in those two immensely powerful societies could, in this area, be decisive;

(b) an absolute prohibition on the acquisition of nuclear weapons by States which do not already possess them; this by means of treaty and of embargo on the export of related preparatory materials and processes;

(c) the establishment of nuclear-free zones in particular continents and regions; the possession of nuclear weapons or bases for their use to be prohibited, by treaty, within such areas;

(d) prohibition of the introduction of any new weapons systems, of a nuclear type, into areas already possessing older systems;

(e) initiatives by individual States, which now possess or provide bases for nuclear weapons, to remove and renounce them.

In the diverse and dangerous conditions within which any of these proposals has to be made and worked for, there are inevitably differences of emphasis and priority. In Europe the most significant campaigns are of types (d) – resistance to the planned introduction of 'cruise' missiles and the neutron bomb – and (c) – nuclear-free regions such as Scandinavia and Central Europe, as steps towards a nuclear-free 'Europe from Poland to Portugal'. There are also urgent responsibilities in Europe in type (b) campaigns. All these campaigns are currently becoming more vigorous, more extended and more expert.

Yet, in the urgency of all these actions, there is in Britain especially an overlap, and at times a confusion, with campaigns of type (e): that is, an overlap with both a residual and a revived 'unilateralism'. The current meanings of this concept have now to be carefully examined.

'Unilateralism' must first be distinguished, historically, from pacifism, which has always, and coherently, proposed the unilateral pacific act, including the renunciation of all weapons, as the first move to break the dangerous deadlock of armed confrontation. But 'unilateralism' acquired more specific and more limited meanings in a particular period – the late 1950s – in which certain special conditions obtained. Britain was at that time the only state other than the superpowers to possess nuclear weapons, so that on the one hand unilateral British renunciation could be argued as the first necessary practical step to prevent the proliferation of nuclear-weapons states, and on the other hand as a moral example, to all states including the superpowers. Furthermore, there was some desire to get out from under this dangerous superpower rivalry, whether positively as a 'non-aligned' state, or negatively as 'leaving them to get on with it'. In either case, though with differences of emphasis, the assumption was that Britain could be independent and autonomous, at the most basic levels.

But what matters now, within a resurgence which is also in some respects a continuity, is to re-examine circumstances before we simply resume old responses. Thus the argument against proliferation is significantly different in the 1980s as compared with the 1950s. It has in any case now to include attention to the problems of superpower monopoly ('hegemonism') which, quite apart from being insufficiently analysed in that earlier phase, are now major political realities. Deprived of this immediate practical bearing, the argument of moral example has, in my view, no reasonable resting place short of pacifism, which remains, in the multiplying dangers of international violence, one of the most profound and accessible responses to evil in our world and culture.

Thus unilateralism of a non-pacifist kind, in the 1980s, has either to be coherently political, with all its consequences followed through, or to resign itself to rhetorical evasiveness. It is clear that the loose assembly of diverse political forces around unilateralism, which for a time held but then failed to hold in the late 1950s and early 1960s, cannot now be responsibly reconstituted on the old terms. What has always been insufficient in its arguments is any realistic facing of the full significance of such an act by a state like Britain. It is significantly often at this point, when in any political campaign aiming for majority support the most stringent realism is an absolute requirement, that there is a rhetorical loop back to the undoubted evils and dangers of nuclear war and to the abstraction of 'the Bomb'.

What then must we really face? The central fact is that Britain (the UK), at every level – military, political, economic and cultural – has been locked into 'the alliance', which is at once a life-or-death military system and a powerful organisation of the most developed capitalist states and economies. To take Britain out of that alliance, to make even the preliminary moves, would be a major shift in the balance of forces, and therefore at once a confrontation of the most serious kind. Every kind of counterforce, certainly economic and political, would be deployed against it, and there could be no restriction of the resulting struggle to the theoretically separable issue of nuclear weapons. Thus a theoretically restricted campaign, based on an eventual popular refusal of the dangers of nuclear war, would arrive, in reality, at a stage of general struggle for which, while it had kept its campaign specialised and selective, it would be quite unprepared.

At the same time the general notion of the unilateral act, now commonly construed as 'renunciation', has in practice to be divided into separable political acts and stages. What most immediately enters the political argument is, first, on a European scale, the decision about medium-range missiles specifically designed for a 'limited' nuclear war on our own territories; and second, in Britain, the decision about the renewal, into a third 'generation', of the so-called independent nuclear capability, by the purchase of Trident missiles from the United States. Political campaigns around each of these decisions can but need not be conducted in terms of old-style unilateralism. It is significant that there seems already to be more political support for the refusal of these stages of escalation than for a general and indiscriminate 'unilateralism'. Many who have taken the full measure of the existing dangers of nuclear weapons and nuclear-alliance strategy insist on absolute positions, which can alone express a full moral sense. They then reject or even despise more limited positions as mere political calculation. It is certainly important to try to shift opinion to the *abolition* of all nuclear weapons, rather than to those versions of control or limitation within which, as in recent agreements, actual rearmament can occur. But since the dangers are so great, there is also a case for saying that we must advance wherever we can, and that campaigns against Cruise and Trident need not, in these critical years, involve and often be politically limited by the unilateralist case, which is itself only a very limited step towards abolition.

For to refuse the siting of Cruise missiles on our territories, as part of a process of demanding multilateral European negotiations for the removal of all such missiles and the related bomber and submarine bases from the territories of 'Europe from Poland to Portugal', is not, in any ordinary sense, 'unilateralism'. It is the exercise of independence and sovereignty as a stage in a negotiating process for which there is still (just) time. Similarly in the case of the Trident purchase; it can be a conscious entry into the negotiating process of strategic arms reductions, by refusing the (in fact unilateral) escalation of British-based missile-nuclear systems. Positive campaigns for these specific initiatives can then in practice be very different from the relatively unfocused demand for 'unilateral renunciation', and should, in all public argument, be kept rationally distinct.

What remains to be faced, although at a different level from old-style unilateralism, is the full consequence of such positive refusals and initiatives. For these more specific moves would not only challenge existing strategic dispositions and calculations but would also, just as radically, challenge the logic of superpower hegemonism. The consequent political struggles would be on an even wider stage than that of the consequences of old-style British unilateralism. But that the stage would be wider is an opportunity as well as a problem, and it is in this context that we must examine one of the deeper structures of British unilateralism.

8

It is noticeable now that there is a congruence, within that spectrum of opinion which we can describe, broadly, as the Labour Left, between economic, political and peace campaigns which are all, in a general sense, unilateralist. Proposals for a siege or near-siege economy, protected by the strongest version of import controls; proposals for the recovery of political sovereignty or actual withdrawal from the EEC; proposals for the unnegotiated unilateral renunciation of nuclear weapons and bases: all have this common style. There are strong arguments within each of the positions, but the decisive common factors seem to be a radical overestimate of Britain's capacity and effect in independent action, and a radical underestimate of the degree of actual penetration of British economy and society by both international capitalism and the military-political alliance which exists to defend it. There can be no question that we have to find ways to contain this penetration and to roll it back, but it is then a matter of very intricate and realistic economic and political argument to find the most effective ways.

The 'Labour Left' position, at its simplest public level, seems to be not only an abstract short-cut through all these actual difficulties, but based in a very deep political structure which characteristically idealizes desirable conditions and forces and, as a protection against more radical perspectives, reduces real opposing forces to abstract and alien entities. For the question is never what we could legally do, or find some temporary majority for doing. The question is one of broad struggle. And if the question is one of struggle, the political campaign must be a matter of mobilising real forces, on the most favourable possible ground. It would be unfair to say that the passing of resolutions, even within relatively etiolated structures, is a deliberate evasion of this much harder political reality. Properly understood, it can be part of the process of actual mobilization. But what does seem to be an evasion is the simple rhetoric of 'go it alone'. For as this attempts to supply itself with at least some realistic alternative programmes, there is a very strong and, for some, irresistible tendency to cut through the difficulties with the powerful underlying impulse of reversion to the *status quo ante*.

There is one obvious test case. If we seriously support a collaborative movement for European nuclear disarmament, is it sensible at the same time to propose simple withdrawal from the EEC? What is necessary and possible, in both cases, is a radical negotiation, and this can only really be undertaken on a European rather than simply a British scale. None of the actual negotiating steps is easy, but I have found in discussion that the dominant mood thus far, on the EEC as on nuclear weapons, is an impatient insistence on the 'swift, decisive unilateral act'. After such an act, all the radical consequences, and the radical struggles, for which a maximum of carefully prepared collaboration and alliance would undoubtedly be necessary, would be faced *ad hoc*. Yet in any of these struggles, and especially in the struggle against the polarised hegemonism of the nuclear alliances, only combined action, on a European scale (of course based on what are also nationally conducted and to some extent uneven and differently inflected campaigns) has any realistic chance of success. Thus in Europe we should consistently advance *European* rather than British-unilateralist arguments and objectives.

9

Yet never only European arguments and objectives. The most dangerous nuclear arena is indeed in Europe, but the crucial political struggles and dangers are very much more widespread. At the same time, in a world order dominated from North America, West and East Europe and Japan, there are particular responsibilities for the general peace within these 'metropolitan' societies.

There is, first, the chaotic debris of the old Empires, with their often arbitrary frontiers, their confusion of peoples, their implantation of alien and alienated minorities. Regional, local and civil wars still flow, bloodily, from these. There is, further, the powerful penetration of other societies by the internationalist capitalist economy, often impoverishing, indebting or distorting their economies, destabilising their societies, and implanting local, often military, forms of dependent dominance. One of the key forms of this penetration is the direct training and arming of military forces, which are intended to control the poor of their own countries. But these forces learn also a fully developed militarism from the old centres and academies, and armed competitively from the advanced military technologies can develop wars of other kinds and proliferate the arms race, up to and including, in the worst cases, the threshold of nuclear weapons.

Within the armed establishments of such states, imposed or client-dependent, all ordinary processes of social change and political development can be savagely blocked. The move, within such blocked societies, to armed popular resistance or insurrection is then as probable as it is tragic. There is a clear duty of solidarity with such struggles, but this has always to be interpreted within a wider perspective, in which vicarious support or romanticisation is very much less to the point than action to end the lines of supply – military, economic and political – of the cruel and exploiting regimes that are being opposed. The dangers of any revolutionary rising deteriorating into a new armed camp are now beyond speculation;

they have repeatedly become actual. Armed popular struggles can be questioned, in good faith, only if everything has been done to weaken the lines of supply – the profitable connecting interests – which run from us to the regimes they are attacking. Correspondingly they should be supported, directly or indirectly, only while they are unambiguously linked with the necessary peaceful development of their own lands and peoples. These distinctions are often in practice very difficult to make, confused as they repeatedly are by the enrolment of such struggles, as of the regimes they oppose, in fundamentally external causes and interests.

It is false to look out from Europe or North America at this turbulent world and propose a complacent contrast with now relatively settled and peaceful older societies. It is not only a matter of old and new political and economic interventions, from these apparently peaceful centres, but the direct and unforgivable criminality of the modern arms trade, which is presented to its own peoples as simply a specialised and advantageous kind of export. It can be fairly argued that to stop the international arms trade, at these official government levels (which are now significantly more dangerous than the underworld of private arms dealers) would be likely, on the odds, to save more lives, in the next ten years, than even the most determined campaign against nuclear weapons in Europe. There is, fortunately, no competition between the two objectives. Both are necessary for peace, and each is wholly compatible with and in the end dependent on the other.

Yet there may be some risk of becoming so preoccupied with the nuclear threat to our own peoples that we define peace campaigning only in its terms. One of the worst moments in the Falklands/ Malvinas crisis of 1982 was the realisation – if the opinion polls were to be believed – that many people in Britain who had opposed Cruise and Trident missiles, in figures up to 40 and 50 per cent, were approving and applauding, even in the hardest terms – accepting the deaths of our own soldiers – the war to recapture the islands, which got supporting figures of up to 80 per cent. Some elements of this can be explained or explained away, but there is clearly a risk of interpreting peace as the mere distancing of danger, whatever the consequences to others. This risk is heightened when we observe the still extraordinarily powerful hold of militarism – again very evident in Britain in that crisis – in the popular as well as in the official culture. We have become accustomed to the integral militarism of the modern nation-state, at its most formal and official levels. It is not surprising that this has spread to stain the whole society. But we may also now be facing something worse than this: a vigorous spectacular and consumerist militarism, extending from the toy-missile flashes of the children's shops and the games arcades, to the military tournaments and air displays of general public entertainment, and finally to the televised images of safely distant wars. Nobody can purge that acceptance and enjoyment of violence by declaring against 'the Bomb' which might destroy his or her own home and family. War, anywhere, is now the last enemy, and it cannot be opposed or ended with one hand in the export ledger or on the battle-entertainment video switch.

Over and above all this, meanwhile, is the relentless extension of the conflict between the superpower alliances to lands which are basically selected, indifferent to their own needs and natures, from the strategic maps. Enmeshed with this, from the Gulf to Latin America, is the use of military force to maintain systems of power and exploitation beyond even the ravenous terms of this military-strategic deployment. If we are to understand and explain this fully, we have to move on from the known facts of the international economic order to the now rapidly emerging facts of the crisis of resources. It has become an absolute duty to prepare, in good time, the positions from which we can oppose and defeat attempts to secure scarce resources – the case of oil is the most urgent current example – by military interventions direct and indirect. Such interventions will of course attempt to recruit popular opinion by appeals for the protection of our (privileged) 'way of life'. And then, given the simultaneous crisis of imposed unemployment and deprivation on the working peoples of the West, and the resulting frustration and anger which patriotic militarism, rather than any socialism, now most clearly offers to articulate, nobody can suppose that these attempts will be easy to defeat. But there is then no contradiction between a predictive ecology and campaigns for disarmament. Indeed unless the economic assessments and alternatives are developed, in practical ways, the more isolated peace campaigns could be simply overwhelmed.

Such considerations are also relevant to what is now the major problem of the traditional linkage between opposition to rearmament and opposition to unemployment and social deprivation. There are still real links between essentially wasteful military spending and poverty and deprivation in the rest of the social order. But here, as elsewhere, there is not going to be any simple return to the *status quo ante*. We may have to face the old problem of a reactionary connection between rearmament and the revival of employment. But beyond this there are new and quite major problems of change, if both peace and decent living standards are to be maintained – at our own expense, rather than at the expense or by the exploitation of others – in the old capitalist world. It is not just a matter of cancelling useless or horrific military expenditure, nor even of redirecting investment to preceding kinds of civilian manufacture. The changes will have to involve radical transformations, internally and externally, rather than simple cancellations or reversions.

Thus the issues and the arguments converge. It is fortunately still possible to generate movements for peace and for disarmament on the most general human grounds. That these are again growing is a significant gain, against the culture and politics of violence. Yet alike for their intellectual adequacy and for extension of their support it is necessary to reach beyond the moving and honourable refusals on which many of them still characteristically depend. To build peace, now more than ever, it is necessary to build more than peace. To refuse nuclear weapons, we have to refuse much more than nuclear weapons. Unless the refusals can be connected with such building, unless protest can be connected with and surpassed by significant practical construction, our strength will be insufficient. It is then in making hope practical, rather than despair convincing, that the ways to peace can be entered.

V

RESOURCES FOR A JOURNEY OF HOPE

RESOURCES FOR
A JOURNEY OF HOPE

___

I

It is usually taken for granted that to think about the future, as a way of changing the present, is a generous activity, by people who are not only seriously concerned but also, in those familiar adjectives, forward-looking, reforming, progressive. All the good ideas are on this side; all the bad or disappointing practice on the other. There is a question of how far we can go on with this easy assumption. As things now are, all the good ideas, and especially the ways in which they connect or might connect with how people are actually living, have to be rigorously re-examined.

Yet there is also another check to the assumption. It used to be taken for granted that the opposing forces were not themselves forward-looking: that they were, in those equally familiar adjectives, conservative, regressive, reactionary. Many of them indeed still are, but we misread the current situation if we rely on this easy contrast. There is now a very important intellectual tendency, with some real bases in political power, which is as closely concerned with thinking and planning the future as any reforming or progressive group. Within this tendency the signals are not being jammed but are being carefully listened to. Yet there is then the deliberate choice of a very different path: not towards sharing the information and the problems, or towards the development of general capacities to resolve them. What is chosen instead, intellectually and politically, is a new hard line on the future: a new politics of strategic advantage.

I call this new politics 'Plan X'. It is indeed a plan, as distinct from the unthinking reproduction of distraction. But it is different from other kinds of planning, and from all other important ways of thinking about the future, in that its objective is indeed 'X': a willed and deliberate unknown, in which the only defining factor is advantage. It is obvious that this has connections with much older forms of competitive scheming and fighting, and with a more systematised power politics. There are all too many precedents for its crudeness and harshness. But what is new in 'Plan X' politics is that it has genuinely incorporated a reading of the future, and one which is quite as deeply pessimistic, in general terms, as the most extreme readings of those who are now campaigning against the nuclear arms race or the extending damage of the ecological crisis.

The difference of 'Plan X' people is that they do not believe that any of these dangerous developments can be halted or turned back. Even where there are technical ways they do not believe that there are possible political ways. Thus while as a matter of public relations they still talk of solutions, or of possible stabilities, their real politics and planning are not centred on these, but on an acceptance of the indefinite continuation of extreme crisis and extreme danger. Within this harsh perspective, all their plans are for phased advantage, an effective even if temporary edge, which will always keep them at least one step ahead in what is called, accurately enough, the game plan.

The first obvious signs of Plan X politics were in the nuclear arms race, in its renewal from the mid-1970s. It was by then clear to everyone that neither staged mutual disarmament (the professed ultimate aim) nor any stable strategic parity (the more regular political ratification) could be achieved by the development of radically new weapons systems and new levels of overkill. Many sane people called these new developments insane, but within Plan X thinking they are wholly rational. For the real objective is neither disarmament nor parity, but temporary competitive advantage, within a permanent and inevitable danger.

There were further signs of Plan X in some of the dominant responses to the rise in oil prices. Other groups proposed a reduction in energy consumption, or a reduction in dependence on oil, or negotiations for some general stability in oil and other commodity prices. Plan X people think differently. Their chosen policy is to weaken, divide and reduce the power of the oil producers, whatever the long-run effects on supply, so that a competitive advantage can be retained. To argue that this cannot be a lasting solution is to miss the point. It is not meant to be a lasting solution, but the gaining of edge and advantage for what is accepted, in advance, as the inevitable next round.

Again, Plan X has appeared recently in British politics. As distinct from policies of incorporating the working class in a welfare state, or of negotiating some new and hopefully stable relationship between state, employers and unions (the two dominant policies of post-1945 governments), Plan X has read the future as the certainty of a decline in capitalist profitability unless the existing organisations and expectations of wage-earners are significantly reduced. Given this reading, Plan X operates not only by ordinary pressures but where necessary by the decimation of British industrial capital itself. This was a heavy and (in ordinary terms) unexpected price to pay, but one which had to be paid if the necessary edge of advantage was to be gained or regained. Again many sane people say that this policy is insane, but this is only an unfamiliarity with the nature of Plan X thinking. Its people have not only a familiar hard drive, but one which is genuinely combined with a rational analysis of the future of capitalism and of its unavoidable requirements.

In this kind of combination, Plan X people resemble the hardest kinds of revolutionary, who drive through at any cost to their perceived objectives. But the difference of Plan X from revolution is that no transformed society, no new order, no lasting liberation seriously enters these new calculations, though their rhetoric may be retained. A phase at a time, a decade at a time, a generation at a time, the people who play by Plan X are calculating relative advantage, in what is accepted from the beginning as an unending and unavoidable struggle. For this is percentage politics, and within its tough terms there is absolute contempt for those who believe that the present and the future can be managed in any other way, and especially for those who try to fudge or qualify the problems or who refuse the necessary costs. These wet old muddlers, like all old idealists, are simply irrelevant, unless they get in the way.

Does it need to be said that Plan X is dangerous? It is almost childish to say so, since it is, in its own terms, a rational mutation within an already existing and clearly foreseeable extremity of

danger. There is often a surprising overlap between the clearest
exponents of Plan X and their most determined political opponents.
The need for constant attention to the same kinds of problem, and
for urgent and where necessary disturbing action in response to
them, is a common self-definition by both groups. The difference,
and it ought to be fundamental, is that Plan X is determined solely by
its players' advantage. Any more general condition is left deliberately undefined, while the alternative movements see solutions in terms
of stable mutual advantage, which is then the principle of a definable
and attainable general condition: the practical condition which re-
places the unknown and undefined X.

If we put it in this way the general choice ought to be simple. Yet
we are speaking about real choices, under pressures, and we have
then to notice how many elements there are, in contemporary
culture and society, which support or at least do not oppose Plan X.
Thus the plan is often presented in terms of national competitive
advantage: 'keeping our country a step ahead'. In these terms it
naturally draws on simple kinds of patriotism or chauvinism. Any of
its damaging consequences to others can be mediated by xenophobia, or by milder forms of resentment and distrust of foreigners.
Very similar feelings can be recruited into the interests of a broader
alliance, as now commonly in military policy. Again, at a substantial
level, there is a deep natural concern with the welfare of our own
families and our own people. That they at least should be all right,
come what may, inspires extraordinary effort, and this, in certain
conditions, can appear as Plan X. Moreover, from the long experience of capitalist society, there is a widespread common sense that
we have always to look to our own advantage or we shall suffer and
may go under. This daily reality produces and reproduces the
conditions for seeing Plan X as inevitable. It has then made deep
inroads into the labour movement, which was basically founded on
the alternative ethic of common well-being. When a trade union
argues for a particular wage level, not in terms of the social usefulnes
of the work but, for example, in terms of improving its position in
the 'wages league table', it is in tune with Plan X.

There are also deeper supporting cultural conditions. Plan X is
sharp politics and high-risk politics. It is easily presented as a version
of masculinity. Plan X is a mode of assessing odds and of determining a game plan. As such it fits, culturally, with the widespread

habits of gambling and its calculations. At its highest levels, Plan X draws on certain kinds of high operative (including scientific and technical) intelligence, and on certain highly specialised game-plan skills. But then much education, and especially higher education (not only in the versions that are called business studies) already defines professionalism in terms of competitive advantage. It promotes a deliberately narrowed attention to the skill as such, to be enjoyed in its mere exercise rather than in any full sense of the human purposes it is serving or the social effects it may be having. The now gross mutual flattery of military professionalism, financial professionalism, media professionalism and advertising professionalism indicates very clearly how far this has gone. Thus both the social and cultural conditions for the adoption of Plan X, as the only possible strategy for the future, are very powerful indeed.

At the same time Plan X is more than any one of these tendencies; it is also more than their simple sum. To emerge as dominant it has to rid itself, in practice, whatever covering phrases may be retained, of still powerful feelings and habits of mutual concern and responsibility, and of the very varied institutions which support and encourage these. Moreover, to be Plan X, it has to be more than a congeries of habits of advantage, risk and professional play. This is most evident in the fact that its real practitioners, still a very small minority, have to lift themselves above the muddle of miscellaneous local tendencies, to determine and assign genuine major priorities. At the levels at which Plan X is already being played, in nuclear-arms strategy, in high-capital advanced technologies (and especially information technologies), in world-market investment policies, and in anti-union strategies, the mere habits of struggling and competing individuals and families, the mere entertainment of ordinary gambling, the simplicities of local and national loyalties (which Plan X, at some of its levels, is bound to override wherever rationally necessary) are in quite another world. Plan X, that is to say, is by its nature not for everybody. It is the emerging rationality of self-conscious elites, taking its origin from the urgent experiences of crisis-management but deliberately lifting its attention from what is often that mere hand-to-mouth behaviour. It is in seeing the crises coming, preparing positions for them, devising and testing alternative scenarios of response, moving resources and standbys into position, that it becomes the sophisticated Plan X.

To name this powerful tendency, and to examine it, is not to propose what is loosely called a conspiracy theory. There are many political conspiracies, as we eventually learn when at least some of them are exposed, usually after the event. Elements of Plan X are inherently conspiratorial. But we shall underestimate its dangers if we reduce it to mere conspiracy. On the contrary, it is its emergence as the open common sense of high-level politics which is really serious. As distinct from mere greedy muddle, and from shuffling day-to-day management, it is a way – a limited but powerful way – of grasping and attempting to control the future. In a deepening world crisis, it is certain to strengthen, as against an older, less rational, less informed and planned politics. But then the only serious alternative to it is a way of thinking about the future, and of planning, which is at least as rational and as informed in all its specific policies, and which is not only morally much stronger, in its concern for a common wellbeing, but at this most general level is *more* rational and *better* informed. For the highest rationality and the widest information should indicate a concern for common wellbeing, and for stable kinds of mutual general interest, as the most practical bases for particular well-being and indeed for survival.

2

This is where the real political problems start. We can begin by trying to assess the actual and immediately potential resources for any radical changes of direction. Two sectors are at once apparent. There is now a growing body of detailed professional research, most of it dependent on the still expanding scientific community, in the key areas of ecology, alternative technologies and disarmament. There is also a rapidly growing movement of specific campaigns, most visible in the peace movement and in ecological initiatives but also extending over a very wide social and cultural range. Here, certainly, are actual and immediately potential resources for radically new kinds of politics.

Yet it has to be recognised that in some ways these are two very different groups of people. In some of their forms of activity they are quite distinct and unconnecting. Thus much of the most useful scientific work is directed, as if it were still orthodox research, at existing political leaders or generalised public opinion. Because by current definitions much of it is 'not political', but rather an objective assessment of physical facts, there is a tendency to resist its involvement with the simplifications of politics or with the street cries and emotionalism of demonstrations. Again, by their own best values, many of the campaigns are concerned primarily with forms of public witness and protest, with direct personal involvement in opposition to some evil, or with the growth of immediate relationships of an alternative kind. They can then be generalised, by some of their representatives, as movements of conversion, analogous to early religious movements, and as such disdainful both of what is seen as mere intellectualism and of the whole system of organised politics.

These differences have to be recognised. Yet the most remarkable fact about both the peace and the ecology movements of recent years has been their relative success in combining scientific information, at quite new levels of practical development, with the direct action, in witness and exposure, of both small-group protests and huge public demonstrations. This is never either an easy or a stable combination, but in the degree it has practically reached, in many countries, it is already a new political factor.

A similar kind of combination has been evident in the most recent phases of feminism. There is now a remarkable and growing body of distinctively feminist scholarship and argument, shifting our intellectual perspectives in many fields, while at the same time there has been a major expansion of supportive groups and initiatives, as well as sharp public and private challenges to old dominative and subordinating habits. This degree of combination is relatively stable, resting as it does on more immediate identities and bondings than are available in the peace and ecology movements. At the same time, as is evident from the quality of the intellectual work, the specific directions of what is called 'the women's movement', but is more often an association of distinctive movements with different bases and intentions, are still being formed and are subject to crucial interactions with other forms of political organisation, many of these not yet resolved.

It would be possible to project, from these humane and growing movements – peace, ecology and feminism – an immediately potential and effective political majority. Yet the general situation is not really like that. The potential cannot reasonably be doubted. It is the immediacy that is the problem. There is now a major risk that there will be a jump from this sense of potential, centred in the reasonable belief that these movements represent the deepest interests of large human majorities, to an option of indifference towards all other organised and institutionalised political and social forms. The jump seems irresistible, time and again, as we look from these dimensions of concern and possibility to the mechanical thinking and manoeuvring practice of most of these forms for most of their time. Yet this is still not a jump that can be reasonably made, especially by some loose analogy with early religious movements or with heroic minorities whose objective time will come. That option should already have been rejected in the experiences of the sixties, even if there were not such clear intellectual arguments against it.

For it is not only in the movements of peace, ecology and feminism that the shift has begun. It is also in the vigorous movement of what is called an alternative culture but at its best is always an oppositional culture: new work in theatre, film, community writing and publishing, and in cultural analysis. But what has been learned very clearly in all this work, and in new kinds of political and ideological analysis, is that the relations between small-group initiatives and potentials and a dominant system are at the very centre of the problem. It is there that we have learned how new work can be incorporated, specialised, labelled: pushed into corners of the society where the very fact that it becomes known brings with it its own displacements. It is possible here also to persist as a minority, but in the cultural system as a whole it is soon clear that the central institutions are not residual – to be disregarded, for their often residual content, until the emergent minority's time has come – but are dominant and active, directing and controlling a whole connected process towards which it is impossible to be indifferent. And if this is true of the cultural system, it is even more strongly true of the general social and political system which the institutionalised forms control and direct.

At the practical centre of this problem are the existing political parties. For it is clear that at all effective levels it is towards such parties that the system now directs us. Yet it is equally clear that the central function of these parties is to reproduce the existing definitions of issues and interests. When they extend to new issues and interests, they usually lead them back into a system which will isolate, dilute and eventually compromise them. If there is one thing that should have been learned in the years since 1945, it is this. Indeed in Britain, where in the early 1960s the popular cause of nuclear disarmament was entrusted to an apparently welcoming Labour Party, only then to sink without trace, for some fifteen years, at either effective popular or institutional levels, the lesson has been very sharp and should be unmistakeable. Moreover, it is not of a kind that can be reversed by the now systematic apologias for such events, assigning merely local and proximate causes and assuring everyone that it is bound to be different next time. In their present forms the parties are practically constituted to be like this. They absorb and deflect new issues and interests in their more fundamental process of reproducing and maximising their shares of the existing and governing dispositions.

It need not stay like this. For comparable in importance to the growth of new issues and movements is a steady withdrawal of assent to orthodox politics by what is in all relevant societies a sizeable minority of a different kind, and in some societies an already practical majority. Thus except in conditions of unusual stability, which are not going to be there, the pressures on existing political forms and institutions will in any case become irresistible. It is because one likely outcome of these pressures is a harsh movement beyond the now familiar forms, into new and more open kinds of control and repression, that there can be no jump to any kind of indifference to the institutions. On the contrary, just because there will be so many pressures of a negative, cynical and apathetic kind, it is essential that the carriers of the new and positive issues and interests should move in on the institutions, but in their own still autonomous ways.

This point has special reference to the institutions of the labour movement. It is clear that these began, in all or most of their original impulses, beyond the terms of what were then the governing definitions. They were genuine popular responses, slowly built over generations, to changes in the social and economic order which were at least as fundamental as those which we are now beginning to experience. Yet any comparative measure of degrees of change has to be assessed also in two further scales. First, the relative speed of current transfers of employment beyond the societies in which the institutions were shaped, and the interaction of this with internally generated structural unemployment. Second, the basic orientation of the institutions to predominantly male, predominantly stable, and above all nationally-based and nationally-conceived economic processes.

In both these respects the existing institutions have become not only insufficient but at certain key points actually resistant to new kinds of issue. The new issues of peace and of feminism have been included in certain ways: the former as a commitment to nuclear disarmament, but characteristically of a 'unilateral', nationally-based kind; the latter as a limited responsibility to women workers as trade unionists, but largely omitting, in theory and especially practice, response to the wider critique of hierarchy and dominance. The relative indifference of the institutions to the new cultural movements is notorious. Their confidence in their sets of received ideas – keeping new kinds of thinking at a distance ratified by the disdain for 'intellectuals' and 'academics' which they share with their capitalist masters – has ensured that at the broadest public levels they have been losing the decisive intellectual arguments. In relation to the ex-colonial world, the political affiliations of an earlier epoch have been sustained but there has been a radical unwillingness to face the consequences of the contemporary domination of the international economic order by capitalist trading forms within which, from positions of advantage, their own 'labourist' economic policies and assumptions are still based.

It is possible and necessary to believe that substantial changes can be made, on each of these issues, in the general direction of the existing institutions. Yet by their nature this cannot be done by any form of intellectual affiliation to them. On the contrary, the only relevant approach is one of challenge. This is especially important in what is often the most urgent practical area, that of elections. There is an orthodox electoral rhythm in the society as a whole. But there is also a rhythm of radical thought, in which periods of intense activity on the decisive long-term issues are punctuated by silences, compromises, evasions, expressions of meaningless goodwill and artificial solidarity, which are thought appropriate because an election is imminent. It is not only that much of this is in any case vanity. What a radical minority does or does not do in these large spectacular events, dominated by the deployment of competitive leaderships, is not in practice very important. But what is much more serious is the practical surrender of the real agenda of issues to just that version of politics which the critique has shown to be deceptive and is offering to supersede.

There are some elections which are genuinely decisive: especially some which it is important not to lose, with all the evident consequences of some reactionary or repressive tendency being strengthened. Specific decisions to be electorally active in these terms are entirely reasonable. There are also some rarer occasions when an election can be much more positively worked for, because it contains the probability of some coherent advance. But even in these cases there can be no intellectual affiliation to the adequacy of the processes themselves, and no defensible temporary pretence that they are other than they are. The challenging move towards the existing institutions, which can be effectively made only if there are already alternative institutions and campaigns on a different issue-based orientation, is in no way reducible to elections, or even to party programmes and manifestos. The central approach is always to the actual people inside them, but then on the same terms as the much wider approach to the significant number of people who are at their edges or who are leaving or have left them.

This approach, by definition, has to be in good faith, candid, open to learn as well as to teach: in all those real senses comradely. But we should now have reached the end of a period in which campaigners and intellectuals acquired the habit of going as petitioners or suppliants, touched by guilt or by an assumed deference to so much accumulated wisdom. There is hardly anything of that kind to go to any longer, and any of it that is genuinely wise will not require deference or sidelong flattery. If it is indeed the case, as now seems likely, that the most the existing institutions can do, in their fixed terms, is conduct losing defensive battles, then much deeper loyalties are in question, in the survival and welfare of actual people.

3

The toughest element in all the changes that will need to be made is in the economy. It is significant that the new movements are active and substantial in almost every area of life except this. It is as if everything that was excluded by the economic dominance and specialisations of the capitalist order has been grasped and worked on: in the real issues of peace, of ecology, of relations between men and women, and of creative artistic and intellectual work. Movements of a new kind race ahead in these areas, with new bodies of argument and action. But meanwhile, back in the strongholds of the economic order itself, there are not only the dominant institutions and their shadow subordinates. There are, for most of the time, most of the people.

Thus it has been possible to move relatively large numbers of people on popular versions of the issues of disarmament, protection of the environment, the rights of women. There is then an apparent asymmetry between these real advances and persistent majorities of a different kind: conservative (in more than one party); nationalist; consumerist. Some people make desperate attempts to prove that this is not so, seizing on all the exceptions, all the local breaks, all the local resistances. But while these must of course be respected, there is no real point in pretending that the capitalist social order has not done its main job of implanting a deep assent to capitalism even in a period of its most evident economic failures. On the old assumptions it would have been impossible to have four million people unemployed in Britain, and most of our common services in crisis or breaking down, and yet for the social order itself to be so weakly challenged or political support for it so readily mobilised. Yet that is where we now are.

It is then no time for disappointment or recrimination. All that matters is to understand how this can happen, and this is not in fact difficult. All the decisive pressures of a capitalist social order are exerted at very short range and in the very short term. There is a job that has to be kept, a debt that has to be repaid, a family that has to be supported. Many will fail in these accepted obligations after all their best efforts. Some will default on them. But still an effective majority, whatever they may do in other parts of their minds or in other areas of their lives, will stick in these binding relations, because they have no practical alternative. The significance of predominantly middle-class leadership or membership of the new movements and campaigns is not to be found in some reductive analysis of the determined agencies of change. It is, first, in the fact of some available social distance, an area for affordable dissent. It is, second, in the fact that many of the most important elements of the new movements and campaigns are radically dependent on access to independent information, typically though not exclusively through higher education, and that some of the most decisive facts cannot be generated from immediate experience but only from conscious analysis.

What is then quite absurd is to dismiss or underplay these movements as 'middle-class issues'. It is a consequence of the social order itself that these issues are qualified and refracted in these ways. It is similarly absurd to push the issues away as not relevant to the central interests of the working-class. In all real senses they belong to these central interests. It is workers who are most exposed to dangerous industrial processes and environmental damage. It is working-class women who have most need of new women's rights. The need for peace in which to live and to bring up our families is entirely general. But then it is a consequence of the social order that, lacking the privileges of relative social distance and mobility, or of independent (often publicly funded) access to extended learning, the majority of employed people – a significantly wider population than the working-class in any of its definitions – have still primarily to relate to short-range and short-term determinations.

Even the issues that get a widening response are marginalised as they encounter this hard social core. Moreover what is repeatedly experienced within it, and has been put there to be experienced, is a prudence, a practical and limited set of interests, an unwillingness to be further disturbed, a cautious reckoning and settling of close-up accounts. Whatever movement there may be on issues at some distance from these local and decisive relations, there is no possibility of it becoming fully effective until there are serious and detailed alternatives at these everyday points where a central consciousness is generated. Yet it is at just these points, for historically understandable reasons, that all alternative policies are weakest.

4

The hard issues come together on two grounds: the ecological argument, and changes in the international economic order. There are times when all that seems to flow from these decisive issues is a series of evident and visible disadvantages, losses of position, to the employed majorities in the old industrial economies. Some campaigners still race ahead, on defensible grounds of universal need or justice. But they can hardly then be surprised that they are not followed. Indeed what often happens is that their proposals soon become even more unrealistic. There is at times an indiscriminate rejection of all or most industrial production, supported by some option for local crafts or for subsistence agriculture. It is not that these are unavailable ways of life. It is that they are unavailable as whole ways of life for the existing populations of urban industrial societies. The association of such wholly unrealistic proposals with the central critique of industrial-capitalist society is then either an indulgence or a betrayal. It can still be either of these when it is accompanied by talk of an imminent moral conversion.

The means of livelihood of the old industrial societies will in any case change; are indeed already changing. But there is then need for more qualified, more rational and more informed accounts. The intellectual problem, however, is that while certain principles can be established, all actual policies have to depend on new and difficult audits of resources, which must by definition be specific. We can look first at the principles, but their full practical bearings cannot be set down except in this place and that, by this enquiry and that, in a sustained and necessarily negotiated process.

The principles that matter are as follows. First, we have to begin, wherever we can, the long and difficult movement beyond a market economy. Second, we have to begin to shift production towards new governing standards of durability, quality and economy in the use of non-renewable resources. Third, and as a condition of either of the former, we have to move towards new kinds of monetary institutions, placing capital at the service of these new ends.

These principles are very general, but some specific cases look different in their light. Thus, if we begin the movement beyond a market economy, it is by no means inevitable, as the capitalist order now threatens, that many or even most industrial assembly processes should be moved out of the old economies. Nor is it inevitable that transformation-manufacturing processes should be similarly moved out. On the contrary, the decisions about any of these would be subject to a different kind of accounting. The most obvious new reference point would be the relation of any of these processes to indigenous resources. It is only the capitalist accounting of cheap labour elsewhere that is exporting many kinds of assembly. On the other hand, processes which centrally depend on the import of major raw materials would be among the first to be transferred to those economies which could radically improve their own livelihoods by their own indigenous manufacturing and processing. There would doubtless be exceptions and anomalies, as these long shifts were negotiated, but if the principle of moving beyond the market economy is taken seriously such shifts have to be made. They can be accounted as losses in the old industrial economies, as many of them would necessarily be. But there can be corresponding gains, not only in some productive transfers to new advanced technologies, developed in relation to actual indigenous resources, but also in the retention of many kinds of assembly and manufacture which would otherwise, by the operations of the now dominant global market, be transferred elsewhere. They often become a false priority in those other societies, which could better determine alternative kinds of development from their own resources and needs. It follows, inevitably, that equitable kinds of mutual protection would then have to be negotiated, as alternatives to the destructive interventions which the market, following only its own criteria, would otherwise quickly impose.

Again, in the new emphases on durability, reclamation, maintenance and economy of resources, there are some immediate losses that would have to be negotiated. A significant part of current production is oriented by the market towards relatively early obsolescence and replacement, and many jobs depend on these cycles. Yet it is only the false accounting of the market system that makes reclamation now economically marginal, and it is probable that in many processes the result of the different emphases would be a broadly comparable area of work but with many quite basic real savings. The examples of badly-made and short-term houses, furniture, toys, cars and a whole range of everyday equipment are already clear, from our experience as users. There have been sharp declines in quality over a range even of genuine short-term goods, from bread to ironmongery. The market pressures for cheap standardised production based on minimal adequacy and early replacement have distorted the common sense of a whole economy. In certain sectors of the market, of a relatively privileged kind, this lesson has already been learned and there has been a movement towards greater quality and durability, avoiding the selling routines and devices of the 'mass' market. But to generalise this would mean gaining control over the central production processes, rather than the best that is now, within market terms, foreseen, of extending the 'quality' market. This is not, except in a very few areas, a return to 'crafts'. On the contrary, it is mainly a redirection of available and new advanced technologies to the priorities of production rather than the priorities of marketing. A wholly unreasonable proportion of technical development has been assigned to improvements in marketing – now the leading edge of the whole system – rather than to the improvements in production – durability, quality, economy – which will be centrally necessary in the material conditions which lie ahead of us.

There can be no changes of these kinds unless there is a successful challenge to the monetary institutions which, centred on a financial rather than a material world, and predominantly oriented to short-term profit, now sustain what should be seen as obsolescent economies. A large part of contemporary capital is now socially generated, through taxation, savings, insurance and pension funds, over and above the direct capitalist generation through surplus value. It should then be axiomatic that these are subject to direct social controls, for investment in a different kind of economy. But it is very doubtful if this can be achieved by any of the older socialist methods, and especially by procedures of state centralisation. The most promising way forward is through a combination of new kinds of auditing of resources, within self-determining political areas, with a related auditing of available monetary resources of these kinds. Instead of the existing and uninviting alternatives of state or corporate appropriation, there should be a linked process, democratically discussed and determined, of the actual planning of physical investment and the allocation of funds. Production and service decisions should be determined by locally agreed needs, and monetary investment similarly determined by local retention of its own self-generated funds. In the long and complex negotiations towards this radically alternative system there would undoubtedly have to be arrangements for transfers between relatively advantaged and disadvantaged areas. This process, structurally very similar to the complex negotiation of income transfers in quite new conditions of employment, will be the central political problem of the coming generations. But it has only to be compared with the predictable results of the existing alienations and appropriations of capital, and of the consequent dislocations and widening inequalities within and between societies, to stand out as necessary, and to generate the will to find new procedures.

All these changes would be occurring within the radical changes in working habits already discussed. The market economy, left to itself, will continue to produce massive redundancies, including of whole societies, which it has not the least chance of regulating and compensating by any orthodox political means. At the same time, in its current dominance, it is inducing fatalism by its ideological insistence that its processes, and its alone, are 'economic'. In fact, through the linked development of shorter working time and of new schemes of education and retraining, and through the new procedures of locally audited decisions on the kinds of work undertaken, there is every chance of making, even in very diverse and sometimes unfavourable circumstances, stable and equitable economies in which all necessary work is reasonably shared. Genuine labour-saving in certain kinds of production could be linked with a necessary expansion in all the caring services – themselves typically labour-intensive and relatively economical in resources and especially imported resources. But this can happen only if there are new kinds of linkage between production and expenditure, cutting out the institutions that now appropriate and distribute them by their own alienated priorities. What could be a major opportunity for easing the strains of work without discarding large numbers of people will be seized only if this kind of commitment to a directly determined social order, rather than to either corporate capitalism or a centralised socialist command economy, begins to grow from a popular base.

It is here that the assessment of political resources for so different a social order is at its most critical point. There is really only one sector in which these alternative kinds of thinking and planning can be effectively developed, and that is in the trade unions and professional associations. Many kinds of expert help – scientific, technical and economic – will be needed. But none of it can happen, in the necessary practical ways, unless trade-union organisation, now typically oriented to corporate-capitalist and national scales, becomes more flexible in two new directions: first in direct relations with effective smaller-scale political communities; and second, in extended relations with the international labour movement.

There are already some signs of such developments. But there is bound to be a long and difficult transition from the existing kinds of state-centred and industry-centred organisations and priorities. The

signs of change, understandably, are occurring in crisis-hit enterprises – as in the alternative production plans of the Lucas Aerospace
shop stewards – or in areas which already have some distinctive
political identity and have been especially hard hit by the current
depression – Scotland, Wales, London, the English North–East.
The political problem is to extend and generalise these early shifts of
direction, beyond the emergencies which now govern them, until
there is a labour movement of a new kind, determined to take direct
responsibility for the organisation of work and resources, and
capable of taking such responsibility, through new kinds of open and
qualified research and planning.

In fact the extension of the trade-union movement to workers in
some of the most complex areas of technology, management and
finance offers a real possibility of this kind of cooperative transformation. At every level this would be very different from the
reproductive and defensive strategies which are still dominant.
These old strategies, excluding broader public considerations or
merely projecting them to an incompetent all-purpose political
party, now hold the movement back from the real work it has to do.

It is in what will happen in this central economic area that the
future of the social order will be determined. Once there is significant movement here, the alternative movements and campaigns
which can alone make general sense of the kind of society which an
alternative economic order must serve will move into a radically
different set of political relationships and possibilities.

5

What is now beginning to emerge, to support these changes, is at
least the outline of a unified alternative social theory. This involves
three changes of mind.

First, as I argued in my analysis of the industrial revolution, the
connection between the forces and the relations of production has to
be restated. It is evidently false to abstract the forces of production, as
in technological determinism. But it is equally false to abstract the
relations of production, as if they were an independent variable. It is
no longer reasonable to believe, as in most modern forms of
socialism, that these can be independently altered or transformed.
On the contrary, what is at issue within both the forces and the

relations of production is a set of alternatives at a more fundamental level of decision. The dominant version has been a basic orientation to the world as available raw material. What has been steadily learned and imposed is a way of seeing the world not as life forms and land forms, in an intricate interdependence, but as a range of opportunities for their profitable exploitation. It is then true that this has been most damaging within a capitalist economy, in its relentless drives for profit and for the accumulation of capital. But this cannot reduce the argument to one against the property and wage forms of capitalism. If that were true, we would have no way of explaining the continuing appropriation and exploitation of the world as raw material in the 'communist' or 'actually existing socialist' economies.

The necessary new position is that this orientation to the world as raw material necessarily includes an attitude to people as raw material. It is this use and direction of actual majorities of other people as a generalised input of 'labour' which alone makes possible the processes of generalised capital and technology. Thus the drive to use the earth as raw material has involved, from the beginning, the practical subordination of such majorities by a variety of means: military, political, economic, ideological. The system of capitalist property and wage relations is only one such form. Slavery and serfdom preceded it. Modern forms of the mobilisation and direction of labour can succeed it. In any of these cases, what is most at issue is the basic orientation itself, in which relations to other people and to the physical world have changed and developed in a connected process, within which the variations are important but neither absolute nor, in our present situation, decisive.

It is clear from our material history that what we can now see as a basic orientation was developed through several critical stages, each increasing its practical effects. Its first stage can be seen in the complex of changes which are summarised as the Neolithic and Bronze Age revolutions, in which, with the development of farming, stockbreeding and metalwork, decisive interventions in a constituted nature were successfully made. Yet this stage, which was indeed the appropriation and transformation of certain life forms and land forms as raw material, was still highly selective and coexisted with other forms of social and natural orientation. We can see this very clearly if we compare it with the last stages of this orientation, through which we are now living. In the development of much more powerful technologies, and in their capture by a class which defined its whole relationship to the world as one of appropriation, what was once selective and guided by conscious affinities with natural processes has been replaced by a totalitarian and triumphalist practice in which, to the extent that it succeeds, there is nothing but raw material: in the earth, in other people, and finally in the self.

The early interventions in a constituted nature were, in the strict sense, new means of livelihood. It has taken a very long time to transform these reasonable intentions and practices to the stage at which we now find ourselves. There has been a remarkable increase in such means of livelihood but *as part of the same process* (which we are now in a position to observe) a remarkable increase also in forms of death and destruction. Each part of the process is beyond the terms of a constituted nature.

It is then tempting to try to revert, if only in principle, to a stage before these conscious interventions. But this is neither possible nor necessary. We are now in a position where we can monitor our interventions, and control them accordingly. We can select those many interventions which support and enhance life, in continuing ways, and reject those many other interventions which have been shown to be damaging or to involve the reasonable possibility of damage. This is the central ecological argument. But it can only prevail if we unite it with the political and economic argument, in ways that then change what we have become used to as politics and economics. For it is the ways in which human beings have been seen as raw material, for schemes of profit or power, that have most radically to be changed. Some of these changes are already inscribed in the deepest meanings and movements of democracy and socialism. But not all of them are, and the exclusions now limit and even threaten to destroy these two most hopeful forces of our world.

What is most totalitarian about the now dominant orientation is its extension beyond the basic system of an extraction of labour to a practical invasion of the whole human personality. The evidence of treating people as raw material is not to be gathered only in accounts of wages and conditions, or of real absolute poverty, serious and often grave as these are. It is present also in an area which has been conventionally excluded from both politics and economics. It is quite clear, for example, in those sexual attitudes and practices which have been correctly identified, principally by feminists, as treating people as 'sex objects'. There is now a major interpretation of sexual relationship as finding, in another person, the raw material for private sensations. This has been profitably institutionalised in pornography, but there are much more serious effects in the actual physical treatment of others, with women and children especially vulnerable.

Failure in such versions of relationship is wholly predictable since relationship is precisely an alternative to the use of others as raw material. But what is most totalitarian about this failure is that it extends not only to the cruel punishment of others, who indeed in these terms cannot yield the lasting satisfactions that are sought, but also to the cruel punishment of self: in alcoholism, in addiction to damaging drugs, in obesities and damaging asceticisms. For the very self is then only raw material in the production of sensations and identities. In this final reach of the orientation, human beings themselves are decentred.

Thus there are profound interconnections in the whole process of production – that version of relations with others and with the physical world – to which the now dominant social orders have committed themselves. The way forward is in the neglected, often repressed but still surviving alternative, which includes many conscious interventions in a constituted nature but which selects and directs these by a fundamental sense of the necessary connections with nature and of these connections as interactive and dynamic. This can emerge, in practice, only if it is grounded in a conception of other people in the same connected terms. But this is where the intellectual difficulties of uniting the ecological and economic arguments, in a new kind of politics, are most evident. This brings us to the second necessary change of mind.

The concept of a 'mode of production' has been a major explanatory element of the dominant social orders through which we have been living. It has enabled us to understand many stages of our social and material history, showing that the central ways in which production is organised have major and changing effects on the ways in which we relate to each other and learn to see the world. But what has now to be observed is that the concept itself is at some important points a prisoner of the social orders which it is offering to analyse. It has been most successful and enlightening in its analysis of capitalism, and this is not accidental, for in its own conceptual form it seized the decisive element of capitalism: that this is a mode of production which comes to dominate both society as a whole and – which is less often stressed – the physical world. The eventual inadequacy of the concept is then that it has selected a particular historical and material orientation as essential and permanent. It can illuminate variations of this orientation, but it can never really look beyond it. This fact has emerged in the most practical way, in that the great explanatory power of Marxism, where this concept has been most active, has not been accompanied by any successful projective capacity. For all that follows from one mode of production is another, when the real problem is radical change, in hard social and material terms, in the idea of production itself.

Thus it is not surprising to find that Marx shared with his capitalist enemies an open triumphalism in the transformation of nature, from the basic orientation to it as raw material. He then radically dissented from the related and cruel uses of people as raw material, and looked for ways in which they could organise to transcend this condition and control production for themselves. This is his lasting and extra-ordinarily valuable contribution. Yet in basing his thought on an inherited concept of production – one which is in no way a neces-sary outcome of the most rigorous historical materialism – Marx was unable to outline any fully alternative society. It is not only the attempts and failures to find such alternatives, in the name of such thinking however diluted or distorted, which confirm this conclu-sion. The problem and the obstacle are in the concept itself.

For the abstraction of production is a specialised and eventually ideological version of what is really in question, which is the form of human social relationships within a physical world. In his justly influential idea of 'man making himself' Marx seized one specialised moment which connected with the developed processes he was observing in his own time: the intervention in nature to transform it as new means of livelihood: that is, to *produce*. Yet 'man' – actual men and women – had been 'making themselves', developing their social and material skills and capacities, long before this specialised and conscious intervention. Living within a constituted nature, in the hunting and gathering societies, they had already developed high social and technical skills. The long subsequent shift, through successive stages of intervention and production, altered both nature and people but was nevertheless in some major respects continuous with that earlier human phase. The sense of a connection with constituted nature was still the ground of the most successful innovations, in that selective breeding of plants and animals which positively depended on continuing interactive observation. It is in the major interventions we now class as technological – from metal-working to modern chemistry and physics – that the sense of transforming intervention is strongest, but all these, in practice, at their most useful, have similarly depended on continuing interactive observation, within both a physical and a social world. It is then only at the point when these processes are abstracted and generalised as 'production', and when production in this sense is made the central priority over all other human and natural processes and conditions, that the mode of intervention – at once material and social – becomes questionable. The decisive question is not only about intervention – 'production' – itself, but about its diverse practical effects on nature and on people.

It is this which social analysis based only on a 'mode of production' prevents us from seeing or from taking seriously. For, just as capitalist production, in practice, attempted to substitute itself for the broader and more necessary principle of human societies in a natural world, so this concept, in theory, attempted to substitute itself for the broader bases of human social and material activities. It was common to see human history before such specialist interventionist production as a mere prehistory; almost in effect pre-human. What has now to be seen, at this most intense stage of the isolation and dominance of interventionist production, spreading rapidly over the entire planet and beyond it, is another stage of prehistory, or, better, a second but now concluding stage of history, as active but also as limited as that which preceded it.

For the consciousness of the possibilities of intervention, which inaugurated that phase of history which connects to our own time, is now, at a point of great danger, being succeeded by a new consciousness of its full effects. They are at once its real and sustainable advantages and its at first inextricable recklessness and damage to people and to the earth. It is in this new consciousness that we again have the opportunity to make and remake ourselves, by a different kind of intervention. This is no longer the specialised intervention to produce. The very success of the best and most sustainable interventions has made that specialised and overriding drive containable. Where the new intervention comes from is a broader sense of human need and a closer sense of the physical world. The old orientation of raw material for production is rejected, and in its place there is the new orientation of livelihood: of practical, self-managing, self-renewing societies, in which people care first for each other, in a living world.

A third change of mind follows, when we have replaced the concept of 'society as production' with the broader concept of a form of human relationships within a physical world: in the full sense, a way of *life*. This change appears in one special way, in the current movement beyond the specialisation and contrast of 'emotion' and 'intelligence'. It is understandable that people still trapped in the old consciousness really do see the new movements of our time – peace, ecology, feminism – as primarily 'emotional'. Those who have most to lose exaggerate this to 'hysterical', but even 'emotional' is intended to make its point. The implied or stated contrast is with the rational intelligence of the prevailing systems. In reaction to this there is often a great business of showing how rational and intelligent, in comparable ways, the campaigns themselves are. Moreover, and increasingly, this is true. But a crucial position may then be conceded. For it is in what it dismisses as 'emotional' – a direct and intransigent concern with actual people – that the old consciousness most clearly shows its bankruptcy. Emotions, it is true, do not produce commodities. Emotions don't make the accounts add up differently. Emotions don't alter the hard relations of power. But where people actually live, what is specialised as 'emotional' has an absolute and primary significance.

This is where the new broad concept most matters. If our central attention is on whole ways of life, there can be no reasonable contrast between emotions and rational intelligence. The concern with forms of whole relationship excludes these specialised and separated projections. There are still good and bad emotions, just as there are good and bad forms of rational intelligence. But the habit of separating the different kinds of good from each other is entirely a consequence of a deformed social order, in which rational intelligence has so often to try to justify emotionally unacceptable or repulsive actions.

The deformed order itself is not particularly rational or intelligent. It can be sharp enough in its specialised and separated areas, but in its aggregates it is usually stupid and muddled. It is also, in some of its central drives, an active generator of bad emotions, especially aggressiveness and greed. In its worst forms it has magnified these to extraordinary scales of war and crime. It has succeeded in the hitherto improbable combination of affluent consumption and widespread emotional distress.

Informed reason and inquiry can explore these complex forms, but it is not surprising that the strongest response to them has appeared at the most general 'emotional' levels. Before any secondary reasons or informed intelligence can be brought to bear, there is an initial and wholly reasonable reaction, carrying great emotional force, against being used, in all the ways that are now possible, as mere raw material. This response can develop in several different directions, but where it is rooted in new concepts, now being steadily shaped, and in many kinds of relationship – forms of genuine bonding which are now being steadily renewed and explored – it is already generating the energies and the practical means of an alternative social order.

It can then make a difference that this alternative is being clarified theoretically. The central element is the shift from 'production' to 'livelihood': from an alienated generality to direct and practical ways of life. These are the real bases from which cooperative relationships can grow, and the rooted forms which are wholly compatible with, rather than contradictory to, other major energies and interests. They are also, at just this historical stage, in the very development of the means of production, the shifts that most people will in any case have to make.

6

It is reasonable to see many dangers in the years towards 2000, but it is also reasonable to see many grounds for hope. There is more eager and constructive work, more active caring and responsibility, than the official forms of the culture permit us to recognise. It is true that these are shadowed by the most general and active dangers. They are shadowed also by the suspicion – which the official culture propagates but which also comes on its own – that as the demonstration disperses, as the talk fades, as the book is put down, there is an old hard centre – the reproduction of a restricted everyday reality – which we have temporarily bypassed or ideally superseded but which is there and settled and is what we have really to believe.

Two things have then to be said. First, that the objective changes which are now so rapidly developing are not only confusing and bewildering; they are also profoundly unsettling. The ways now being offered to live with these unprecedented dangers and these increasingly harsh dislocations are having many short-term successes and effects, but they are also, in the long term, forms of further danger and dislocation. For this, if we allow it, will be a period in which, after a quarter of a century of both real and manufactured expectations, there will be a long series of harshly administered checks; of deliberately organised reductions of conditions and chances; of intensively prepared emergencies of war and disorder, offering only crude programmes of rearmament, surveillance and mutually hostile controls. It is a sequence which Plan X can live with, and for which it was designed, but which no active and resilient people should be content to live with for long.

Secondly, there are very strong reasons why we should challenge what now most controls and constrains us: the idea of such a world as an inevitable future. It is not some unavoidable real world, with its laws of economy and laws of war, that is now blocking us. It is a set of identifiable processes of *realpolitik* and *force majeure*, of nameable agencies of power and capital, distraction and disinformation, and all these interlocking with the embedded short-term pressures and the interwoven subordinations of an adaptive common sense. It is not in staring at these blocks that there is any chance of movement past them. They have been named so often that they are not even, for most people, news. The dynamic moment is elsewhere, in the difficult business of gaining confidence in *our own* energies and capacities.

I mean that supposing the real chances of making a different kind of future are fifty-fifty, they are still usually fifty-fifty after the most detailed restatement of the problems. Indeed, sometimes, in one kind of detailed restatement, there is even an adverse tilt. It is only in a shared belief and insistence that there are practical alternatives that the balance of forces and chances begins to alter. Once the inevitabilities are challenged, we begin gathering our resources for a journey of hope. If there are no easy answers there are still available and discoverable hard answers, and it is these that we can now learn to make and share. This has been, from the beginning, the sense and the impulse of the long revolution.

INDEX

ABOUT THE AUTHOR

Raymond Williams, who was born in 1921, is a Fellow of Jesus College, Cambridge.

The Year 2000 follows in the tradition of his pioneering works of cultural and political analysis, *Culture and Society, 1780–1950,* which Frank Kermode called "a book of quite radical importance" when it was published in 1958, and *The Long Revolution* (1961), described by Richard Crossman as "the first book to break through the thought barrier into a new epoch of Socialist ideas."

Among Mr. Williams's other books are *Communications;* a study of George Orwell; four works of cultural analysis—*Drama from Ibsen to Brecht, Modern Tragedy, The English Novel from Dickens to Lawrence,* and *The Country and the City;* and three novels set in his native Wales—*Border Country, Second Generation,* and *The Fight for Manod.*